Toward a Biocritical Sociology

John William Neuhaus

Toward a Biocritical Sociology

PETER LANG
New York • Washington, D.C./Baltimore
Bern • Frankfurt am Main • Berlin • Vienna • Paris

Library of Congress Cataloging-in-Publication Data

Toward a biocritical sociology / John William Neuhaus.
p. cm.
Includes bibliographical references and index.
1. Sociobiology. 2. Social problems. 3. Social ethics. I. Title.
GN365.9.N48 304.5—dc20 95-44341
ISBN 0-8204-3081-1

Die Deutsche Bibliothek-CIP-Einheitsaufnahme

Toward a biocritical sociology / John William Neuhaus. – New York;
Washington, D.C./Baltimore; Bern; Frankfurt am Main;
Berlin; Vienna; Paris: Lang.
ISBN 0-8204-3081-1

Sue Townsend, *The Adrian Mole Diaries,* Grove. Copyright © 1986.
Reprinted with permission of Sheil Land Associates.

Martha Nussbaum, "Human Functioning & Social Justice," *Political Theory* 20.2,
pp. 202–246, Copyright © 1992 by Sage Publications, Inc.
Reprinted by permission of Sage Publications, Inc.

Extracts from *Sociobiology* by Edward O. Wilson, Copyright © 1975 by the President
and Fellows of Harvard College. Reprinted by permission of Harvard University Press.

Extracts from *On Human Nature* by Edward O. Wilson,
Copyright © 1978 by the President and Fellows of Harvard College.
Reprinted by permission of Harvard University Press.

Extracts from *Darwin & the Emergence of Evolutionary Theories of Mind & Behavior* by
Robert J. Richards, The University of Chicago Press, Copyright © 1987.
Reprinted by permission of The University of Chicago Press.

Cover design by James F. Brisson.

The paper in this book meets the guidelines for permanence and durability
of the Committee on Production Guidelines for Book Longevity
of the Council of Library Resources.

© 1996 Peter Lang Publishing, Inc., New York

Printed in the United States of America.

For Lori, Alison and Jessamyn,
who define the meaning of family

and

For Chris, Jing and Wes,
lifetime friends nonpareil

ACKNOWLEDGMENTS

As the social psychology of George Herbert Mead makes very clear, every book is inevitably the result of a lifelong social and educational process. In particular, I want to acknowledge the many efforts made by my Mother and Father to encourage and finance my education. This book is one result of that encouragement. Two of the outstanding and inspirational teachers I encountered during that process were Paul Green, who made sociological theory more interesting than perhaps even most sociologists believe is possible, and Louis Junker, whose work in Institutional Economics profoundly affected my own intellectual orientation and development.

I would also like to gratefully acknowledge the friendship and wisdom of Dr. Richard Means of Kalamazoo College who cheerfully endured a very early version of the entire manuscript. Dr. Douglas Davidson and Dr. Ronald Kramer of Western Michigan University made a great many helpful suggestions during every stage of my work.

I want to especially recognize the constant guidance and support of Dr. Gerald Markle. Western Michigan University is enriched by his presence. I was the fortunate recipient of his continual encouragement and incisive critique. My indebtedness and gratitude to him are very, very great. His cosmopolitan perspective and intellectual craftsmanship represent the university at its best.

Finally, I want to express my sincere gratitude to two people: Heidi Burns, my Editor at Peter Lang, whose enthusiasm and diligence were greatly appreciated; and Karen Rice, of Western Michigan University, who prepared the entire manuscript with a speed and dedication which bordered on the miraculous.

CONTENTS

INTRODUCTION

This book is a critical discourse with three prominent trends within contemporary sociology. Elaborating on what I term a "biocritical" perspective, I carry on a critical conversation with Emile Durkheim over his philosophy of dualism and his insistence that sociology foundationally requires absence of concern with individual psychological or biological characteristics. Second, I provide a critical or Left reading of current biosocial and sociobiological research. Contrary to the prevailing orthodoxy in sociology that a biosocial or evolutionary perspective is inherently conservative or Social Darwinist in its implications, I show that the possibilities for a critical sociobiology have been woefully undertheorized and misunderstood by mainstream sociology. Utilizing biosocial evidence need not produce the misguided and conceptually muddled analysis of best sellers such as Richard Herrnstein and Charles Murray's *The Bell Curve* (1994). On the contrary, by assuming a necessary link between biosocial evidence and reactionary political positions, social scientists have ignored vast quantities of data which suggest the importance of human commonalities. A biocritical sociology is long overdue.

After demonstrating the relevance of a biocritical approach for sociological analysis, I will then demonstrate its utility in a re-reading of the communitarian works of Robert Bellah et al. (1985, 1991). The utilization of a biocritical perspective expands the possibility of discourse and "spirit of community" that Bellah and other communitarians seek (Etzioni, 1993). Unfortunately, the ghost of Durkheim haunts Bellah's *Habits of the Heart* (1985). Broadening the range of privileged sociological data would enable the communitarians to more adequately respond to their critics (Phillips, 1993). Sociology most certainly does not need an updated, foundationalist version of Newtonian physics. But a contemporary understanding of evolutionary psychology and biology would do wonders for our hubristic myopia.

This book demonstrates the necessity of expanding the boundaries of what is "normal" or taken for granted within sociology. It demonstrates the importance of utilizing what William Durham (1991) terms a "coevolutionary" perspective. It shows that one aspect of major importance in this perspective for sociology is its relevance for any discussion of human needs. Including the concept of human needs in sociological discourse enables me to develop a biocritical approach to sociological analysis.

I will show that "biocritique" is one potentially helpful way of approaching— not resolving—some of the major conflicts which seem to have paralyzed much of sociology. I emphasize "approach" as opposed to "resolution" because I believe, along with John Dewey and the pragmatists, that knowledge is best viewed as a *process* which is emergent over time. It is never complete and should be linguistically understood as both a verb and a noun (West, 1989; Diggins, 1994). I assume that there are no eternal, a priori verities and that sociology should develop a pragmatic, biosocial approach to knowledge which takes into account a wide range of material neglected or ignored by many social scientists.

In Robert Trivers' seminal article "The Evolution of Reciprocal Altruism" (1971), one discovers a wide range of interdisciplinary references. Presumably Trivers, even though he is a biologist and the article was published in the *Quarterly Review of Biology*, feels free to refer to whatever source he believes has merit. Included in this classic piece of biosocial theorizing are references to Alvin Gouldner, Robert Friedrichs (sociology), Gabriel Almond (political science), Albert Bandura, Fritz Heider, Lawrence Kohlberg (psychology), Richard Lee, Ivan DeVore, Ashley Montagu (anthropology), Anatol Rapoport (game theory), and Jean Jacques Rousseau (philosophy), as well as the expected references to biologists and ethologists. It is a singularly catholic list.

Sociologists, however, have often felt that one could, with impunity, ignore the biological. In what authors Stephen Sanderson and Lee Ellis say is the only study of "theroetical preferences of sociologists...undertaken since the onset of the present state of threoretical fragmentation in the mid-1960s," we find that 1.9% of the respondents listed "sociobiology" as their "primary theoretical perspective" and *none* listed "evolutionism" (Sanderson and Ellis, 1992, p. 31). As a "secondary theoretical perspective," 1.2% indicated "evolutionism" and one additional person answered "sociobiology." Altogether, the percentage of sociogists indicating either a "primary" or "secondary" preference for "sociobiology" was 2.5% and for "evolutionism" 1.2% (Sanderson and Ellis, 1992, pp. 32–33). Very few sociologists have seriously considered the kinds of information I analyze in this book.

Indeed the suggestion has often been made that sociology as a discipline requires a kind of intellectual bifurcation: nature/nurture, innate/learned or biological/social. Durkheim, for example, argued that "social" facts "should not be confused with biological phenomena" and that "if...we begin with the individual, we shall be able to understand nothing of what takes place in the group" (Durkheim, 1966 [1895], pp. 3, 104)

Leslie White argued in *The Evolution of Culture* that social analysis would not "be aided in the slightest degree by taking the biological organism into consideration," and that, furthermore "the biological factor is irrelevant, and consequently, it should be disregarded" (1959, p. 14). William Ogburn presented the crux of the sociological argument with his seemingly irrefutable statement that "a change cannot be explained by a constant" (Ogburn, 1964, p. 22). That is, since the basic physiology/predispositions of *Homo sapiens* as a species— what sociobiologists call our "biogram"— changes very slowly compared to cultural change, one cannot explain a change (i.e., cultural evolution) by a constant (i.e., genetic inheritance). What could be more obvious? Dennis Wrong's suggestion that "*In the beginning there is the body*" is either ignored or considered sociologically trivial (Wrong, 1961, p. 191, emphasis in original).

It has been over seventy years since John Dewey argued in *Reconstruction in Philosophy* (1920). that one should always be suspicious of apodictic pronouncements.[1] I will argue in this book that the current sociological rejection of the biosocial—a kind of aversive ideological tropism towards any biological consideration—is not intellectually warranted. Durkheim's insistence on "the dualism of human nature" (Durkheim, 1960 [1914]) is unthinkingly imbibed by sociological neophytes and has contributed to the contemporary intellectual isolation of sociology. As indicated by his references to Anatol Rapoport (1965, 1967), Robert Trivers was able to quickly determine the relevance of game theory and probability theory for his discussion of reciprocal altruism. Trivers' reasoning was later extended and popularized by Robert Axelrod (1984). One wonders how quickly sociologists would perceive the sociological relevance of research carried out in such divergent disciplines.

In *The Sociology of Knowledge* (1958, p. 156) Werner Stark refers to "the fallacy of *pars pro toto*," of "taking the part for the whole." The same phenomenon has also been termed "the synechdochaic fallacy" or "the error of nothing but" (Griffin, 1992, p. 118). This suggests that knowledge is always obtained in a fallible and incremental fashion. Different perspectives provide different (temporary) "truths." Knowledge is emergent and not predetermined or teleologically foreordained. The necessary result, as Dewey pointed out in *The Quest for Certainty* (1929), is that the accumulation of "warranted knowledge" is an unending process. By its knee-jerk rejection of the biosocial, however, sociology *ipso facto* excludes potentially relevant information. What we are left with is "taking the part for the whole" or "theory" by way of presuppositional fiat.

Advocates of a biosocial perspective are aware of what might be termed "Ogburn's Theorem" (i.e., "You can't explain a change with a constant"). Edward O. Wilson, who is unquestionably the best-known (or perhaps notorious) of the "sociobiologists" noted in 1978 that it was "demonstrably not the case" that contemporary hunter-gatherers differed genetically in any significant way from people in "advanced" industrial nations (Wilson, 1978, p. 35). One could not, therefore, explain differences between the "primitive" and the "modern" on the basis of genetic evolution. Wilson knows this. What, then, is he trying to do? As he clearly states in *On Human Nature*: "The sociobiological hypothesis does not therefore account for differences among societies, but it can explain why human beings differ from other mammals" (1978, p. 160). Wilson is trying to get at what ethologists call "species-specific characteristics." What, in other words, do humans *have in common*? A great deal of the mutual incomprehension between sociology and biology relates to this simple difference in objectives. Sociologists and cultural anthropologists are normally looking for differences between groups and cultures. A bioevolutionary perspective looks for commonalities (Brown, 1991). The differing logics and paradigms produce distrust and what might be termed a kind of "out-of-sight-out-of-mind" sociological autarky.

I argue throughout this book that the results of a presumed biological/ social binary in the explanation of behavior has produced many negative results for sociological theory and analysis. If one wants an empirical science, one should look at things empirically, as well as with a useful and adequate theoretical perspective.

According to Robert Merton, a "theoretical framework" indicates "types" of variables which are "taken into account" (Merton, 1967, p. 142). The "chief function" of a theoretical framework "is to provide a general context for inquiry" (Merton, 1967, p. 142). Merton, for example, refers specifically to Durkheim's admonition to only use "social facts" to explain other "social facts," as a kind of macro-methodological statement at the highest level of generalization. In this book I argue that a theoretical framework which excludes all biological evidence is limiting itself unnecessarily in several fundamental ways with respect to its taken-for-granted assumptions concerning the etiology of "social facts."

Referring to a "familiar dispute" in sociobiology, Philip Kitcher suggests that the two theoretical extremes in the "nature/nurture" controversy are a genetic "iron grip" on behavior and "no genetic constraints at all" (Kitcher, 1993, p. 164). He suggests that "As soon as the extreme positions are articulated, they are quickly disavowed: everybody agrees that there are two important determinants" (Kitcher, 1993, p. 164).

"Everybody," however, most certainly does not agree that "there are two important determinants" of social action. In particular, as suggested above, Durkheim believed sociologists should feel free to ignore all biological considerations as irrelevant to social facts by definition. I maintain that the consideration of biological evidence by sociologists will lead to what Kitcher terms "conceptual" and "explanatory" progress (Kitcher, 1993, pp. 95–112). Durkheim's insistence that sociology is a discipline or an approach to knowledge "*sui generis*" leads to a theoretical and empirical cul-de-sac.

What difference does it make if we actually accept Wrong's idea that sociology should take into account individual biological and psychological characteristics? (Wrong, 1961). What sociological difference does it make, as Edward Wilson argues in *On Human Nature*, that people *as a species* do not accept slavery, that "slaves under great stress insist on behaving like human beings instead of slave ants, gibbons, mandrills, or any other species"? (Wilson, 1978, p. 84). What difference does it make if, in our research, we *look for* commonalities as opposed to differences? In the discussion which follows, I will show the importance and relevance of these questions and issues for sociological analysis.

I also argue that the utilization of biological evidence provides one way of moving forward on such seemingly intractable problems in sociology as the question of "values" or the "fact/value" dichotomy and the debate in social problems over social constructionism. One of the virtues of a biocritical approach to sociological analysis is a rejection of simplistic binary reasoning. Part of the problem with the a priori rejection of biological reasoning by sociologists is the resulting Cartesian split between "nature" and "nurture" or "fact" and "value." One of the principal objectives of this book is a demonstration that the utilization of biosocial evidence provides a potentially useful way of moving beyond current theoretical and empirical controversies.

There have been a number of works which have stressed the desirability of a more naturalistic approach for social science. In my initial chapter I will look at the logic of a biosocial approach to sociology. What is the "face validity" of biological or evolutionary considerations? *Why* should we be concerned with the biosocial? What types of research have been carried out in this area? What has the most potential for utilization by sociologists? Looking at specific areas of prior research, what do they suggest with respect to potential sociological applications?

Having established the potential, if generally unexploited, relevance of the biosocial for sociology, I will then examine two works by Edward O. Wilson which might be taken as "exemplars" (Kuhn, 1970) for the field of "sociobiology" (Wilson, 1975, 1978). It is important to examine the work of Wilson in detail, because the "politically correct" reaction to his work within social science obscures both its positive and negative aspects. Any examination of sociobiology needs to take Wilson into account. I will then critically examine the supposedly invariant relationship between a biosocial approach and political conservatism (Hubbard and Wald, 1993; Lerner, 1992).

One sociologist who has examined the work of Wilson suggests that Wilson's sociobiology should be seen as "natural theology" (Kayc, 1986). Wilson, for example, argues that, assuming the truth of sociobiology "challenges the traditional belief that we cannot deduce values from facts or moral prescriptions from scientific information" (Kaye, 1986, p. 99). Accepting the accuracy of this position clearly challenges the positivistic shibboleth that there is an absolute or qualitative distinction between "facts" and "values" (Bryant, 1985) and suggests that there is an important relationship between sociobiology and what has been termed "evolutionary ethics" (Nitecki and Nitecki, 1993).

In his definitive study *Darwin and the Emergence of Evolutionary Theories of Mind and Behavior* (1987), Robert Richards outlines a sophisticated case for "evolutionary ethics" (Richards, 1987, pp. 595–627). His arguments have received extensive examination and debate (Hughes, 1986; Williams, 1990; Nitecki and Nitecki (1993), as well as commentary on the commentary by Richards (1986a, 1986b, 1989, 1993). If his argument is valid, it would seem to have extremely significant implications for sociology and serve as a validation of the importance of evolutionary and biological considerations for the social sciences. I will therefore look at the strengths and weaknesses of Richards' evolutionary perspective in some detail.

Lacking in almost all sociological discourse, as well as not being adequately elaborated by Richards, is any consideration of specific human needs. Basing the discussion primarily on the works of Braybrooke (1987), Nussbaum (1992, 1993), and Midgley (1978, 1983a, 1983b, 1985), I argue that this is the key theoretical move if sociology is to advance beyond senseless polemics and develop a comprehensive biosocial, empirically warranted perspective. Adding the concept of human needs to the biosocial perspective provides the opportunity of a theoretical "site" or "space" for my development of biocritique.

I also argue that a biocritical perspective based on a biosocial elaboration of human needs enables us to usefully analyze current controversies over social constructionism and the definition of social problems. While it appears from a review of the social problems literature that opposing viewpoints are at a theoretical dead end, I will demonstrate that a biocritical perspective allows us to think about and examine these issues and go beyond approaches that now give the impression of being irreconcilable "polar opposites" (Miller and Holstein, 1993).

Having analyzed the basic elements of a biocritical perspective, I will then put it to use with a detailed re-reading of the well-known work of Robert Bellah and his co-authors in *Habits of the Heart* (1985). Bellah is a major proponent of the communitarian approach to social theory (MacIntyre, 1984; Etzioni, 1993). It is my contention that biocritique provides a much-needed theoretical and analytical extension of the kinds of criticisms of individualism and contemporary society made by Bellah et al. The re-reading of Bellah will provide a case study of the utility of the biocritical approach and its relationship to a specific sociological tradition.

The biocritical perspective usefully extends the analysis of the authors of *Habits of the Heart*. It helps to concretize, and, as I will demonstrate, to further elaborate and justify their criticisms (i.e., their critique of individualistic self-absorption; their discussions of our lack of "commonality" and/or "communities of memory"). The complementarity of Bellah's and the biocritical approach is in itself a useful example of *extending the boundaries of the permissible* with respect to presumed disciplinary "territories" or research techniques. A broader and more flexible orientation towards the explanation of human behavior is warranted. A fresh reexamination of biosocial evidence by sociology is long overdue.

Sociology, like all other academic disciplines, will continue to develop and change. The kind of "disciplinary pessimism" evident in current works on "the sociology of sociology" is not justified (Horowitz, 1993; Faia, 1993).[2] I will show in this book that the utilization of a naturalistic, biosocial, and biocritical perspective is one way of proceeding which offers much hope for the reduction of our current intellectual ethnocentrism.

The use of biological and evolutionary reasoning need not imply an atavistic or misogynistic ideology which should be summarily dismissed by all "proper" sociologists. There is no necessary relationship between political conservatism and biological or evolutionary arguments. Sociologists, however, often assume the opposite. This *precludes by definition* the sociological consideration of biosocial data. In a recent survey of the "theoretical and political perspectives of American sociologists in the 1990s," over three-fourths of the respondents identified themselves as "liberal, radical, or somewhere in between." Only 3% of the sample identified themselves as "conservatives" (Sanderson and Ellis, 1992, p. 34).

If all "biological" reasoning is labeled as *ipso facto* "conservative," it is easy to understand why sociology as a discipline has almost entirely ignored biosocial perspectives. A basic objective of this book is to demonstrate that biological and evolutionary reasoning are by no means necessarily "reactionary." Disconnecting the supposedly inevitable biological/conservative political relationship would allow sociologists to more adequately consider the importance of biosocial logic and evidence. I argue throughout this book that we need to move in that direction.

I

THE THEORETICAL AND PRACTICAL UTILITY OF A BIOSOCIAL PERSPECTIVE

A. THE BIOSOCIAL PERSPECTIVE

In her extended discussion on "the roots of human nature," philosopher Mary Midgley has argued that "*What counts as a fact depends on the concepts you use, on the questions you ask*" (Midgley, 1978, p. 5, emphasis in original). By ignoring what has been termed a "biosocial" or a "coevolutionary" perspective (Fox, 1989; Durham, 1991), sociology excludes by definition areas of research which need to be taken into account in any adequate explanation of human behavior. Pierre L. van den Berghe has suggested that the sociological aversion to biology "is in large part *trained* incompetence" and that "sociologists are not merely oblivious" towards biology but that "they are militantly and proudly ignorant. They *know* biology to be irrelevant to their interests, so they are determined not to make the effort to learn about it" (Van den Berghe, 1990, p. 177, emphasis in original).

Sociologists "know" about the presumed irrelevance of biology to sociology for several major reasons which have historically been taken-for-granted assumptions of the discipline:

1. Sociologists and anthropologists study culture as a reality *sui generis*.
2. Each culture is distinct. Cultural evolution causes and explains each culture's differences and unique qualities.
3. Biological explanations of behavior have been proposed in the past and have resulted in political conservatism, Social Darwinism, and, ultimately, genocide.
4. Any "critical" sociology should, therefore, exclude a biosocial level of analysis for both theoretical and political (i.e., "politically correct") reasons.

Beginning with Durkheim, sociology has viewed the cultural level of analysis as its exclusive domain. In carving out a distinct space for sociological discourse, the discipline justified its own existence: We are, claimed Durkheim, dealing with a *qualitatively distinct* method of structuring reality which no one else employs. Sociology should be a separate and epistemologically distinct academic discipline (Durkheim, 1966 [1895]). Its special emphasis was to analyze and understand what William Graham Sumner called our "folkways" and "mores": all our taken-for-granted cultural traditions and habits (Sumner, 1960 [1906]).

It seemed self-evident to Sumner, for example, that cultural differences are what distinguished every society from each other and that the subject matter of sociology consisted of cross-cultural comparisons of these differing characteristics. Sumner also proposed a tautological definition of what was later to be called "cultural relativism": "Everything in the mores of a time and place must be regarded as justified with regard to that time and place" (Sumner, 1960 [1906], p. 65). Due to the fact that "the standards of good and right are in the mores," it follows that "for the people of a time and place, their own mores are always good" (Sumner, 1960 [1906], p. 65). Sumner, however, found it difficult to consistently follow his own definitions. In what was a typical example of Social Darwinist rhetoric, he proclaimed that:

So long as we do not know whether acquired modifications are inheritable or not, we are not prepared to elaborate a policy of marriage which can be dogmatically taught or civilly enforced. This much, however, is certain—the interests of society are more at stake in these things than in anything else. All other projects of reform and amelioration are trivial compared with the interests which lie in the propagation of the species, if these can be so treated as to breed out predispositions to evils of body and mind, and to breed in vigor of mind and body. (Sumner, 1960 [1906], p. 414)

So much for "their own mores are always good." It appeared to Sumner that our "breeding" mores were significantly deficient. Cultural relativism evidently did not begin at home. Some "projects of reform" are "trivial" and others are absolutely necessary, no matter whatever the current "mores" of those involved. Sumner's words also demonstrate the Social Darwinist implications of his presumably "biological" approach to social reform. He was clearly advocating a kind of eugenics policy to "cure" social problems. We see here an early example of why a biosocial orientation is considered so undesirable today.   Many contemporary sociologists seem to feel that Sumner's political positions are necessarily reflected in any consideration of biological evidence.   They are mistaken.   By ignoring contemporary developments in the biological sciences we are unnecessarily distorting and limiting our sociological analyses and, most importantly, trivializing or ignoring cross-cultural similarities.   By concentrating on the particular, we ignore what Roland Robertson has termed "global culture" or "globalization" (Robertson, 1992).

Perhaps it is no longer true, as Ruth Benedict argued in *Patterns of Culture*, that "Social thinking...has no more important task before it than that of taking adequate account of cultural relativity" (Benedict, 1934, p. 239).   In a time of increasingly violent ultra-nationalism and "ethnic cleansing," the political implications of biosocial approaches which stress human commonalities are not the Social Darwinist shibboleths of William Graham Sumner but a new appreciation of transcultural similarities and common concerns.

Anthropologist John Tooby and psychologist Leda Cosmides maintain that recent research in evolutionary psychology and other disciplines has strengthened arguments for commonalities:

> There are strong reasons to believe that selection usually tends to make complex adaptations universal or nearly universal, so humans must share a complex, species-typical and species-specific architecture of adaptations, however much variation there might be in minor, superficial...traits.   As long-lived sexual reproducers, complex adaptations would be destroyed by the random process of sexual recombination every generation if the genes that underlie our complex adaptations varied from individual to individual. (Tooby and Cosmides, 1992, p. 38)

This logic of the biosocial is lacking in most current sociology.   Its implications are contrary to much current thinking.   Sociology has acted as a kind of theoretical flashlight illuminating one small area and ignoring whatever was outside its "cultural" beam of light (Degler, 1991, pp. 187–211).   If, as a popular introductory text tells us, sociology is defined as "the systematic study of human social interaction" (Brinkerhoff and White, 1991, p. 4), one should be prepared to take into account whatever influences that interaction. One may realistically argue that it is time to broaden the beam. As Donald Griffin argues in *Animal Minds*, "Recognizing our ignorance is a necessary first step toward reducing it" (Griffin, 1992, p. 5).

There have been several kinds of research which have stressed the importance of biological considerations for reaching any adequate understanding of human behavior. There are, for example, the entire range of ethological studies which suggest that naturally occurring animal behavior may offer analogies or insights into human social interaction (Darwin, 1981 [1871]; 1965 [1872]). By the 1950s, the work of Nikolaus Tinbergen and Karl Lorenz gained a popular audience (Evans, 1975; Lorenz, 1952). By 1973, their work, along with Karl von Frisch's studies of the "language" of the honeybee, resulted in Nobel Prizes for all three men, even though "ethology" was not a recognized category for awards (Degler, 1991, p. 227). A number of popular best-sellers using the ethological perspective appeared during the same time period (Ardrey, 1966; Morris, 1967; Tiger, 1969).

More recent ethological work avoids the simplistic and unsupported generalizations made by writers like Ardrey (Kuper, 1994; Dawkins, M., 1993). There is, for example, the remarkable volume by Dorothy Cheney and Robert Seyfarth called *How Monkeys See the World* (1990). While this book contains a great deal of information about other ethological research, it is principally a recounting of their thirteen-year study of vervet monkeys in Kenya. Cheney and Seyfarth discovered that vervets have specific vocalizations indicating the approach of different predators (Cheney and Seyfarth, 1990, pp. 139–74). An encounter with a leopard produces a loud bark, and the monkeys run up trees. Sighting an eagle results in short coughs, and the monkeys run into bushes. A snake produces another distinct call, and the monkeys stand on their legs and look down towards the ground. Tape recorded playback of the different sounds produced similar responses compared to naturally occurring behaviors (i.e., the "leopard call" caused the monkeys to run up trees). Cheney and Seyfarth also varied a number of their experiments chronologically and concluded that "Vocal developments in primates exhibit many parallels with the early stages of speech development in young children" (Cheney and Seyfarth, 1990, p. 138).

Language, of course, is one of the principal attributes which has historically been viewed as an inviolate difference in kind between humans and all other forms of life. Cheney and Seyfarth's work suggests that the distinction may be more gradualistic or part of a continuum. Sue Savage-Rumbaugh's recently successful attempt at teaching a pygmy chimp to make stone tools strongly suggests the same (Savage-Rumbaugh and Lewin, 1994). If that is in fact the case, it is clear that ethological research may have more utility in suggesting analogies or homologies than most sociologists recognize. Part of the problem, as Griffin notes, is simple ignorance. Sociologists simply do not know what is being done in current ethological research. We "know" we do not need to know because humankind is presumably defined solely by its cultural activities.

Anthropologist Donald Brown has suggested that our reluctance to accept the potential usefulness of ethological work for the social sciences is ultimately due to a profound historical and cultural bias. He argues that the nature/nurture dichotomy is related to the flesh/spirit distinction which has been a feature of Western thought for millennia (Brown, 1991, p. 86). The idealization of the "spirit" and the denigration of the "flesh" suggests that we have little to learn from "mere brutes." Brown believes that this material "denigration" shapes Western thought to this day. As Joseph Wood Krutch has observed, however, a continuum between humans and other species may just as easily be viewed as conferring a *more* impressive status on other beings as opposed to necessarily denigrating humans (Krutch, 1954, pp. 98–99).

Sociology needs to incorporate a new reading of the work of such writers as Griffin (1992), Marian Dawkins (1993), and Francine Patterson and Eugene Linden (1981). One of the reasons for the lack of biosocial evidence in sociology is a taken-for-granted assumption that the differences between "us" and "them" are without question *differences in kind*. It does no good, according to this line of reasoning, to utilize ethological data because the differences between species are so great that any comparison is thereby invalid. As Leslie White argued, a necessary and sufficient "social science" is always and only "the science of culture" (1969). What I am suggesting, however, is that many such "differences," as they are enumerated by social scientists, are merely the result of unexamined, taken-for-granted assumptions and reflect a nearly total ignorance of developments in such fields as ethology, biology, and genetics (Cavalieri and Singer, 1993). Mary Midgley (1983a, p. 11) traces such "reasoning" back to Descartes, "who identified the human soul or consciousness so completely with reason as to conclude that animals could not be conscious at all, and were in fact just automata." Many social scientists believe that a similar "Cartesian Gap" still obtains today. Such a "gap" also helps to define an avowedly distinct subject matter for sociology, thereby providing yet another example of Marx's insistence that ideologies inevitably serve one's own self-interest.

Sociologists might ponder the significance of recent research in molecular biology and DNA hybridization which has shown that the genetic distance between humans and both the common and pygmy chimpanzee is 1.6% (Diamond, 1992, pp. 20 –24). As Jared Diamond notes, "The remaining 98.4% of DNA is just normal chimp DNA. For example, our principal hemoglobin...is identical in all of its 287 units with chimp hemoglobin" (Diamond, 1992, p. 23). As measured by genetic similarity or distance from a common ancestor, there is a closer relationship between chimpanzees and humans than between chimpanzees and gorillas (Diamond, 1992, pp. 23 –24). As Richard Dawkins (1993) and R.I.M. Dunbar (1993) have argued, it is clear that taxonomic classifications are not based solely on logic, but also on anthropocentric considerations and what Dawkins terms the "discontinuous mind" (Dawkins, 1993, pp. 81 –82). We exaggerate the "gaps" and refuse to see obvious shared characteristics. One of the principal achievements of anthropologists earlier in this century was the description of "ethnocentrism" and the valuation of all cultural differences (Degler, 1991, pp. 59 –104). Today sociology and anthropology demonstrate an opposite kind of bias which might be termed "commonophobia" or the fear of identifying the common transcultural similarities of diverse peoples.

Given the degree of genetic similarity between humans and other species, the ethological perspective has, I believe, more "face validity" than many sociologists recognize. In their history of evolution, Johanson and Edey note that "The interior of the cell revealed a wonderful unity in all living things; all use the same four bases to make the same 20 amino acids. The triplet code is the same.... That unity speaks with a thundering voice for the validity of evolution theory" (Edey and Johanson, 1989, p. 277). It seemed obvious to Joseph Wood Krutch that "If our consciousness 'evolved' it must have evolved from something in some degree like it. If we have thoughts and feelings, it seems at least probable that something analogous exists in those from whom we are descended" (Krutch, 1956, pp. x-xi). Current research on our closest relatives certainly suggests as much.

We have already seen the remarkable genetic similarities between the chimpanzee and what Diamond calls "the third chimpanzee" or "the human animal" (Diamond, 1992). For example, a number of researchers have made impressive, longitudinal efforts to teach various apes American Sign Language or ASL (Griffin, 1992). These have included chimpanzees (Fouts and Fouts, 1993), gorillas (Patterson and Lindsen, 1981; Patterson and Gordon, 1993) and orangutans (Miles, 1993). The results have called into question the linguistic Cartesian split assumed to be self-evident for so many years in the Western intellectual tradition.

It is true that much controversy surrounds this research, and some of those working in the field have tempered their original enthusiasm and questioned their earlier results (Terrace, 1979). Controversy surrounds interpretations of the results and the similarity or dissimilarity of ASL used by other species compared to human speech. It is clear, however, that apes are capable of doing something which is more complex and indicates in some sense more intelligence than what they have been given credit for in the past. As Mary Midgley has remarked, "*if they are not talking, what are they doing?*" (Midgley, 1978, p. 216, emphasis in original). That is, even if there are obvious differences between written/spoken languages as used by human beings and ASL as used by chimps/gorillas/orangutans, what is it that these apes are doing when they use sign language if not in some sense communicating?

Perhaps the best-known example of this research is that of Francine Patterson with the female gorilla Koko (Patterson and Linden, 1981). Since 1972 she has worked constantly with Koko. From September 1972, to May 1977 she administered various IQ tests to Koko including the Cattell Infant Intelligence Scale, the Peabody Picture Vocabulary Test, and the Stanford-Binet Intelligence Test (Patterson and Linden, 1981, pp. 126–130; Patterson and Gordon 1993, pp. 58–62). Koko has consistently scored between 70 and 90 on different IQ scales. She has a working vocabulary of about 500 signs which she combines in statements of three to six signs in length (Patterson and Gordon, 1993, p. 59). She engages in "self-directed behavior in front of a mirror," "lies to avoid the consequences of her own misbehavior," and "becomes fidgety and uncomfortable when asked to discuss her own death" (Patterson and Gordon, 1993, pp. 58–59).

Washoe, the famous chimp raised by R.A. and B.T. Gardner, spontaneously taught ASL to young chimps and used signs to communicate with other adult chimpanzees (Fouts and Fouts, 1993, pp. 31–32). The Fouts, who succeeded the Gardners in their work with Washoe, in one study "recorded over 5,200 instances of chimpanzee to chimpanzee signing" (Fouts and Fouts, 1993, p. 33). The videos were analyzed by category, and it was found that "food" was *not* a prevalent topic, accounting for only 5% of the conversations. Eighty-eight percent were in the categories of "play," "social interaction," and "reassurance" (Fouts and Fouts, 1993, p. 33).

After not seeing the Gardners for a period of eleven years, Washoe, when they finally did visit, "looked at the Gardners and signed their name signs.... Then Washoe signed 'COME MRS G' to Beatrice Gardner and led her into an adjoining room and began to play a game with her that she had not been observed to play since she was a five-year-old" (Fouts and Fouts, 1993, pp. 37 –38). A lack of retained memory images was seen as part of the "essential" distinction between "man" and animals in the Western intellectual tradition (Fouts and Fouts, 1993, pp. 37 –38). Washoe is clearly an outstanding counter example.

H. Lyn White Miles has carried out another long-range project with orangutans. Her work is particularly interesting insofar as this ape is believed to be less closely related to us genetically than gorillas or chimpanzees (Miles, 1993, p. 44). Miles argues, however, that orangutans in "gestation period, brain hemispheric asymmetry, characteristics of dentition, sexual physiology, copulatory behavior, hormonal levels, hair pattern, mammary gland placement and insightful style of cognition" are closer to humans than are the other apes (Miles, 1993, pp. 44 –45). The orangutan Chantek eventually used 150 different signs "forming a vocabulary similar to that of a very young child" (Miles, 1993, p. 47). He learned to be deceptive, to use a mirror for grooming, to paint, and to sign for things which were not present. He developed "sign-speech correspondences without intentional training" (Miles, pp. 46 –50). Additional research has recorded "altruistic behavior in rhesus monkeys" (Masserman, Wechkin and Terris, 1964), "cooperative communication" between chimpanzees required to achieve a common task (Griffin, 1992, pp. 227 –230), and pygmy chimpanzees (bonobos) at the Yerkes Laboratory in Atlanta "who have learned to use a combination of gestures and the Yerkes keyboard to achieve a fluent two-way communication with their human companions" (Griffin, 1992, p. 231).

The presumed line of demarcation between "us" and "them" grows weaker by the moment. Indeed, like the Maginot Line in France, it represents the illusion of collective human security—safe from infestation from the "beasts from below." Although the arguments against a biosocial perspective are, I believe, as ineffective as the Maginot Line proved to be in wartime, they still linger and hinder our ability to understand and explain human interaction. To the extent that current research demonstrates similar capabilities and commonalities *between* species, the argument against using interspecies analogies in social science is weakened. If, for example, the great apes are much closer to us in certain abilities than was previously recognized, it is more difficult logically and theoretically to exclude all research on apes as being inherently useless for the explanation of human behavior. The face validity of ethological studies is enhanced. Perhaps, as Midgley argues (1978, 1985, 1992), we still need to learn to ask relevant questions when conducting social science research.

The biosocial approach to social analysis assumes that human beings, as is the case with all other species, have an evolutionary past (Darwin, 1981 [1871]; Leakey and Lewin, 1977; Willis, 1989; Mayr, 1991; Lloyd, 1994). The principal force behind evolutionary change is "natural selection" which Mayr defines as the argument that:

> change comes about through the abundant production of genetic variation in every generation. The relatively few individuals who survive, owing to a particularly well-adapted combination of inheritable characters, give rise to the next generation. (Mayr, 1991, p. 37)

The result, in the famous phrase coined by Herbert Spencer, is "the survival of the fittest" (Rachels, 1990, p. 30). According to Darwin in his *Autobiography*, the final inspiration for his theory came from social science, not biology:

> In October 1838, that is fifteen months after I had begun my systematic enquiry, I happened to read for amusement Malthus on *Population*, and being well prepared to appreciate the struggle for existence which everywhere goes on from long-continued observation of the habits of animals and plants, it at once struck me that under these circumstances favorable variations would tend to be preserved, and unfavorable ones to be destroyed. The result of this would be the formulation of new species. (Darwin, 1958 [1887] p. 120)

Although there has been considerable debate over the "real" origins of Darwin's theories (Eiseley, 1961; Himmelfarb, 1968; Gruber, 1974; Richards, 1987), let us, to some extent, accept his own account. Surely it would be difficult to find a more momentous example in modern intellectual history of the utility of interdisciplinary study. The Theory of Natural Selection, which, while endlessly debated in its details (Gould, 1977; Eldredge, 1985), is the foundation of modern biological theory, was, at least in part, inspired by Malthus's early version of *The Population Bomb* (Ehrlich, 1971). Those who argue that sociology needs to broaden its "traditional" or "cultural" boundaries are in very good company. The ability to *think the unthinkable* was clearly instrumental in Darwin's success. For example, he was able to accept the possibility that the common earthworm showed signs of intelligence and carried out experiments to test "the mental powers of worms" (Rachels, 1990, p. 134). Sociologists are not inclined to demonstrate such presuppositional flexibility. What is defined as "hard-headed" or "realistic" is often merely narrowness of vision.

A number of social scientists have argued that a more naturalistic or biosocial approach to social science is absolutely essential for any realistic explanation of human behavior (Mazur and Robertson, 1972; Van den Berghe, 1975; Konner, 1982; Eaton, Shostak and Konner, 1988; Brown, 1991; Degler, 1991; Wilson, 1990; Durham, 1991; Crippin, 1992, 1994). They argue that sociology should take seriously the implications of evolutionary history with respect to *Homo sapiens*. Consider, for example, the fact that "100,000 generations of humans have been hunters and gatherers; 500 generations have been agriculturalists; ten have lived in the industrial age; and only one has been exposed to the world of computers" (Eaton, Shostak and Konner, 1988, p. 26). Using an evolutionary time frame implies that *whatever* adaptations developed throughout our evolutionary history may have little relationship to the situations we encounter today.

The rate and magnitude of technological/social change is exceptionally rapid compared to changes in the human genotype. This implies the possibility of what has been termed "the discordance hypothesis," which suggests "that nearly all our biochemistry and physiology are fine-tuned to conditions of life that existed before 10,000 years ago" (Eaton, Shostak and Konner, 1988, pp. 38 –68). The biosocial perspective suggests that within contemporary society our wants may have very little relationships to our needs (Fox, 1989, pp. 46–47). As I will show later in the chapter on "human needs" and social constructionism, recognition of this possibility allows us to approach the area of "social problems" with something other than complete cultural relativism (Edel, 1955, 1980; Midgley, 1993).

The biosocial perspective argues for the similarity of human cultures. Robin Fox believes that social scientists have been suffering from "ethnographic dazzle" (Fox, 1989, p. 18). We have been taught to always look for *differences* between cultures and tend to ignore similarities or take them for granted. Having earned an M.A. in Latin American Studies, I know about the differences *between* Latin American countries and between all of them and the United States. The economies are different. The religions are different. The languages are different. The customs are different. The histories are different. "Master/servant" relationships are different. What Edward Hall made famous as "the silent language" or the taken-for-granted assumptions of each country are different (Hall, 1959). And yet we tend to see only what we are looking for.

Marriage customs differ cross-culturally, and yet every culture has some system of marriage. "Biology cannot explain the differences," says the cultural anthropologist. One cannot explain a variable with a constant. But perhaps sex and our biology help to explain why *every* culture experiences marriage, as well as adultery. As Fox argues, "are societies and cultures really so different at the level of forms and processes?" (Fox, 1989, p. 18). Don't people everywhere live in families, raise children, and try to make a living? If we look for cross-cultural similarities, won't they too be obvious?

The biosocial perspective suggests that such similarities are indeed obvious and that they are ultimately a result of our specific evolutionary history. Writers like Fox argue that the presumed culture/nature binary in social science has caused a great deal of harm and misunderstanding. Culture is constitutive of our evolutionary background and species-specific characteristics. It is the name for a process or behavior which ultimately depends on our specialized brain (Fox, 1989, p. 28; Restak, 1984, 1991; Wills, 1993). For human beings, separating "nature" and "culture" is like separating "dog" and "barking" or "fish" and "swimming." The fundamental reason human beings share similarities is that they share a similar biosocial evolutionary history. Perhaps it would be more obvious if biosocial was always written— like Foucault's knowledge/power binary—as bio/social (Foucault, 1979). The terms are constitutive of each other and are inseparable. Humankind shares this condition. We are therefore capable of recognition of our common characteristics. We perceive similarities along with differences.

As was originally stated by Franklin Giddings, "The original and elementary subjective fact in society is the *consciousness of kind*" (Giddings, 1986, p. 17, emphasis in original). This occurs when an individual "recognizes another conscious being of like kind with itself" (Giddings, 1896, p. 17). (Giddings also assumed that "Human nature is the preeminently social nature" and "the cycle of social causation begins and ends in the physical process" [Giddings, 1896, pp. 20, 225]). In spite of all the prevailing ethnocentrism, racism, and sexism, we all may potentially "recognize" each other because we are all members of the same species. In a phenomenological sense, it is ultimately the biological similarities of "the other" which lead to a "consciousness of kind."

If "the other" is considered more and more divergent—for whatever reasons—"consciousness of kind decreases. For example, Michael Root has made the interesting observation that "functional" analysis in social science is related to the "strangeness" of the group being observed (Root, 1993, pp. 78–99). If the "other" is similar to ourselves, we tend to accept *their own version* of their motives and actions (an "emic explanation"). If the group is much "different"—the proverbial Trobriand Islanders—we use a "functional" or "etic" approach. "They" give explanations, but not the "real" or "right" explanations for their behavior. Hence the "real" reasons are supplied by the anthropologist. As the degree of cultural differences increase, the less likely we are to develop a consciousness of kind or accept an emic explanation.

Conversely, circumstances sometimes force recognition. An extension or transcultural expansion of consciousness of kind is brought about by unusual conditions. In emergency situations, our perceptions of "otherness" dramatically decrease, and our recognition of common characteristics grows exponentially. Consider, for example, the French during World War II who hid downed American flyers. Discovery of this "crime" was punishable by death during the Nazi regime. Consider the Quakers in 19th-century America who hid runaway slaves (the slave being, perhaps, the classic example of "the other"). Consider the casual bystander who dives into a river to rescue a drowning stranger. Consider the African-Americans who came to the rescue of seriously injured and beaten white truck driver Reginel Denney during the riots in Los Angeles in April 1992. Consider people who donate blood for complete strangers year after year. Ultimately, such actions are based on a recognition of transcultural *human* characteristics and needs. One does not jump into a lake to rescue a drowning chicken.

B. THE LOGIC OF BIOSOCIAL RESEARCH

Proponents of biosocial approaches to social science have utilized a number of arguments to advance their position. One principal method is to suggest the possibility of analogous behavior between *Homo sapiens* and other species. For example, given the close genetic similarities between humankind and the apes, ethologists have argued that similarities exist between various species (Cheney and Seyfarth, 1990; Griffin, 1992). Activities of free-ranging chimpanzees, for example, manifest some similarities or analogies compared to our own behavior (Goodall, 1986). By examining the activities of other species we are given clues as to the possible evolutionary development of our own species.

Arguments concerning analogies between humans and other species have been the subject of much debate and criticism (Ruse, 1978; Kitcher, 1985). Sociobiologists, as I will show in the next chapter, have often made unwarranted analogies between their own "favorite" species, or area of research interest, and human beings. As Carl Sagan has argued in his history of evolution, "chimps are not rats" (Sagan and Druyan, 1992, p. 302). Under conditions of crowding and overpopulation, for example, rats and chimps react very differently. Rats become exceedingly aggressive and exhibit other abnormal behavior (Sagan and Druyan, 1992, pp. 184–187). Chimps, on the other hand, "make extraordinary efforts to be more friendly, to be slower to anger" (Sagan and Druyan, 1992, p. 302). *Ceteris paribus*, it is reasonable to assume that the closer the genetic relationships between humans and other species, the more likely any analogy is valid. What Kitcher terms "pop sociobiology" has often ignored this proposition. Sociobiologist David Barash, for example, has been heavily criticized for his discussion of "rape" in mallard ducks (Kitcher, 1985, pp. 184–201). The presumption of the critics is that this is a clearly *false* analogy. Their arguments are indeed persuasive. As Kitcher rightly observes, Barash's speculations on rape among humans "are not fit for serious discussion" (Kitcher, 1985, p. 186). One cannot make analogies between completely dissimilar circumstances when one totally misunderstands both of them.

Let us look more closely at the evidence presented by those arguing for a biosocial perspective. The argument that it is reasonable to assume that the closer the genetic relationship between species the more likely the validity of analogies between the species presupposes that some behavioral consequences are the results of genetic background and evolutionary history. One need not make this assumption. Behaviorists such as Skinner (1971) or cultural materialists such as Harris (1989) certainly do not. They claim that the "argument from analogy" is tautological: One *assumes* some genetic "analogy" and forces empirical evidence into preconceived categories. "Culturologists," such as Leslie White, argue that we need go no further than culture to explain all behavior (White, 1969). Where is the empirical evidence, they wonder, which supports the importance of the biosocial? What does social science gain from the utilization of biological or ethological investigations?

One of the intriguing areas of investigation in biosocial research which provides some *prima facie* evidence supporting genetic influence is the study of identical twins (Cummings, 1991, pp. 348–356). Interviewing twins raised separately, for example, suggests a possible approach to research on the nature/nurture controversy. There are two classifications of twins: monozygotic (identical) or dizygotic (fraternal). The "genetic relatedness" of identical twins is 100%. Francis Galton, the "father" of eugenics, expressed these relationships in correlation coefficients so that the correlation coefficient of identical twins is 1.0 (Cummings, pp. 350–352). Dizygotic twins, on the other hand, have on the average 50% of their genes in common, or have a correlation coefficient of .5. These relationships have been used to explore the interactions and influences of heredity and environment.

An alternative but related approach is to compare adopted children with biological siblings. Even Richard Lewontin, who is exceptionally critical of nearly all efforts to relate heredity to behavior (Lewontin, 1991), notes that "The practice of adoption makes possible, at least in theory, a separation of genetic from environmental transmission" (Lewontin, Rose and Kamin, 1984, p. 110). For example, a researcher can make comparisons of IQ correlations between biological parents and their children and stepparents and their adoptive children. One study reported by Lewontin showed a correlation of .15 between adoptive parents and their stepchildren as opposed to a correlation of .48 between a "matched control group" of consanguine families

(Lewontin, Rose and Kamin, 1984, p. 110). Other studies have suggested that "the risk of schizophrenia is greater in an adopted child if a biological parent also has been diagnosed as schizophrenic" (Sutton and Wagner, 1985, p. 351).

In spite of the criticism directed towards almost any attempt to connect genetics and specific areas of human behavior (Levins and Lewontin, 1985), it is possible to see the logic behind this approach to research. Lewontin, for example, suggests another possibility: One could compare the IQ of an adopted child and of a biological child who lives in the same family with a parent's IQ. The two children have lived in the same house with the same parents. As Lewontin states, "To the extent that genes determine IQ, the correlation between parent and biological child should obviously be larger than that between parent and adoptive child" (Lewontin, Rose and Kamin, 1984, p. 112). The important point to note is that even one of the harshest critics of such things as the Human Genome Project (Lewontin, 1991, pp. 61 –83) and "genetic determinism" has in this case outlined a *logical possibility* with respect to determining the influence of genetics on behavior.

One of the most extensive studies of this type has been carried out by Thomas Bouchard and David Lykken at the Minnesota Center for Twin and Adoption Research (Bouchard, et al., 1990, pp. 223–228). Bouchard and his colleagues believe they have conclusively demonstrated the significance of "heritability"—"that proportion of total variance caused by genetic differences" (Cummings, 1991, p. 348)—for behavior and have answered the usual complaints against the methods utilized in "twin" and "adoption" studies. Their work, I believe, is one of the most suggestive and coherent empirical studies now available arguing for the significance of genetic influences on behavior. If their conclusions are even partially correct, they demonstrate the short-sightedness and lack of realism in all sociological studies which implicitly assume that environmental conditions are *all* that need concern sociologists.

The Minnesota Center has worked with 348 sets of twins, including 44 pairs of identical twins raised separately, since 1979 (Wellborn, 1987, p. 58). One way of determining heritability is to look at the average correlation within a twin pair raised apart, "where all similarities are presumed genetic since the environment they share is no more similar than that of two individuals selected at random" (Holden, 1987, p. 599). Another method is to compare "the average correlation of a group of fraternal twin pairs to that obtained from identical twins" (Holden, 1987, p. 599).

The Minnesota studies resulted in a median correlation for nine classes of variables of .49 for identical twins raised apart and .52 for those raised together.[3] The results for fraternal twins raised apart was about .23, or approximately half the correlation of identical twins. As Holden notes, this is "about what would be predicted if calculations were based solely on the proportions of genes shared by the twin pairs" (Holden, 1987, p. 599). Bouchard and Lykken also argue that the small differences in correlation between identical twins raised separately and together, answer the arguments of critics like Lewontin (Lewontin, Rose and Kamin, 1984, pp. 214–220) who suggest that environmental influences are confounding the results of twin studies. Lewontin, for example, argues that being reared together increases similarity in twins. They are treated similarly and thereby experience similar environmental influences compared to other siblings who are not raised together. Certainly this seems a likely and common-sense observation.

Bouchard and his co-workers, however, have found similarities in traits "regardless of rearing status" (Bouchard, et al., p. 226). This significant finding has major importance for advocates of a biosocial approach to social science. One assumes that the environmental influences on identical twins raised apart are different from those raised together. Why the similarity in test results regardless of being reared apart or together? Bouchard counters the obvious objection that the families that adopted the twins are more similar to each other than what might be expected at random with the results of surveys of the "Moos Family Environment Scale" which gives each twin's "retrospective impression of treatment and rearing during childhood and adolescence" (Bouchard, et al., p. 225). In addition, he developed a "checklist of available household facilities" which provided an "index of cultural and intellectual resources in the adoptive home" (Bouchard, et al., p. 225). The result was "the absence of any significant effect due to SES or other environmental influences on the I.Q. scores of these adult adopted twins" (Bouchard, et al., p. 225). One must entertain the possibility that the similarity in identical twins raised together or separately, as well as the average difference in correlation of traits between identical and fraternal twins—a correlation of traits approximately twice as great for identical twins— is due to interaction between genetic and environmental factors. This is a conclusion which is unpalatable to much current sociology.

It should be noted that Bouchard et al. speak of *interaction, not determination*. They suggest the possibility that "MZA twins (monozygotic twins raised apart) are so similar because their identical genomes make it probable that their effective environments are similar" (Bouchard, et al., p. 227). Bouchard argues that it is "a plausible conjecture" that the influence of genes on behavior is "indirect" (Bouchard et al., 1990, p. 227). That is, what we are looking at in these studies at what William Durham calls "coevolution" (1991), or the mingling of diverse environmental and genetic influences. Durham convincingly shows that it is impossible to understand such things as the epidemiology of sickle-cell anemia in West Africa without taking into account both cultural and genetic influences. Both factors influence each other. Culture also influences genotypes (Durham, 1991, pp. 103 – 153; Duster and Garrett, 1984).

That we still talk in the Cartesian language of either/or is simply an unwarranted and unfortunate result of our Western intellectual heritage. A social scientist who suggests any biological or genetic influences on behavior is viewed with "politically correct" suspicion. Sociologists engage in "sociological gerrymandering" similar to the process of "religious gerry-mandering" described by Walter Kaufmann (Kaufmann, 1978, pp. 219 – 227). We pick out the *weakest* of our opponents' arguments and declare them "representative" or "the best they can offer." No one should be surprised that it takes such a small breath to blow away the resulting straw men.

C. TAKING EVOLUTION INTO ACCOUNT

If we accept the foregoing argument that biosocial interaction is at least a possibility, we will discover that this supposition can make a considerable difference in the way we carry out research. An impressive example—indeed almost an "exemplar" (Kuhn, 1970)—of the biosocial perspective is the article by anthropologist Lars Rodseth et al., "The Human Community as a Primate Society" (Rodseth et al., 1991, pp. 221 – 241). Rodseth and his co-authors argue that cross-cultural studies of diverse societies have "no independent measures of variation...without considering nonhuman organisms" (Rodseth et al., 1991, p. 241). That is, if we only look at divergent cultural patterns of *Homo sapiens*, we "are likely to see only enormous differences across the range of human societies, never noticing the common themes" (Rodseth et al., 1991, p. 241).

For example, if one makes comparisons between humans and other primates, one notices that humans are the only species "to maintain lifelong consanguinial relationships, despite sex-biased dispersal from their natal groups" (Rodseth et al., 1991, p. 223). Ideally we *keep in touch* with our children, no matter what sex or wherever their location. As is true of all primates, "Sex and kinship...are encompassing dimensions of sociality" (Rodseth et al., 1991, p. 223). Unlike all other primate species, however, humans have developed a "release from proximity" in their family relationships (Rodseth et al., 1991, p. 240). Our primary group relationships, in other words, are not determined by spatial proximity. No matter the sex or location of our children, we stay in touch.

The analysis provided by Rodseth et al. suggests that we should view intergenerational communication, irrespective of spatial propinquity, as an area of unique significance for human beings. Its significance is accentuated by the kind of comparative perspective they present. We are the only species which has developed in this fashion.

We also see in this example the "coevolutionary" perspective favored by Durham (1991). Clearly what allows us to "keep in touch" are cultural instruments of communication. That is, it is only because of our technology/culture that the "release from proximity" is able to occur. What has been viewed as the nature/culture "duality" cannot be coherently separated as if they were two antithetical "essences." As Fox argues, "culture is an aspect of man's [sic] biological differences from other species. It is the name for a kind of behavior found in the human species that ultimately depends on...the brain" (Fox, 1989, p. 28). In naturalistic terms, we have not somehow "overcome" our "primate nature," but we are "a different kind of primate with a different kind of nature" (Fox, 1989, p. 28). That one can make ultimate or qualitative distinctions between "nature" and "culture" is simply an unjustified and self-serving presumption of a social science determined to carve out its own ecological "niche." Each implies, supports, and is constitutive of the other.

As I am suggesting, the reasoning behind the presumed biological-social chasm is ideological and "political." We will explore these connections in more detail later. I might simply note at this point that the presumed "necessary" political connections between biology and politics are not somehow etched in stone. A sociologist, for example, may include some awareness of evolutionary processes in his or her discussion without adopting a conservative or reactionary political stance. Even the "scientific" conclusions presented by Rodseth and others are not what social scientists might presume they would be. For example, after their review of the ethological evidence concerning violence and aggression in other primate species, they wonder why "males seem to monopolize violence in human societies *and not in those of most other primates*" (Rodseth et al., 1991, p. 232, emphasis in original). They note that "females in these [other primate] groups regularly engage in violent competition with females" (Rodseth et al., 1991, p. 232). This at least suggests the possibility that the disparity in violent acts in human society between males and females is influenced by processes very broadly defined as "cultural." Thus the *ethological evidence itself* suggests the plausibility of cultural influences on violent behavior. If we have *trained* males to be violent and females to resist violent solutions, we may clearly alter that training in the future. A consideration of genetic/evolutionary influences does not necessitate simplistic genetic determinism. The use of glasses or insulin does not determine one's political position, even if it does indicate biosocial influence.

Leda Cosmides has made the interesting observation that "an evolutionary perspective can help eliminate biases against women" (Cosmides, quoted in Allman, 1994, p. 46). She notes that "male scientists" have generally proposed that gender-based "differences" in some fashion indicated female inferiority. In contrast, evolutionary psychology suggests that one would expect to find some differences if the problems and tasks that the two sexes dealt with over time were in any way distinct, but "you would not find sex differences, when their problems were the same" (Cosmides, quoted in Allman, 1994, p. 47). The point is that any "differences" are exactly that: differences—not "better" or "worse" qualities.

I am arguing that a consideration of biological and evolutionary evidence may cause fundamental alterations in viewpoints and that such alterations are long overdue in the work of most sociologists. Suppose, for instance, that we took Rodseth et al. seriously and we *were inclined to look for* the commonalities we see among differing "lifestyles." Assume we wanted to outline the common features of *Homo sapiens* as a species, as contrasted to other species. Using the comparative framework of Rodseth allows us to perceive what "may appear to a narrower perspective as enormous differences" as, in fact, "variations on a theme" (Rodseth et al., 1991, p. 241).

Part of the difficulty in perceiving "variations on a theme" is the result of the kind of training typically provided by academic sociology. One can sympathize with Pierre L. van den Berghe's complaint that "sociologists, individually and collectively, spend an astonishingly small proportion of their professional activities learning about the real world" (van den Berghe, 1975, p. 14). We do not, according to van den Berghe, live our sociology. We do not, in general, do much participant observation. We do not necessarily learn other languages or spend time in foreign cultures. *Of course* the "foreigner" is viewed as "the other." We consider strange what we have never seen or understood. We are instantly aware of differences and unaware of "common themes."

If we more easily shared and perceived our commonalities, we might be less inclined in our research to develop "us" vs. "them" kinds of categories of analysis. In *The Truly Disadvantaged* (1987), for example, William Julius Wilson presents a cogent analysis of recent economic trends in inner-city areas. He argues in his chapter on "Race-specific Policies and the Truly Disadvantaged" that only a "universal" program of social change and reform offers any real hope for changing current conditions (Wilson, 1987, pp. 109 –124). According to Wilson, an emphasis on "race" per se limits the attractiveness of reform programs for other segments of the population whose support Wilson views as essential to their success. What we need, Wilson suggests, is a kind of "Marshall Plan" for the cities which people may universally view as helpful to their common situations. He believes that one "minimal required change" is a *"national AFDC benefit standard adjusted yearly for inflation"* (Wilson, 1987, p. 152, emphasis added). Clearly Wilson seems prepared to argue that in some sense *all people* are affected by what happens in central cities and share a common interest in their city's improvement and prosperity. His approach is "universalistic": We are all in this together.

How is it possible, however, to truly share a concern with someone who is qualitatively distinct? I suggest that this is the problem with the term "underclass" which Wilson has made famous. Furthermore, the use of biosocial perspectives which emphasize human commonalities would, contrary to many of the platitudinous assumptions of social science, make one less likely to draw such qualitative distinctions between the "good guys" (us) and the "bad guys" (them).

Wilson states that he uses the term "underclass" for:

> individuals who lack training and skills and either experience long-term unemployment or are not members of the labor force, individuals who are engaged in street crime and other forms of aberrant behavior, and *families that experience long-term effects of poverty* [sic] and/or welfare dependency. (Wilson, 1987, p. 8, emphasis added)

Wilson argues that his use of "underclass" suggests that "groups that have been left behind are *collectively different* from those that lived in these [inner-city] neighborhoods in earlier years" (Wilson, 1987, p. 8, emphasis added). He heatedly criticizes liberals who "relate these characteristics [of the "underclass] to the broader problems of society" (Wilson, 1987, p. 6). Wilson claims that "one cannot deny" that the behavior of the "underclass" "contrasts sharply with that of mainstream America" (Wilson, 1987, p. 7). We simply "obscure these differences by eschewing the term *underclass*" (Wilson, 1987, p. 7, emphasis in original).

"Under," of course, suggests someone less valuable or even "sub-human" compared with those "over." It suggests a master/servant relationship. It implies that those who are left behind are indeed "collectively different" compared with those who are part of the "overclass." It implies the "us vs. them" distinction that can be ultimately traced to the dualism of Descartes. It, as opposed to a biosocial perception of species commonalities, implies that the "underclass" is so much "the other" that concentrating on the "broader problems of society" obscures the qualitative distinctions between the "underclass" and "mainstream America." Wilson's classificatory distinctions in this case distort and contradict his general political orientation—which is clearly universalistic. One could simply talk about people in different circumstances. One could talk about people who experience wildly different conditions, incomes, or status. Why do we need a specific, emotive, Cartesian label at all? Why assume those on welfare belong to a qualitatively distinct taxonomic category? People as *a species*, as demonstrated, for example, in the work of Rodseth et al., *all* share a multitude of commonalities.

A concern with commonalities and ethological comparisons would also enhance the work that has been done on adolescence. As an example, consider the classic work by Edgar Friedenberg *The Vanishing Adolescent*

(1959). David Riesman claimed in his Introduction that "of all the wide-ranging diagnoses of our time, it is one of the most profound...grounded in the social-psychological studies of adolescent character" (Riesman, 1959, p. 7). I am interested, however, not so much in its specific prescriptions, but in its taken-for-granted social science assumptions. Postmodernists have argued that *what is left out* of an argument is often as significant as what is being said. That is, we need to examine the "aporias" or "material gaps" in any text (Pfohl, 1994, p. 477). What does this kind of analysis suggest about Friedenberg's classic best-seller?

A glaring omission is that there is very little discussion of adolescent sex. This appears not to be due to any reluctance to discuss the topic of sex in general, insofar as there is an extensive analysis of the possibility of adolescents serving as a "homoerotic" threat to adults (Friedenberg, 1959, pp. 181–190). Presumably this was even more "shocking" to his readers than any discussion of adolescent sexuality per se might have been at the time. From the first paragraph of the work, however, we are informed that "Adolescence is not simply a physical process; there is more to it than sexual maturation. It is also—and primarily—a social process, *whose fundamental task is clear and stable self-identification*" (Friedenberg, 1959, p. 17, emphasis added).

Friedenberg provides a clear statement of the putative culture/nature dualism: Adolescence must be viewed as either a "physical" or a "social" process and, in this case, is "primarily" a "social" event. He argues that adolescent sexuality "must be regarded in somewhat the same light as photosynthesis in the study of ecology" (Friedenberg, 1959, p. 52).
Friedenberg suggests that for photosynthesis/adolescent sexuality "the process is benign, and it seems fortunate that it can be carried on successfully under so wide a variety of circumstances" (Friedenberg, 1959, p. 52). One conjures up images of leisurely, sun-drenched tranquility—a kind of botanical/sexual Garden of Eden. It is not surprising when Friedenberg develops a forty-three question sentence-completion test to give to adolescents that the only question which—decorously—refers to sex begins "Love is:" (Friedenberg, 1959, pp. 150–155). If one assumes that culture = "higher" and sex = "lower," one naturally tends to concentrate on the more positive of the two evaluations. Who wants to be accused of writing pornography?

If, however, sexual/family relationships are, as Rodseth et al. argue, "encompassing dimensions of sociality" in all other primates (Rodseth et al., 1991, p. 223), perhaps we should begin at that point in any analysis of adolescence. Perhaps we should assume that sexual relationships are of overwhelming importance for all adolescents and that the "five exemplary boys" who Friedenberg analyzes as examples of differing ideal-typical patterns of adolescent behavior share that particular distinction. We also note the absence of "exemplary" girls in his discussion. He states that for the boys, the school was a "source of difficulty," but "for the girls it was not one" (Friedenberg, 1959, p. 147). Lucky for the girls.

Schools, according to Friedenberg, accomplish four principal things. They teach adolescents "to be an American"; they serve to divide us by social class; they transmit "some of the knowledge and some of the intellectual skills and attitudes" we need as a culture; and each school "functions as an administrative and records center" (Friedenberg, 1959, pp. 72–75).

Schools, however, are also the places where adolescents learn about, experience, and try to come to grips with sex. The "clear and stable self-identification" that Friedenberg discusses in his opening paragraph is not somehow opposed to sexual relationships and exclusively "cultural." As any realistic description of high school life in America would show, they are inextricably intertwined. One does not achieve "self-identification" by ignoring hormones. They are, at any rate, impossible to ignore and are part of the biosocial development of every adolescent.

If we examine some of the popular literary works on adolescence, we obtain a vastly different perspective on "growing up" compared to the sanitized version of photosynthetic socialization presented by Friedenberg. Looking at well-known works such as *The Catcher in the Rye, Red Sky at Morning, Summer of '42, The Adrian Mole Diaries*, and the popular novels of Judy Blume, what stands out above all else is the omnipresent, demanding, overwhelming, pulsating presence of sex. It is the primary area of concern—the underpinning upon which all other social and cultural relationships are based and develop. Certainly this would not be surprising to comparative ethologists.

In *The Adrian Mole Diaries*, the principal character is a fourteen-year-old British adolescent who records his overwhelming and lengthy infatuation with his beloved Pandora in a series of ruminations in his diary. There is no placid botanical garden here. A more typical reaction to Pandora's presence is that "My heart was beating so loudly in my throat that I felt like a stereo loudspeaker, so I left before she heard me" (Townsend, 1986, p. 38). Also typical is the constant poetic stream of musings inspired by Pandora:

Saturday July 25

PANDORA! PANDORA! PANDORA!

Oh! my love,
My heart is yearning,
My mouth is dry,
My soul is burning.
You're in Tunisia,
I am here.
Remember me and shed a tear.
Come back tanned and brown and healthy.
You're lucky that your dad is wealthy.

She will be back in six days.
(Townsend, 1986, p. 91)

It is, of course, easy to ridicule this type of material and all the other poetic doggerel scattered throughout the book as "unrealistic" or merely humorous. I suggest, however, that the "dry" and "burning" kinds of sensations mentioned are a more realistic description of high school life than the more "scientific" descriptions of Friedenberg. Adrian Mole's remark that "Pandora and I indulged in extremely heavy petting; so heavy that I felt a weight fall from me. If I don't pass my exams it won't matter" (Townsend, 1986, p. 335) rings true to anyone who has been involved in a high school romance: What is important are the social, sexual, and interpersonal aspects of high school. One cannot separate "sex" and "culture" into airtight, mutually exclusive categories.

Works like *Catcher in the Rye* and *The Adrian Mole Diaries* bridge the gap between "nature" and "culture" and are therefore inherently more accurate in their presentations than works of social scientists which ignore such fundamental human characteristics as the overarching preoccupation with sex. We respond to their work—according to the dust jacket, *The Adrian Mole Diaries* sold five million copies in England alone during its first three years of publication—because we *recognize ourselves* in their descriptions and dilemmas. We know that we experienced similar things and that the "manifest" or "official" purposes of high schools often have almost no relationship to what is significant for the students who attend them.

If we refuse to recognize the obvious significance of such biosocial preoccupations as sexual relationships, we will necessarily produce studies lacking in verisimilitude. Even in studies which are generally "qualitative," such as Friedenberg's *The Vanishing Adolescent*, the students involved would have a hard time recognizing themselves. And with reason. As was the case with the term "underclass," why is it essential to have a separate and implicitly derogatory classification (i.e., "That's typical of adolescent behavior") at all? Aren't we merely talking about people of younger ages? Does the term "adolescent" imply a qualitative distinction which obscures more than it illuminates? Of course we need to develop separate categories to talk about anything. But we should be aware of what they imply. Why should social science embrace unnecessarily invidious and condescending comparisons?

I have argued throughout this chapter that a biosocial approach to social science research is one way of overcoming a number of shortcomings which are the result of an exclusive emphasis on "cultural" levels of analysis. We have seen that current research on monozygotic twins strongly supports biosocial explanations of behavior. It is also evident that work being done in ethology has demonstrated that many of the presumed "absolutes" or differences between humans and other species do not represent rigid or qualitative differences.

In the next chapter I will examine in some detail the theories and sociological implications of the work of Edward O. Wilson, who is the best-known — or most infamous and reviled— sociobiologist. We have seen, however, that an emphasis on human similarities may decrease the likelihood of invidious comparisons. Is the lack of sociological interest in Wilson justified? Does his work offer a new "reading" of social behavior? Wilson strongly supports the argument that the presumably "qualitative" distinctions between *Homo sapiens* and other species have gradually disappeared as ethological and sociobiological research has advanced over the past twenty-five years. Is Wilson therefore an implicit or explicit Social Darwinist?

II

THE SOCIOBIOLOGICAL PERSPECTIVE OF E. O. WILSON

A. INTRODUCTION

Edward O. Wilson, the author of the massive and authoritative *Sociobiology: The New Synthesis* (1975), is the central intellectual figure in the development of sociobiology (Ritzer, 1983, p. 402). In this chapter, I will look at the sociological implications of his work and the controversies which it has generated. Until the publication of *Sociobiology: The New Synthesis*, Wilson was a respected entomologist who was recognized as a leading expert on ants (Ritzer, 1983, p. 402). After 1975, however, Wilson was viewed as the *enfant terrible* of a new and dangerous academic discipline.

The initial sociological reaction to his book was actually quite positive. Marion Blute called it an "exceptionally fine book" (Blute, 1976, p. 731). Allan Mazur, while critical of aspects of Wilson's work, suggested that he "has both the visibility and credibility to legitimate the biological approach to sociology" (Mazur, 1976, p. 700). Edward Tiryakian labeled it "an imposing attempt to update Darwinian-derived evolutionary theory" (Tiryakian, 1976, p. 701). While all of the sociological reviewers had specific criticisms of Wilson, none condemned him outright. All of them suggested that the book was important and deserved to be taken seriously as "a stimulating prodding of the sociological imagination" (Tiryakian, 1976, p. 705).

What George Ritzer terms the "firestorm of criticism"—Wilson being "harangued and jeered at professional meetings, including at least one professional sociological meeting"—came later (Ritzer, 1983, p. 402). An examination of Wilson's writing in *Sociobiology*, as well as his more popularized works *On Human Nature* (1978) and *Promethean Fire* (1983), will demonstrate the complexity of what is often viewed in simplistic, Manichean dualities. Wilson is neither the proto-Nazi pilloried by his most vehement critics (Alper, Beckwith and Miller, 1978) or the political "innocent" he sometimes seems to appear in his own defense.[4] Wilson raises important issues which should be taken into account by contemporary sociology.

The secondary literature dealing with Wilson and sociobiology is massive and detailed (Sahlins, 1976; Caplan, 1978; Gregory, Silvers and Sutch, 1978; Barlow and Silverberg, 1980; Singer, 1981; Lewontin, Rose, and Kamin, 1984; Kitcher, 1985; Lewontin, 1993; Hubbard and Wald, 1993). Despite this outpouring of material, I agree with Walter Gove's forthright statement that "Most sociologists who are critical of sociobiology lack a clear understanding of what sociobiology is and how it relates to recent developments in biological theory and research" (Gove, 1987, p. 258). As a result, according to Gove, "most have rejected sociobiology largely on metaphysical grounds" (Gove, 1987, p. 258). But if critics are going to accuse a major intellectual figure of a "sexist synthesis" (Chasin, 1977) or of providing a theory which produces "specific political consequences" (Alper, Beckwith, and Miller, 1978, p. 5), they should be able to offer coherent reasons for their criticism. In this chapter I will examine some of Wilson's major themes and their sociological significance. There are indeed good reasons for sociologists to be critical of Wilson, but the issue is much more complex than the automatic and inevitable sociological rejection of "biological determinism" would suggest.[5]

In *Sociobiology: The New Synthesis* (1975), Wilson defines sociobiology as "the systematic study of the biological basis of all social behavior" (Wilson, 1975, p. 4). While Wilson claims that sociobiology "for the present" deals with other species and ethological concerns, it is clear throughout *Sociobiology* that Wilson's agenda is broader and includes humankind. It has often been suggested that his *magnum opus* is perfectly acceptable to sociology excluding the final chapter which attempts to "biologicize" sociology. Bruce Eckland, in a review in the *American Journal of Sociology*, states that "only the last of 27 chapters deals directly with man" (Eckland, 1976, p. 693). This statement, however, is somewhat misleading. Part of the explanation for the adverse responses to *Sociobiology* is due to Wilson's continual extension of his ethological descriptions onto *Homo sapiens*. Like the waves of criticism which greeted Darwin's *On the Origin of Species* (Himmelfarb, 1962, pp. 268–309), it was clear from the beginning that Wilson's book is of immense significance for our understandings and images of "the human."

Donna Haraway suggests in *Primate Visions* (1989) that "evolutionary discourse" is "highly narrative" and that "story-telling is central" to its "scientific project" (Haraway, 1989, p. 188). She believes that evolutionary narratives deal with "ontological statuses" and "framing myths" about our origins (Haraway, 1989, p. 146). In a more reflexive and complex fashion, she agrees with Gove's statement that sociologists have rejected Wilson "largely on metaphysical grounds." Haraway argues that in order to understand "metaphysical" conflicts, one must look at the kinds of evolutionary narratives and stories about human beings which the various authors present. If one wants to begin to understand the negative reaction to Wilson's arguments, one must examine the "framing myths" he provides and the tales he tells. We need to be aware of what is excluded as well as what is present. Let us examine three statements Wilson makes about "man,"[6] all preceding his controversial final chapter, which provides some insight into his evolutionary "tales."

In Chapter 5 on "Group Selection and Altruism" Wilson concludes by suggesting that:

a science of sociobiology, if coupled with neurophysiology, might transform the insights of ancient religions into a precise account of the evolutionary origin of ethics and hence explain the reasons why we make certain moral choices instead of others at particular times. Whether such understanding will then produce the Rule remains to be seen. For the moment, perhaps it is enough to establish that a single strong thread does indeed run from the conduct of termite colonies and turkey brotherhoods to the social behavior of man. (Wilson, 1975, p. 129)

In Chapter 11 on "Aggression" he writes that "the lesson for man" is:

If we wish to reduce our own aggressive behavior, and lower our cholamine and corticosteroid titers to levels that make us all happier, we should design our population densities and social systems in such a way as to make aggression inappropriate in most conceivable daily circumstances and, hence, less adaptive. (Wilson, 1975, p. 255)

In Chapter 14 on "Roles and Casts" he writes that:

When too many human beings enter one occupation, their personal cost-to-benefit ratios raise, and some individuals transfer to less crowded fields for selfish reasons.... Nonhuman vertebrates lack the basic machinery to achieve advanced division of labor by either the insect or the human methods. Human societies are therefore unique in a qualitative sense. They have equaled and in many cultures far exceeded insect societies in the amount of division of labor they contain. (Wilson, 1975, p. 313)

In his comment on religion and ethics from Chapter 5, Wilson makes absolutely clear that he is interested in examining broad philosophical issues which are of major significance for human beings. He wants to explain "the reasons why we make certain moral choices instead of others at particular times." He suggests that we need to examine "the evolutionary origin of ethics." And he explicitly argues that *there is no qualitative distinction between Homo sapiens and other species* (i.e., "a single strong thread does indeed run from the conduct of termite colonies...to the social behavior of man"). In *On Human Nature* (1978) and *Promethean Fire* (1983) Wilson made his attitude toward the significance of religion and "mind" much clearer. He begins his chapter on religion with the statement that "The predisposition to religious belief is the most complex and powerful force in the human mind and in all probability is an ineradicable part of human nature" (Wilson, 1978, p. 176). Wilson wants us to understand what he terms "the material basis of moral feeling" (Ruse and Wilson, 1986, p. 174). He suggests that our religious sentiments, like all our other species characteristics, were formed by natural selection and our evolutionary history (Wilson, 1978, pp. 176–201). If we want to adequately explain our current religious feelings we need to understand how they originally developed.

Speaking of the nature and development of "mind," Wilson states:

At the center of the neurophysiological recall and self-assembly, a maximally intense and coherent activity comprises conscious thought.... If and when we are able to characterize the organization of these various processes and identify their physical basis in some detail, it will be possible to define in a declarative and unambiguous manner the urgent but still elusive phenomenon of mind, as well as self and consciousness. (Lumsden and Wilson, 1983, p. 3)

In order to understand the development of "mind" and religion, we must look at the evolutionary sequences which lead to their formation. These have formed what Wilson terms "epigenetic rules" or "various regularities of development" (Lumsden and Wilson, 1983, p. 70). The "mind" is not a tabula rasa (Wilson, 1978, p. 69). We are predisposed towards certain kinds of mental activities and feelings. Thus, for example, with respect to classifying colors, "The epigenetic rules of color vision and classification are stringent enough to direct cultures around the world towards the central clusters of color classification as revealed by the Berlin-Kay experiments" (Lumsden and Wilson, 1983, p. 71).[7]

Wilson views "epigenetic rules" as a kind of Rosetta Stone of the mind. If we understand their origins and development, we will have unlocked the door to understanding all of nature. We will have produced what his quotation on ethics terms "the Rule." We will have demonstrated that it is "possible to proceed from a knowledge of the material basis of moral feeling to generally accepted rules of conduct. To do so will be to escape—not a minute too soon—from the debilitating absolute distinction between *is and ought*" (Ruse and Wilson, 1986, p. 174, emphasis in original).

Human beings, according to Wilson, really have no choice in the matter. If we ignore the "epigenetic rules"—assuming, for the moment, their validity[8]— they will nevertheless "navigate" our behavior: "A society that chooses to ignore the existence of innate epigenetic rules will nevertheless continue to navigate by them and at each moment of decision yield to their dictates by default" (Lumsden and Wilson, 1983, p. 184).

What Wilson terms "scientific materialism" or "scientific naturalism" will enable us to proceed in the fashion he proposes (Wilson, 1978, pp. 200–201). This results from the fact that "the final decisive edge enjoyed by scientific naturalism will come from its capacity to explain traditional religion, its chief competitor, as a wholly material phenomenon" (Wilson, 1986, p. 201). Scientific materialism will allow us to sustain the "blind hopes that the journey on which we are now embarked will be further and better than the one just completed" (Wilson, 1978, p. 217). All this depends, as suggested above, on an evolutionary history of ethics and moral choices. Sociobiology will finally allow us to overcome the "Cartesian Gap" between "is" and "ought."

In the second quotation from Wilson on "aggression," we see a number of other themes which have driven critics of sociobiology to distraction. On the one hand, it is clear that Wilson assumes that it is possible to alter environmental conditions and that the resulting changes will influence behavior ("We should *design our populates densities and social systems*" [emphasis added]). On the other hand, the reason we need to change that environment is to reduce hormonal levels and their negative effects ("cholamine and corticosteroid titers") which, according to Wilson, are the "proximate" causes of aggression. But is the individualistic level of analysis implied in the "cure" of hormone reduction an adequate "framing" of the etiology of aggression? Surely more social or institutional factors need to be considered. At the least, the reasons for their exclusion need to be explained and considered. Perhaps the problem is that Wilson defines "mind" as "an epiphenomenon of the neuronal machinery of the brain" (Wilson, 1978, p. 202). How then is it possible to talk of a conscious plan—"designing social systems"—at all? To "design" a social system presupposes an architect capable of more than "epiphenomenal" thought.

Wilson assumes in his discussion of aggression that one may legitimately make valid interspecies comparisons and analogies. Immediately preceding the discussion of aggression quoted above, Wilson concludes a detailed discussion of experiments on overcrowding in cats and its "bizarre effects" with the statement that the experimentally induced feline behavior has "close parallels in certain of the more dreadful aspects of human behavior" (Wilson, 1975, p. 255). The assumption is that the effects on human behavior of overcrowding are directly analogous to what happens with cats. But why is that the case? Why not birds? Or fish? Or prairie dogs? Wilson doesn't provide the criteria of selection he uses for making valid comparisons. It is reasonable to assume that the closer the evolutionary or genetic relationships and similarities, the more valid the comparison. Sociobiologists should focus their attention on the Cercopithecoidea (Old World monkeys) and the great apes. Similarities abound.

In the third quotation from Chapter 14 of *Sociobiology*, Wilson reveals his entomological background. One of the aspects of his writings which has positively outraged critics is his tendency to make comparisons between the insect order Hymenoptera—or "eusocial" insects—and human beings. Wilson actually admits in the quote that human societies are "unique in a qualitative sense"—contrary to the implied continuum in the quote on religion—but then goes on to assume that one may make meaningful comparisons between humans and insect societies. He states that the division of labor in human societies "far exceeded insect societies in the amount of division of labor they contain." The point is that most social scientists would challenge the validity of the comparison in the first place. It is not self-evident that one can make any valid comparisons between insect "societies" and human societies. If one is going to make that argument, one needs to at least offer reasons and arguments for believing it is possible. Wilson offers none and, in this case, sociologists are not his only critics.

Wilson spends a considerable time in his *Sociobiology* discussing "communication" (Wilson, 1975, pp. 176–241). He quotes with approval Norbert Wiener, who, Wilson says, argued in his classic work on cybernetics that "sociology, *including animal sociobiology*" could be understood as reciprocal exchanges of bits of information (Wilson, 1975, p. 18, emphasis added). According to Wilson, much of sociobiology can be similarly defined as information exchange. Hence the analogy between eusocial insects and humans is certainly proper. They both exchange information.

If, however, we examine Wiener's famous *The Human Use of Human Beings*, we find that he spends a good part of his chapter on "Cybernetics and Society" in an extended critique of exactly the kind of comparison Wilson is trying to make. It is Wiener's position that an "ant society" is qualitatively distinct from human culture and that his cybernetic system does not apply to the insect world. He argues that "a human state based on the model of the ant results from a profound misapprehension both of the nature of the ant and of the nature of man" (Wiener, 1954, p. 51). "Feedback" between ants and between humans are two very different things:

> Thus the insect is rather like the kind of computing machine whose instructions are all set forth in advance on the "tapes," and which has next to no feedback mechanism to see it through the uncertain future. The behavior of an ant is much more a matter of instinct than of intelligence. *The physical strait jacket in which an insect grows up is directly responsible for the mental strait jacket which regulates its pattern of behavior.* (Wiener, 1954, p. 57, emphasis in original)

The distinction between the "mechanical rigidity of the insect" and the "mechanical fluidity of the human being" is, says Wiener, "highly relevant to the point of view of this book" (Wiener, 1954, p. 57). In his selection of Wiener, Wilson picked an unfortunate example. Wiener specifically states that the intellectual discipline which made Wilson justly famous has absolutely no bearing on human affairs. He was totally opposed to the point of view of *Sociobiology* twenty years before it was written. A sociobiologist, or anyone else, needs to take care when claiming intellectual soulmates.

B. EDWARD WILSON AS OBJECTIVE SCIENTIST

A positivistic sociologist would take Wilson to task for his conflation of the indicative and prescriptive levels of analysis (Bryant, 1985). Positivists assume that any commingling of the "is" and the "ought" inevitably produces what G.E. Moore called the "naturalistic fallacy" (Midgley, 1978, pp. 177 –199). One cannot, according to this view, say anything about what *ought* to be based on naturalistic descriptions of what exists. Wilson clearly assumes that Moore's argument is mistaken. He assumes that as "we start to elect a system of values on a more objective basis...our minds at last align with our hearts" (Wilson, 1978, p. 215). As we come to adequately understand evolutionary history, we will understand what needs to be done to reconcile the "whisperings within" (Barash, 1979) with our systems of morality and ethics. An informed and accurate sociobiology leads toward an evolutionary/ ethical Holy Grail. Wilson is in many respects a scientist/prophet attempting to arouse the sociobiologically ignorant.

Looking at the normative elements in Wilson's thought suggests the possibility that one may utilize a biological perspective and not embrace a conservative or reactionary political perspective. Contrary to much "common sense," there is no inevitable conservative connection between the use of biological data and one's political perspective. One sociologist who has examined E.O. Wilson's writings in depth refers to "the potentially radical and transformative elements in Wilson's thought" (Kaye, 1986, p. 100). Even in the notorious final chapter in *Sociobiology*, there are nearly utopian projections of current social and ecological trends. Wilson states, for example, that "When mankind has achieved an ecological steady state, probably at the end of the twenty-first century," the social sciences will be "maturing rapidly" and "biology should be at its peak" (Wilson, 1975, p. 574). He also writes of a "planned society—*the creation of which seems inevitable in the coming century*" (Wilson, 1975, p. 575, emphasis added). Whatever one's political persuasion, it seems unlikely that most of us would predict "an ecological steady state." Surely such things as population increases, resource depletion and environmental pollution point in exactly the opposite direction. Also, the increasing movement towards "privatization" doesn't auger well for Wilson's "inevitable" planned society. Once again, the trend is certainly in the opposite direction. Wilson's "evolutionary optimism" seems singularly misplaced and naive (See Endnote 4). His sociobiology clearly fulfills Mannheim's definition of a "utopian wish" as "all situationally transcendent ideas...which in any way have a transforming effect on the existing historical-social order" (Mannheim, 1936, p. 205). Wilson's writings articulate a desire for extensive social change. As Kaye notes, Wilson "sees modern societies as in a state of crisis" (Kaye, 1986, p. 100).

The biosocial perspective in general, and Wilson in particular, have been perceived as necessarily conservative or worse because of a mistaken belief that biological evidence inevitably results in biological determinism and a consequent devaluation of the effects of differing environments. In its most simplistic form, the assumption is that genetic considerations necessarily lead one to ignore such obvious environmental conditions as poverty or violence in the explanation of human behavior. Lerner, for example, in his discussion of sociobiology, constantly compares and suggests similarities between the Nazis and sociobiologists such as Wilson (Lerner, 1992, pp. 91 – 125).

If sociology as a discipline assumes differences in behavior are explained by differing environmental conditions, and sociobiology, it is believed, assumes that genetics or the "human biogram" explains behavior, it is easy to understand the resulting sociological hostility towards "biologism." Wilson increased the level of sociological discomfort by suggesting that sociology was likely to "merge" with cultural anthropology, economics, and social psychology and that "the transition from purely phenomenological to fundamental theory in sociology must await a full, neuronal explanation of the human brain" (Wilson, 1975, p. 575). A self-interested sociology, of course, would not be ecstatic over either development. No one likes to be told that what they are doing is fundamentally mistaken or that their academic discipline is about to vanish.

Sociologists, however, normally base their critiques of sociobiology on a mistaken notion of identity between "biological" and "conservative." In my development and use of biocritique I will provide an alternative to this point of view. For the moment, with respect to Wilson, I want to show why the assumption of a necessary conservatism with regard to all biological considerations or reasoning is a kind of theoretical *non sequitur*. Sociologists rightly view sociobiology as a threat to "business as usual," but they wrongly assume that their opposition necessarily reflects differences in political philosophies.

As Mary Midgley has argued, "The notion that we 'have a nature,' far from threatening the concept of freedom, is absolutely essential to it. If we were genuinely plastic and indeterminate at birth, there could be no reason why society should not stamp us into any shape that might suit it" (Midgley, 1978, p. xviii). As she has further noted, "Anyone who criticizes existing customs must...do so on the grounds that these customs fail to meet real human needs" (Midgley, 1983b, p. 91, emphasis in original). Wilson argues along similar lines in *On Human Nature* when he analyzes the history of slavery (Wilson, 1978, pp. 82–84). Slaves, according to Wilson, "insist on behaving like human beings instead of slave ants, gibbons, mandrills, or any other species" (Wilson, 1978, p. 84). It is because we are *not* "genuinely plastic" that slavery was ultimately defeated as a viable social arrangement.

Clearly, if *any* environmental condition is acceptable to human beings, slavery could, by definition, be an acceptable, viable, and contemporary reality in North and South America. All social criticism or discussion of "social problems" assumes that particular human needs are not being met. Contrary to the sociological equating of an exclusive emphasis on environmental conditions with "liberal" or "radical" politics, only assumptions about some kinds of human needs enable us to legitimately critique particular political arrangements (Etzioni, 1968).

Sociobiological arguments do not necessitate a reactionary political position. As Robin Fox has pointed out, if a political reformer is confronted by conservative shibboleths such as "You can't change human nature," a perfectly reasonable response is to suggest that the prevailing theories of "human nature" are incorrect. One can maintain "on the basis of evidence and argument, that the version of human nature put forward by the regime is faulty and distorted" (Fox, 1989, p. 69). Herbert Marcuse's arguments in *Eros and Civilization* (1955) and *One-Dimensional Man* (1964) presuppose a theory of human needs which are not being met by the dominant "one-dimensional" society. Erich Fromm makes the same argument in *The Sane Society* (1955). In his insightful study of "critical theory," Douglas Kellner argues that for Max Horkheimer "the concern for human suffering" was a principal determinant of his work" (Kellner, 1989, p. 237). Any analysis of human suffering, however, presupposes that human needs are being adversely affected in some fashion by that suffering. Whatever their other deficiencies, most sociologists would not classify Marcuse, Fromm, or Horkheimer as conservative biological determinists. There is no necessary connection between specific political positions and the use of biological data per se.

Naturalistic arguments can be employed by all political persuasions. Geneticist Steve Jones has proposed that, due to the harmful effects of inbreeding and recessive alleles, someone concerned about congenital genetic defects should marry another person as different genetically as possible: "Since the recessive gene for cystic fibrosis is unknown in Africans and that for sickle-cell anemia unknown in whites, the child of a black-white mating is safe from both diseases" (Jones, 1994, p. 74). The principle is the same, although the consequences are reversed, for harmful "inbreeding." Sociobiologists can logically argue that laws against miscegenation are genetically absurd. This is not a conservative political position.

Donna Haraway has argued that "sociobiological theory can be, really must be, 'female centered' in ways not true of previous paradigms, where the 'mother-infant' unit substituted for females" (Haraway, 1989, p. 178). That is, Wilson's sociobiology posits an equal genetic self-interest for both men and women. According to the sociobiological concepts of "kin selection" and "inclusive fitness," both males and females are equally interested in propagating and extending their genotypes (Wilson, 1975, pp. 117–121, 415–418). Thus the female is defined as "the fully calculating maximizing machine that had defined males already.... The female ceases to be a dependent variable when males and females both are defined as...rational calculators" (Haraway, 1989, pp. 178–179). A similar argument is presented in great detail by sociobiologist Sarah Blaffer Hrdy (1981). Her description of "genetic equality" does not fit the popular notion of a sociobiology which is necessarily misogynistic and ruled by "man the hunter" (Chasin, 1977).

Haraway also observes that sociobiologists may practice a kind of "reverse" rejection of the "naturalistic fallacy" (Haraway, 1991, p. 74). Ethologists and sociobiologists are often excoriated for assuming that *whatever is, is "right."* It is clear, however, that Wilson does not as a general rule subscribe to this belief. Similar to what Haraway writes of sociobiologist David Barash, "'is' is not *ought* for him" (Haraway, 1991, p. 74, emphasis in original). That is, there is no logical necessity for a sociobiologist having to assume that whatever s/he observes is somehow "right" or "positive." Once again, we see that the political implications of sociobiological reasoning are, at best, ambiguous. As Melvin Konner notes, "a gene alone does nothing; context is always important" (Konner, 1991, p. 34).

This is not to suggest that there are no political implications in Wilson's work. As Adam Kuper (1994, p. 102) argues in *The Chosen Primate*, "there are no neutral theories about human beings." Part of the reason Wilson has been attacked so bitterly is that he often seems to deny what his own work so clearly represents: the obvious imbrication of the indicative and the normative. Thus in commenting on "the sociobiology controversy," he argues that sociobiology is not a "politically defined doctrine on human nature" and refers to "the inherent neutrality of the discipline" (Lumsden and Wilson, 1983, pp. 23 and 37). And yet he makes statements such as "The genes hold culture on a leash. The leash is very long, but inevitably values will be constrained in accordance with their effects on the human gene pool" (Wilson, 1978, p. 175). Or "Scientists and humanists should consider together the possibility that the time has come for ethics to be removed temporarily from the hands of philosophers and biologicized" (Wilson, 1975, p. 562). Or "Human beings are absurdly easy to indoctrinate—they *seek* it" (Wilson, 1975, p. 562, emphasis in original). Irrespective of the merits of his arguments, it is self-evident that such statements are profoundly "political."

The statement concerning a genetic "leash" clearly suggests a conservative political orientation. The statement about "indoctrination" would seem to embrace the radical behaviorism he otherwise disavows. The statement about ethics is similar to Wilson's quotation on the significance of developing an evolutionary ethics and the importance of explaining "why we make certain moral choices instead of others" (Wilson, 1975, p. 129). All of these statements are "political" (i.e., may in some way influence political ideologies or processes). Consider Wilson's discussion of the significance of religion.

In *On Human Nature*, Wilson argues that "Self-deception by shamans and priests perfects their own performance and enhances the deception practiced on their constituents" (Wilson, 1975, p. 183). Wilson, while stressing the importance and strength of the "predisposition to religious belief," believes we would all be better off if it were to somehow disappear. He asks "Does a way exist to divert *the power of religion into the services of the great new enterprise [scientific materialism] that lays bare the sources of that power*"? (Wilson, 1978, p. 201, emphasis added). Wilson, I believe, would like us to picture him as a kind of contemporary Voltaire who possesses the "positive" doctrine Voltaire's skepticism lacked (i.e., *Sociobiology: The New Synthesis*). Anyone who seriously proposes the abolition of organized religion in the United States is making a political statement.

C. EDWARD WILSON AS THEORIST AND STORYTELLER

As we have seen in Wilson's discussion of religion, sociobiology is a discipline which presents various theories and narratives, as well as providing ethological and biological comparisons between species. In this section I examine the kinds of stories and metatheory Wilson presents. Part of the reason for the lack of understanding and hostility between sociobiologists and sociologists is the result of differing goals being sought and different stories being told in their separate disciplines.

Wilson makes an important distinction in *Sociobiology* between "proximate" and "ultimate" causation. Proximate causation is defined as:

> The conditions of the environment or internal physiology that trigger the responses of an organism. They are to be distinguished from the environmental forces, referred to as the ultimate causation, that led to the evolution of the response in the first place. (1975, p. 593)

Wilson's formal definition of "ultimate" causation is:

> The conditions of the environment that render certain traits adaptive and others nonadaptive; hence the adaptive traits tend to be retained in the population and are "caused" in this ultimate sense. (1975, p. 597)

He states at the beginning of *Sociobiology* that:

> Ultimate causation consists of the necessities created by the environment: the pressures imposed by weather, predators, and other stressors, and such opportunities as are presented by unfilled living space, new food sources, and accessible mates. The species responds to environmental exigencies by genetic evolution through natural selection, inadvertently shaping the anatomy, physiology, and behavior of the individual organisms.... These prime movers of evolution... are the ultimate biological causes, but they operate only over long spans of time. (1975, p. 23)

Wilson believes that sociobiology should be concerned with demonstrating ultimate causes. His initial discussion of "ultimate" and "proximate" causation analyzes aggression and the "pecking order" of chickens and argues that an earlier analysis is mistaken because the ethologists confuse "proximate" with "ultimate" causes. Wilson believes that dominance hierarchies evolve at the individual level and that "aggression" and "dominance" have "not evolved as proximate devices to provide an orderly society" (Wilson, 1975, p. 23). As Lumsden and Wilson state in *Promethean Fire*: "Sociobiology concentrates more on 'why' questions.... The query 'why' can be answered only by the study of history. And the history of biological process is by definition evolution" (1983, p. 24). Sociobiology is an evolutionary science which provides diachronic explanations of the development of particular species by natural selection. According to Wilson, sociobiologists should examine the evolutionary history of "kin selection," "reciprocal altruism," "gene-culture evolution,"[9] and male and female "reproduction strategies." Sociobiological reasoning is based on evolutionary reconstructions.

In a critique of sociobiology, Stephen Jay Gould has written that sociobiology provides a series of "Just-So" stories similar to those of Kipling: "Rudyard Kipling asked how the leopard got its spots, the rhino its wrinkled skin. He called his answers 'just-so' stories. When evolutionists try to explain form and behavior, they also tell just-so stories—and the agent is natural selection" (Gould, 1980, p. 258). Gould is pessimistic about the possibility of "testing" the theories presented and states that "Virtuosity in invention replaces testability as the criterion for acceptance" (Gould, 1980, p. 258). More recently Philip Kitcher (1993) and Elizabeth Lloyd (1994) have made strong cases for what Lloyd terms the "confirmation of evolutionary theory." Lloyd advocates what she calls a "semantic" view of theory to "establish the plausibility and importance in evolutionary biology of different categories of empirical support" and to "facilitate detailed analysis and comparison of empirical claims" (Lloyd, 1994, p. 159).

Irrespective of the technical controversies in evolutionary theory, Gould's picture of evolutionary theorists as storytellers is important and worth considering in ways which he does not develop. Even conceding, for the moment, the perceived distinction in what Niles Eldredge has termed "time frames" (1985) between social scientists and sociobiologists, it is clear that both groups are engaged in storytelling.

As Secretary of Labor Robert Reich has written, "Every culture has its own parables.... Cultural parables come in a multitude of forms.... What gives them force is their capacity to make sense of, and bring coherence to, common experience" (Reich, 1987, p. 7). Both the sociologist and the sociobiologist are attempting to "make sense of" common experiences. Both are producing what Haraway calls "framing myths." While sociology operates on a more "proximate" time frame, and sociobiology, as defined by Wilson, is primarily concerned with "ultimate" evolutionary history, both are engaged in the interpretation of common experience. We are, as Reich notes, a "meaning-seeking species" (Reich, 1987, p. 7). Wilson clearly believes that his "systematic study of the biological basis of all social behavior" will enable us to understand and interpret our "common experiences" in ways that a more "proximate" analysis misunderstands. Sociologists generally assume that biological factors are a "constant" and may be safely ignored in any contemporary analysis of human behavior. Both groups need to realize that they are telling stories about the same species and, as Wilson writes, "all of the natural sciences and social sciences form a seamless whole" (Lumsden and Wilson, 1983, p. 171).

Much of the hostility which greeted the publication of Wilson's *Sociobiology* may be interpreted as hostility toward the kinds of stories he told. It was not that social scientists denied the existence of an evolutionary past, but they challenged Wilson's interpretations of that past as well as its relevance for contemporary society. And it must be admitted that Wilson himself bears a good deal of the responsibility for the controversies which developed. The problem is that the stories Wilson tells *drastically change over time*. The images presented fluctuate greatly.

Both *Sociobiology* and *On Human Nature* present a starkly materialistic universe in which human happiness is of no consequence in a Darwinian drama designed "to favor the maximum transmission of the controlling genes" (Wilson, 1975, p. 4). For Wilson, as J.B. Schneewind has pointed out, genetic behavior is "a mindless, limitless, compulsive drive toward making copies of oneself" (Schneewind, 1978, p. 237). Wilson's images of genes and genetic influences are similar to Richard Dawkin's notion of "the selfish gene":

Now they [genes] swarm in huge colonies, safe inside gigantic lumbering robots, sealed off from the outside world, communicating with it by tortuous indirect routes, manipulating it by remote control.

They are in you and in me; they created us, body and mind; and their preservation is the ultimate rationale for our existence. They have come a long way, those replicators. Now they go by the name of genes, and we are their survival machines. (Dawkins, 1989, pp. 19 –20)

In this passage there are several themes which are defined by Philip Kitcher as "pop sociobiology" (Kitcher, 1985, pp. 14 –16). Kitcher classifies Wilson, Dawkins, and sociologist Pierre van den Berghe as "pop sociobiologists." He describes passages like the above as "the iron hand [of genetic influence] meets the empty mind" (Kitcher, 1985, p. 18). Dawkins assumes a Cartesian split between genes and environment ("sealed off from the outside world"). Human beings, according to this story, are slaves to molecular behavior. Genetic "preservation" is "the ultimate rationale for our existence." What is lacking in Dawkins is any concern with consciousness or "mind." Wilson states that as sociobiology progresses, "The mind will be more precisely explained as an epiphenomenon of the neuronal machinery of the brain" (Wilson, 1978, p. 202). If *what is missing* from an author's concepts and data is as significant as what is present, it is worth noting that the index for the entire 800-page "sociobiological exemplar" *Sociobiology: The New Synthesis* contains no references to "mind." Wilson refers instead to the "hypothalamic-limbic complex" (Wilson, 1975, p. 3). He suggests that in the case of ethical reasoning, "philosophers intuit the deontological canons of morality by consulting the emotive centers of their own hypothalamic-limbic system" (Wilson, 1975, p. 563).

That "system," however, is, according to Wilson, simply the end result of genetic evolutionary history. Human beings are genetically programmed with "conformer genes" (Wilson, 1975, p. 562) or "altruistic genes" (Wilson, 1975, p. 563). If philosophy = intuition/emotion and the "emotive centers" consulted are genetically predetermined, it is obvious that thought/sociology/philosophy can all be reduced to their biological dimensions. Biological considerations are all that is necessary and sufficient to "explain" Locke, Rousseau, or Kant.[10] Wilson's position on "mind" is a classic example of reductionism. Different levels of analysis (e.g., mind, philosophy, ethics) may be "reduced" or adequately understood and "explained" by a much "simpler" factor: "our innate predispositions" (Wilson, 1978, p. 154). Wilson is explicit in his reductionism in a sociological critique of Durkheim:

Despite the imposing holistic traditions of Durkheim in sociology and Radcliffe-Brown in anthropology, cultures are not super-organisms that evolve by their own dynamics. Rather, cultural change is the statistical product of the separate behavioral responses of large numbers of human beings who cope as best they can with social existence (Wilson, 1978, p. 81).

If "cultural change" is only "the statistical product of the separate behavioral responses of large numbers of human beings," it is self-evident that individual levels of analysis are adequate for understanding social phenomena. Furthermore, if *"biology is the key to human nature"* (Wilson, 1978, p. 14, emphasis added), and genetic or molecular analyses adequately "explain" human behavior, one need go no further in "explaining" human action. As Wilson states, "The genes hold culture on a leash" (Wilson, 1978, p. 175). Dawkins' image of humans as "lumbering robots" is essentially correct. Human beings are composed of molecular forces which are programmed to produce as many other similar molecules as possible. But as J.B. Schneewind protests in his critique of Wilson, "this is not a state of affairs that is intelligible as a goal of human striving" (Schneewind, 1978, p. 238). The story that Wilson strives to tell suggests that conscious "striving" is a neuronal "epiphenomenon." It is not clear within the terms of his own theoretical system how he was able to "break" with his own evolutionary history in such a thorough fashion.[11] Much of sociobiology appears counterintuitive. Wilson suggests, for example, that what he terms "hard-core" altruism simply doesn't exist (Wilson, 1978, p. 162). Even Mother Theresa is out to make a theological buck (Wilson, 1978, pp. 172–173). There is no way for Wilson to explain stranger helping stranger. There is no way, within the "space" provided in his own discourse, that he can adequately explain the examples of "consciousness of kind" and assistance to strangers in wartime or emergencies which I described in Chapter 1.

If everyone else is fundamentally "controlled" by their genes, why is the sociobiologist able to "escape" their impact to such an extent? It would seem to necessarily follow from Wilson's reductionism that people with similar genetic backgrounds would experience the same emotions and "intuitions"— based on their similar "hypothalamic-limbic complexes" and evolutionary history. Why do people think and feel so differently? The story that Wilson tells does not allow us to explain why storytellers tell such different stories.

If we examine the works of Wilson himself over time, we discover that he too tells different stories in different books and articles. There are a great many contradictory elements in his published works. As has been similarly claimed about Marx, there seems to be a "young" Wilson and a "mature" Wilson and their two systems often don't agree with each other. If Wilson's *Sociobiology: The New Synthesis* quickly became the "bible" of sociobiology, it has, since its publication, been subjected to a great deal of contradictory exegesis by its own author.

He argues in *Sociobiology* that one should look at genetic variation between cultures as a possible determinant of societal differences:

> Although the genes have given away most of their sovereignty, they maintain a certain amount of influence in at least the behavioral qualities that underlie variations between cultures.... Even a small portion of this variance invested in population differences might predispose societies toward cultural differences.... In short, *there is a need for a discipline of anthropological genetics.* (Wilson 1975, p. 550, emphasis added)

In an article on the "genetic foundation of human behavior" Wilson considers three possible sociobiological alternatives. One suggestion is that "natural selection exhausted the genetic variability of the species affecting social behavior.... In addition, the brain has been 'freed' from these genes in the sense that all outcomes are determined by culture" (Wilson, 1980, p. 296). A second possibility, according to Wilson, is that "Genetic variability has been exhausted.... But the resulting uniform genotype predisposes psychological development toward certain outcomes as opposed to others...species-specific human traits exist" (Wilson, 1980, p. 296).

Wilson, however, believes "that the evidence appears to lean heavily in favor" of the third possibility: "Genetic variability still exists and...at least some human behavioral traits have a genetic foundation" (Wilson, 1980, p. 296). In addition, "the evidence of genetic variation affecting social behavior is also strong" (Wilson, 1980, p. 299). Sociobiologists, according to this perspective, should be engaged in the cross-cultural determination of genetic variability and the differences in social behavior which they ultimately cause. The shadow of Arthur Jensen crosses the horizon (Gould, 1977, pp. 243–247).

Those who wish to explore sociobiological themes need to practice the "anthropological genetics" Wilson proposes in *Sociobiology*.

On the other hand, in *On Human Nature*, which was written at approximately the same time as the paper on "genetic variations," Wilson makes exactly the opposite claim: "Human social evolution is obviously more cultural than genetic.... *The sociobiological hypothesis does not therefore account for differences among societies*, but it can explain why human beings differ from other mammals" (Wilson, 1978, p. 160, emphasis added). In another quote from the same volume Wilson explicitly denies the logic behind his earlier admonition to explore genetic variability:

> Although genetic evolution of some kind continued during this later, historical sprint [the last 10,000 years], it cannot have fashioned more than a tiny fraction of the traits of human nature. Otherwise surviving hunter-gatherer people would differ genetically to a significant degree from people in advanced industrial nations, but this is demonstrably not the case. (Wilson, 1978, p. 35)

From this alternative and contrasting orientation, it seems obvious that sociobiologists should engage in explorations of what anthropologists at one time called the "psychic unity" of mankind (Harris, 1968, p. 15). One should look for *species commonalities* and *interspecies differences*. From this point of view, sociobiologists are attempting to develop in an empirical fashion what has been termed "philosophical anthropology" or general, taken-for-granted assumptions concerning human beings as a species (Honneth and Joas, 1988). One looks for cross-cultural similarities, not genetic variation. This is the orientation taken by Melvin Konner in *The Tangled Wing* (1982), which is quite possibly the most comprehensive discussion available of the biological foundations of species commonalities.

In their recently published volume *Interactions: The Biological Context of Human Social Systems*, Niles Eldredge and Marjorie Grene specifically propose a "schema for a philosophical anthropology" (Eldredge and Grene, 1992, pp. 184 –201). They argue, for example, that human sociality is structured by "mediated immediacy." Humans learn to perceive everything "through the mediation of linguistic and other cultural devices" (Eldredge and Grene, 1992, p. 185). They quote with approval Rousseau who argued that we need each other "to shape a place for ourselves within a nature that would defeat each of us alone" (Eldredge and Grene, 1992, pp. 184–185). Human culture, according to the coauthor of punctuated equilibria theory, requires a different level of analysis than Wilson's reductionism allows. "Mind" and "culture" are not biological epiphenomena. Obviously cultures change and intellectual history is not somehow frozen in time. On the other hand, we all— simply by being members of the same species—share many similar problems and needs.

It makes a great deal of difference whether a sociobiologist is looking for genetic variation or species commonalities. A number of human characteristics do vary cross-culturally. Skin pigmentation, blood groups, and lactose tolerance are well-known examples (Sutton and Wagner, 1985, pp. 398 –411). According to Sutton and Wagner, the percentage of Thais who are lactase-positive is only 3% of the population. For Sweden, the figure is 97%. Clearly the ability to absorb the nutrients in milk varies by culture and geographical area (Weiss and Mann, 1981, pp. 475–477). On the other hand, these examples are well-known in part simply because they are so well-documented and so unusual. As Wilson himself states, it is "demonstrably not the case" that contemporary hunter-gatherers "differ genetically to a significant degree from people in advanced industrial nations" (Wilson, 1978, p. 35). He observes that "I do not for a moment ascribe the relative performances of modern societies to genetic differences" (Wilson, 1978, p. 82). While Wilson then adds that "there is a limit...beyond which biological evolution will begin to pull cultural evolution back to itself" (Wilson, 1978, p. 82), *this is a completely different issue.* The failure of sociologists to distinguish between these two fundamentally different themes has contributed to the a priori rejection of sociobiology by much of sociology. Wilson has greatly added to the confusion by presenting two completely distinct theoretical positions as the "essence" of his discipline.

Concentrating on species commonalities may lead to a conservative delineation of "limits" to change. As we have seen, this is one of the positions taken by Wilson. But it is clear that whatever "limits" obtain are universal. Sociobiologists, for example, have placed much importance on the research carried out on Israeli kibbutzim which suggests that infants who grow up in close physical proximity generally develop a sexual aversion towards each other. This has important consequences for what is viewed by sociobiologists as the universal "incest taboo" (Wilson, 1978, pp. 37–38). While this research has been subject to criticism (Kitcher, 1985, pp. 270–280), the important theoretical point is that sociobiologists, in this case, are proposing a process and theory of socialization which would apply in any culture which practices it. While the kibbutz may serve as a "natural experiment," it is not being proposed that Israelis somehow differ genetically from other people.

The failure to understand this distinction, along with Wilson's tendency to advocate various and contradictory positions, has helped to contribute to the vehemence with which he has been attacked. Richard Lerner and the group Science for the People have pointed to what they see as similarities between Wilson's work and Nazism (Lerner, 1992; Chasin, 1977; Alper, Beckwith and Miller, 1978). By concentrating on an empirical, cross-cultural analysis of human commonalities, however, Wilson can legitimately claim that his sociobiology is completely contrary to the Nazi classification of "racial" differences. In later chapters we will extend his search for common or cross-cultural human needs and environments. At this point I only wish to note the distinctions in logic and analysis which are implied by looking for any possible differences or any possible commonalities between and across cultures.

By attempting to "force" the data into the taken-for-granted assumption of genetic differences, one may wind up with the pop sociobiological absurdities of University of Western Ontario psychologist J. Philippe Rushton, who argues—incredibly—that blacks and whites in the United States practice different reproductive strategies based on the common Darwinian distinction between "r" and "K" reproductive strategies (Rushton, 1987, 1988a, 1988b). An "r" strategy produces the maximum number of infants with the minimum amount of parental care and involvement. A "K" strategy is the opposite. Rushton seems to actually believe that "Mongoloids are more K-selected than Caucasoids, who in turn are more K-selected than Negroids" (Rushton, 1987, p. 1020). That is, differences in numbers of children between "races" are due to differences in "racial" chromosomes. There is, unfortunately, not "a shred of direct scientific evidence" that different people have different genes which "make them more or less K-like" (Lerner, 1992, pp. 141–142). As Richard Lerner points out, it is also true, of course, that "r" and "K" reproduction strategies are used by biologists to distinguish species, not groups within the same species. To the extent that Wilson looks at common species characteristics, it is unfair and inaccurate to condemn his narratives in the same fashion as a story which contains the crudities and absurdities of Rushton. This is especially true of his more recent writings on "biodiversity" (Wilson, 1992).

As I have previously suggested, the ambiguities in Wilson's own writing are partly responsible for the criticism he has received. In a discussion of "the sociobiology controversy" in 1983, for example, Wilson makes an incredibly damaging, self-critical statement. It now appears that most of *Sociobiology* was fundamentally mistaken:

> But this way of describing human life [as presented in *Sociobiology*], the critics insisted, remains grossly inadequate. Human beings are not automata that perform simply according to the instructions of their genes. They have minds and free will. They can perceive and reflect upon the consequences of their actions. This high level of human mental activity creates culture, which has achieved a life of its own beyond the ordinary limits of biology. The principal habitat of the human mind is the very culture that it creates. Consequently, individual cultures diverge in their evolution and they vary enormously from one society to the next in ways that cannot be explained by traditional reductionistic biological analysis. The questions of importance in the social sciences—of mind, self, culture, and history— *are beyond the reach of sociobiology as that subject matter was originally formulated.* These criticisms of human sociobiology, also forcefully argued by Science for the People, were largely correct (!). *They came to be fully appreciated even by those most optimistic* about the prospects of the new discipline [i.e., Edward Wilson]. (Lumsden and Wilson, 1983, p. 45, emphasis added)

It is as if Mortimer Adler suddenly admitted that Nietzsche had been right all along, but not to worry. His own philosophical system is still intact. One hardly knows what to make of this kind of total self-deprecation. It is clearly effective as a debating technique and rhetorical strategy. Of course I understand what you are saying/have said/mean/did mean. Of course I am taking your arguments into account.[12] Now, let's go on from here. And of course nothing has really changed. To some extent, I think it is fair to say Wilson has followed this approach. It is a kind of tolerant, ecumenical acceptance of all criticism followed by a failure to take it into account in any significant fashion. The stories Wilson tells after 1983 do not seem to indicate a conversion experience. Edward Wilson has not suddenly embraced Herbert Blumer, Alfred Schultz, or Erving Goffman.

For example, an article written by Wilson and Michael Ruse in 1986 argues that "biology shows that internal moral principles do exist.... They are immanent in the unique programmes of the brain that originated during evolution" (Ruse and Wilson, 1986, p. 174). Furthermore, "human thinking is under the influence of 'epigenetic rules,' genetically based processes of development that predispose the individual to adopt one or a few forms of behaviors as opposed to others" (Ruse and Wilson, 1986, p. 180). This sounds suspiciously like the definition of "mind" as a neuronal epiphenomenon of the "hypothalamic-limbic complex—Wilson's original position in 1975. The "largely correct" strictures of Science for the People are forgotten. The reductionism which was evident to critics of *Sociobiology* is once again prominent. Perhaps the subtle nuances of Wilson's self-criticism in 1983 have themselves become victims of a "tough-minded" process of "natural selection" operating within the sociobiological community (see Endnote 11).

Conversely, it is clear that Wilson was never the Nazi-inspired ogre envisioned by Science for the People. As I have tried to make clear, the relationships between political positions and scientific positions are extremely complex and flexible. Once Wilson began to espouse the commonalities of humankind, his position was *ipso facto* contrary to the "Social Darwinist" fantasies of the early eugenicists (Degler, 1991, pp. 32–83; Hofstadter, 1959, pp. 170–200). In his recent work *The Diversity of Life* (1992), Wilson makes his liberal politics absolutely clear. He is very strongly in favor of "an environmental ethic" which would protect "biodiversity" at all costs. If this ethic requires "the strong hand of protective law" and governmental regulation, Wilson argues that this is the government's "moral responsibility" (Wilson, 1992, p. 342). He suggests that the "stewardship of environment" is an issue "where all reflective persons can surely find common ground" (Wilson, 1992, p. 351). Environmental destruction would eliminate "still undeveloped medicines, crops, pharmaceuticals, timber, fibers, pulp, soil-restoring vegetation" as well as untold medical products (Wilson, 1992, p. 347). Wilson believes that only "an enduring environmental ethic" will preserve "access to the world in which the human spirit was born" (Wilson, 1992, p. 351).

As we have seen, Wilson places great stress on religion calling it "the most complex" and "ineradicable" part of "human nature" (Wilson, 1978, p. 176). The problem is that Wilson's conception of "religion" is simplistic in the extreme. As Mary Midgley observes in *Evolution as a Religion*, Wilson "seldom mentions any manifestation of religion which is not openly crude and contemptible" (Midgley, 1985, p. 113). Religion is, above all, "the process by which individuals are persuaded to subordinate their immediate self-interest to the interests of the group" (Wilson, 1978, p. 183). If "society" is viewed ontologically as merely the struggle of all against all—survival of the fittest—than any reference to "the group" per se is illegitimate and illusory. The individualistic, taken-for-granted assumption is that there is always and inevitably a necessary conflict between "society"—which liberal nominalism regards as a dubious level of analysis to begin with—and the individual. But what then becomes of Wilson's "environmental ethic" and his acceptance of institutional means to enforce its acceptance? In this situation he assumes no conflict exists between what is "good" for the individual and what is essential for societal survival. In the case of "environmental" ethics the individual and social levels of analysis require and complement each other. Surely the same is true of much religious activity.

Wilson ignores entire aspects of religious experience with his simplistic "scientific materialism." In a very real sense much of "Liberation Theology" is fundamentally concerned with an "environmental ethic" (Berryman, 1987). Liberation Theology in Latin America sees no necessary conflict between the "real" interests of individuals, social development, and critical education (Garcia, 1987). Religion does not presuppose, as Wilson seems to believe, scientific obscurantism and political tyranny. By denying the complex elements of religious experience, Wilson eliminates one potential source of support for the environmental ethic he wants to implement.

In an important article entitled "Rival Fatalisms: The Hollowness of the Sociobiology Debate" Mary Midgley has analyzed the reductionism evident in Wilson's religious discussion. She compares him to "those sage characters, who, in the French Revolution, enthroned the Goddess of Reason on the altar of Notre Dame and expected the populace to worship her" (Midgley, 1980, p. 24). Wilson believes that if "religion...can be systematically analyzed and explained" its influence as a source of morality "will be gone forever" (Wilson, 1978, p. 208). Explaining religion, however, is qualitatively distinct from experiencing it. Jumping in the water is not the same thing as knowing how and why we are able to swim (i.e., the "evolutionary history" of swimming). Wilson's analysis of religion suffers from an inability to distinguish between mysticism and microscopes. Religion and science are not in all ways commensurable—as Wilson's "scientific materialism" appears to assume.

By propagating a radically individualistic, "genetic" narrative, Wilson constructs a vision of humans as self-sufficient monads each pursuing his or her own "rational" self-interest by as much genetic duplication as possible. There is not, as Darwin stated of his own work in the famous conclusion of *On the Origin of Species*, a "grandeur in this view of life, with its several powers" (Darwin, 1984 [1859], p. 228).   There is only a reductionistic "Scientific Materialism" which excludes all consideration of significant elements of human experience. Wilson's world is cold, hard, and devoid of human meaning and purpose.[13] It is not a place for developing human connections with each other or with other species. There is no sense of wonder. It is the solipsistic universe of "the selfish gene."

By way of contrast, a much different image of the "natural world" and its significance for human beings is provided in the writings of anthropologist and naturalist Loren Eiseley. In such works as "How Flowers Changed the World" (Eiseley, 1959, pp. 61–77) or *The Night Country* (1971) Eiseley convincingly demonstrates that poetry, religion, and science can peacefully and powerfully coexist. Consider the world he describes in "The Mind as Nature":

> Directly stated, the evolution of the entire universe—stars, elements, life, man—is a process of drawing something out of nothing, out of the utter void of nonbeing. The creative element in the mind of man— that latency which can conceive gods, carve statues, move the heart with symbols of great poetry or devise the formulas of modern physics— emerges in as mysterious a fashion as those elementary particles which leap into momentary existence in great cyclotrons, only to vanish again like infinitesimal ghosts. The reality we know in our limited lifetimes is dwarfed by the unseen potential of the abyss where science stops. (Eiseley, 1971, pp. 214–215)

If Wilson's *Sociobiology* is a kind of biological reincarnation of Baron Holbach's systematic materialism (1970), Eiseley represents Thoreau living in Walden and overcome by a sense of wonder and human possibility.[14] To Eiseley much of nature is mysterious, profound, and impossible to adequately understand by "scientific" methods alone. There is, however, no necessary conflict between the various kinds of analyses. Wilson states that he considers the scientific ethos "superior to religion" (Wilson, 1978, p. 208). Eiseley, I believe, would say that neither is "superior" to the other because they have different purposes and serve different functions. At times, if we are lucky, they combine and provide the fortunate onlooker with a synergistic understanding and appreciation of his or her own natural and social universe. Eiseley, to some extent, reminds one of the Darwin who was willing to consider "the mental powers of worms" (Rachels, 1990, p. 134). Wilson's "taxonomic eye" tends to favor a more reductionistic approach.[15]

From the biocritical perspective on human needs which I develop in this book, the major shortcoming of Wilson's *Sociobiology* concerns the kinds of evolutionary narratives he relates and the gaps or "aporias" they contain. Wilson's narratives tend to conflate "proximate" and "ultimate" evolutionary processes in an unwarranted reduction of the complexities of human motivations and actions. As William Allman has observed:

> Human beings love their children because those ancestors who loved their children had more surviving children, and we're descended from them and not the others who didn't love their kids. So in the "grand evolutionary biological" sense, we love our kids because of genes. But in the real sense of *Why do you love your kids*? you love them because it is part of your human nature that evolved as part of our ancestors' brain mechanisms. There is nothing in those brain mechanisms that says that kid has your genes, and so you should love him. (Allman, 1994, p. 49, emphasis in original)

A great many sociobiological narratives seem unrealistic and even absurd because they fail to make the kinds of distinctions Allman suggests are essential. It is not necessary, in other words, to reduce religion to a kind of crude materialistic epiphenomenon. Because "proximate" factors are operative, one is not required to assume that men and women should necessarily be more sexually attracted towards those people who can increase their genetic progeny. The sexual attraction is the same no matter what the "maximization principle" implies. Wilson's reductionism is similar to early varieties of sociological functionalism, but he comes at the data from the opposite direction. Functionalists tended to assume that the current purpose or function of social behavior necessarily explained something about its origin. Wilson's narratives read as if he believes that the ultimate causes of evolutionary development explain proximate human motivations. Both positions are fundamentally reductionistic and mistaken. They confound explanations of evolutionary history with the proximate mechanisms which are the result of that history.

An alternative to the unnecessary reductionism evident in Wilson is provided in the writings of Robert Richards. Richards is the foremost proponent in the United States of what has been termed "evolutionary ethics." Perhaps his writings extend the reductionistic "natural theology" (Kaye, 1986) of Wilson in a productive fashion. If so, Richards' importance for sociology and the development of a biocritical perspective could be considerable and is worth examining at length. In the following chapter we will critically examine his "Revised Version" of evolutionary theory and its relationship to previous work on evolutionary ethics.

III

EVOLUTIONARY ETHICS: THE NATURALISTIC FALLACY AND THE REVISED VERSION OF ROBERT RICHARDS

A. INTRODUCTION

Sociological discussions of facts and values need to take into account the work which has been done in the field of evolutionary ethics on the "naturalistic fallacy." Previous work done in the field of evolutionary ethics has suggested that the debate over values in social science is unnecessary and, in fact, has been resolved. In this chapter I will examine the validity of this position by looking at the evolutionary ethics of philosopher and historian of science Robert Richards. Richards' sophisticated philosophical analysis avoids many of the simplistic assumptions of sociobiologists such as Wilson, although his analysis also begins with our evolutionary past. Richards' work presents an excellent opportunity for sociologists to examine the possibility of an evolutionary ethics. If he has indeed overcome the fact/value dualism, he deserves the widest possible audience.

One of the fundamental distinctions evident in the history of philosophy is the differentiation between a phrase that is prescriptive and a phrase that is descriptive: One cannot legitimately obtain an "ought" from an "is." Max Weber introduced the same distinction into sociological discourse with his description of "Science as a Vocation" (Weber, 1946 [1919], pp. 129 –156). As Weber argued, "To take a practical political stand is one thing, and to analyze political structures and party positions is another" (1946 [1919], p. 145). This presumably inviolable barrier was first described by David Hume in 1739:

> In every system of morality which I have hitherto met with, I have always remarked that the author proceeds in the ordinary way of reasoning...when all of a sudden I am surprised to find that instead of the usual...propositions is and is not, I meet with no proposition that is not connected with an ought and an ought not. This change is

imperceptible, but is, however, of the last consequence. For as this ought or ought not expresses some new relation or affirmation, it is necessary that it should be observed and explained; and at the same time that a reason should be given for what seems altogether inconceivable, how this *new relation can be a deduction from others* which are entirely different from it (Hume, 1739, Treatise III.i.I, emphasis in original).

This is the philosophical reasoning behind the commonplace sociological observation that science is "objective" but values are inherently "subjective." The attempt to derive facts from values is believed to always involve Hume's "naturalistic fallacy" (Midgley, 1978, pp. 177–200). We might, for example, agree on how a particular social problem is described (i.e., the number of homeless), but this tells us nothing about what to do about any specific situation. There is a fundamental difference—a "deduction from others which are entirely different from it"—between a prescriptive and a descriptive sentence (Moore, 1903). In more formal philosophical language, a prescriptive statement must always include a value premise. When this appears not to be the case, it is merely an illegitimately taken-for-granted and unexpressed assumption.

A number of prominent scientists have argued that the Cartesian split between the "is" and the "ought" may be overcome by the use of evolutionary explanations and theory: an "evolutionary ethics" is available which bridges the gap identified by Hume. If true, this has major implications for sociological theory and analysis because the generally accepted sociological distinction between the subjective and the objective is rendered moot. Sociologists no longer need concern themselves with the question of "values" in social science (Friedrichs, 1970; Myrdal, 1969; Bernstein, 1976). Particular values are intrinsic to the evolutionary process. From this perspective, the proper "factual" description includes the values which are an immanent result of our evolutionary history.

In *On Human Nature*, for example, Edward Wilson argues that "a correct application of evolutionary theory also favors diversity in the gene pool as a cardinal value" (Wilson, 1978, p. 205). He suggests that "universal human rights might properly be regarded as a...primary value" (Wilson, 1978, p. 206). As we have seen in the previous chapter, Wilson is very much interested in religion, and he strongly believes that sociobiology has ethical and religious implications (Wilson, 1978, pp. 176 –217). But does Wilson's elaboration of "evolutionary ethics" actually overcome Hume's objections?

It is clear that in the above quotations Wilson is including implicit and unspecified value criteria which therefore make possible the transition from "is" to "ought." "Diversity in the gene pool" is only a "cardinal value" as long as one assumes that is, in fact, the case. Such diversity is clearly a descriptive statement. If one assumes unchanging environmental conditions over extended periods of time, it is evident that a lack of diversity would be the most "efficient" adaptation. In a condition of environmental stasis, a viable response need not presuppose diversity. Thus the "value" of such diversity in our own situation is a value judgment as to its efficiency with respect to *Homo sapiens*.

The statement on "universal human rights" is even more transparent, if also more muddled. Wilson seems to believe that "because we are mammals" and "our societies are based on the mammalian plan," we have a "mammalian imperative" to promote "universal human rights." Mammals promote the reproductive success of their kin and try "to enjoy the benefits of group membership" (Wilson, 1978, p. 206). Therefore, humans "will accede to universal rights because power is too fluid in advanced technological societies to circumvent this mammalian imperative" (Wilson, 1978, p. 206). The best one can say at this point is that Wilson's discussion is unintentionally incoherent. Even if we assume the existence of the "mammalian plan," it is easy to see what value premise is being omitted:

Premise: Mammals share a biological imperative promoting the reproductive success of their kin and group living.

Conclusion: Humans should promote reproductive success and group living by emphasizing universal human rights.

Accepting for the moment the proposed equating of sociality, kin selection and human rights, it is still obvious that a value premise is lacking in Wilson's presentation. He assumes that we should follow our "biological" imperatives, or what David Barash calls "the whisperings within" (1979). We should, in other words, do what our genetic inheritance "prompts" us to do. The missing "value premise," in other words, is the following:

Second Premise: Humans ought to do what their evolutionary history predisposes them to do.

It is the Second Premise which supplies the "ought" which makes the transition possible between the "is" and the "ought" in Wilson's argument. Much of sociobiology makes similar kinds of assumptions, but without specific and explicit theories of human needs, it is unclear why we should pay attention to our genetic inheritance.   As Peter Singer has remarked, "reasoning beings are not bound to do what makes evolutionary sense" (Singer, 1981, p. 81). We need additional criteria which provide reasons for following the proposed dictates of Wilson's sociobiology. One might make the further assumption that evolutionary history and genetic inheritance have given us specific needs as a species. Surprisingly, much of sociobiology ignores the concept of "needs" and assumes that "biological" equals "desirable" equals "socially worthwhile." Many sociobiologists do not see the necessity of making the kinds of distinctions made by Hume. The "fact/value" problem supposedly disappears in a plethora of "Biological Imperatives."

Robert Richards' contemporary attempt to develop an evolutionary ethics has had many historical antecedents. Herbert Spencer (1820 – 1903) was a well-known sociological proponent of the evolutionary perspective. While Spencer has faded from contemporary view, his writings provide clear examples of the strengths and weaknesses of the evolutionary approach. Richards goes so far as to suggest that Spencer developed a kind of "evolutionary Kantianism" which "solved" the ongoing arguments between empiricists such as Locke and the disciples of Kant (Richards, 1987, pp. 285 –286). Spencer, according to Richards, showed that "the structures of thought and perception in each individual were a priori and necessary, but [they were] the evolved consequences of the inheritance of acquired mental habits" (Richards, 1987, p. 286). We each develop with similar "structures of thought" (i.e., Kant's "a priori") but those structures are a result of evolutionary history and do not represent an unchanging "transcendental" consciousness.   As Richards notes, other than the discredited "Lamarckian" or "acquired" theory of inheritance, "we now regard this conclusion as essentially correct" (Richards, 1987, p. 286). He argues that "Spencer deserves at least honorable mention for the Newton prize" for integrating the social sciences in the same fashion as Newton did for physics (Richards, 1987, p. 287). From the point of view of the biocritical perspective I will develop in Chapter 5, one of the advantages of Spencer's analysis was his view of humankind as fundamentally similar in species characteristics and evolutionary history.

Unfortunately Spencer's work also exemplifies many of the shortcomings characteristic of contemporary sociobiologists with respect to the "naturalistic fallacy." He saw evolution as necessarily progressive (Timascheff, 1957, pp. 33–33). He visualized change as "a long-run movement toward increased social harmony and human happiness" (Ashley and Orenstein, 1990, p. 154). Spencer, not Darwin, coined the phrase "survival of the fittest" and believed that "the fittest societies survive, thereby leading to an adaptive upgrading of the world as a whole" (Ritzer, 1983, p. 27). Movement from "homogeneity" to "heterogeneity" resulted in a universal "law of progress" which, like religious theodicies, enabled Spencer to see "goodness even in the face of the most brutal facts" (Oates, 1988, p. 447). As David Ashley and David Michael Orenstein note, *"Evolutionary progress was not an outcome of his sociology; It was a fundamental assumption on which his sociology was constructed* (Ashley and Orenstein, 1990, pp. 167–168, emphasis in original).

If "progress" is inherent in evolutionary development, it seemed self-evident to Spencer that an accurate formulation of human evolution implied positive evaluations. As long as one viewed "progress" as "positive" or "good," one only needed to "let nature run its course." We will, in other words, naturally evolve towards an optimal state. All that is necessary is to let things alone. This, of course, is the justification of Spencer's infamous laissez faire "Social Darwinism." Beyond an absolute minimum of social regulation, "all governmental regulations harmed society" (Ashley and Orenstein, 1990, p. 168). They "unnaturally" interfered with a socially progressive and benevolent evolutionary process. The "proper" mores are intrinsic to social evolution. By merely describing what "is" we imply what "should be." All we need to do is not interfere with "natural" social dynamics.

Unfortunately for Spencer, a number of his contemporaries pointed out various problems with his use of the term "natural" which are still relevant to contemporary discussions of evolutionary ethics. One of the most famous was Thomas Huxley who argued that the "cosmic process" was exactly the opposite of what Spencer claimed. He saw ethical progress as depending on "restraints upon the struggle for existence between men and society" (Huxley, 1993 [1894], p. 44). Ethical progress, according to Huxley, "repudiates the gladiatorial theory of existence" (Huxley, 1993 [1894], p. 67). It is precisely our opposition to the "natural" which, according to Huxley, propels whatever "progress" is discernable in human evolution. As Huxley pointed out, "the thief and the murderer follow nature just as much as the philanthropist" (Huxley, 1993 [1894, p. 66). How do we determine which is more "natural"? Huxley justifiably critiques Spencer's evolutionary utopianism for assuming a Panglossian conception and evaluation of the evolutionary process. This is still a problem for any naturalistic ethics, as we shall see in our analysis of Richards. Natural disasters, disease, plague, cruelty, and murder are seemingly as "natural" as "progressive" evolutionary trends. Whether or not events are given a positive designation depends on a selective and prior evaluation of particular events. A "value premise" is always present. For Huxley, although he used different terminology, the "naturalistic fallacy" is clearly operative in all "positive" conceptions of human evolution. Any naturalistic ethics needs to confront this fundamental criticism.

Several authors have argued that Huxley's arguments can be adequately answered. One of the most famous proponents of an alternative approach was Huxley's own grandson, Julian Huxley. He developed a theoretical perspective he termed "evolutionary humanism" which demonstrated, he believed, the immanent values fundamental to human evolution (Huxley, 1957, pp. 181–212). It seems clear, however, from such works as *Religion Without Revelation* (1957) that Julian Huxley's work exhibits the same mingling of evaluation and description as does Spencer's. Unless one accepts the taken-for-granted assumptions and evaluations presumed by Huxley, his description of evolution is literally non-sense. Huxley argues that "man" is the "highest" form of life. He further suggests that:

> The past history of biological evolution gives us a certain further guidance. We can justifiably extrapolate some of the main trends of progress into the future, and conclude that man should aim at a continued increase of those qualities which have spelt progress in the biological past—efficiency and control of the environment...wholeness and harmony of working...*storage of experience, degree of mental organization*. (Huxley, 1957, p. 193, emphasis added)

We see in Huxley's remarks a specific example of the shift from "is" to "ought" which Hume criticizes. It seems obvious that what Huxley regards as "guidance" and "progress" depend on prior evaluative conceptions of human happiness or morality. In this respect, his grandfather's criticisms of Spencer's position are more justified and coherent than his own writings and evaluations.[16]

A more sophisticated attempt at a naturalistic ethics is presented in the work of Mary Midgley (1978, 1984, 1993). In *Beast and Man: The Roots of Human Nature* (1978) she directly confronts the criticism of Thomas Huxley and others that there is a basic distinction between the "natural" and whatever we evaluate as "good." Midgley argues that what is seen as "natural" is "never just a condition or activity...but a certain *level* of that condition or activity, proportionate to the rest of one's life" (Midgley, 1978, p. 79, emphasis in original). She believes, in other words, that certain combinations of activity are essential to what should be viewed as "natural" and that not every activity which occurs is "natural" in her terms.

Midgley suggests that we may discuss what is natural in a "weak" sense and in a "strong" sense. Using her terminology, cruelty is "natural" in a "weak" sense simply because it occurs (Midgley, 1978, p. 79). She claims that in a "strong" sense it is "unnatural" because, quoting Bishop Joseph Butler, the eighteenth-century English theologian, it is "contrary to the whole constitution of that nature" (Midgley, 1978, p. 79). Certain actions, as Plato and Aristotle believed, are more rewarding and "natural" than others for all human beings as integrated beings, as a result of their common evolutionary background and species characteristics. Midgley argues that there is "some underlying human nature—some structure indicating what kinds of things can be good and bad for human beings" (Midgley, 1993, p. 92, emphasis in original). Particular actions are more likely to "naturally" lead to a satisfying human existence which is "harmonious through time" (Midgley, 1984, p. 186). Certain activities are more likely than others to satisfy human needs.

Any transcultural theory of human needs assumes that Midgley's argument is correct in this respect. Midgley's position begins to seriously address the criticisms of Huxley concerning a "naturalistic" ethics. As it stands, her distinction between a "weak" sense and a "strong" sense of "natural" is not entirely convincing. It is clear that this distinction depends on certain prior philosophical and ethical criteria as to what constitutes a "balanced" life. It also depends on an implied concept of human "potential." Midgley assumes that we are capable of achieving "more" than we usually do but offers few criteria upon which one might make a determination of "lost" potential. How do we compare different ways of achieving what is presumed to be "natural"? How do we decide who is correct when conceptions of "the natural" disagree and conflict? These are some of the questions we will examine in the following chapter, which discusses the concept of "human needs."

While Midgley's analysis raises important questions for any evolutionary ethics, she is unclear in certain areas which are of special interest to Robert Richards. Both Midgley and Richards believe that we have no option but to reason from facts to values. If we ask "how should this institution be altered," according to Midgley, we have "no option but to reason from the facts about human wants and needs"[17] (Midgley, 1978, p. 189). Richards argues similarly that all ethical systems require "empirical assumptions" (Richards, 1987, p. 615). Richards, however, presents an explicit demonstration of how he believes it is possible to move beyond the fact/value dichotomy.

Before we look at Richards' specific arguments concerning the "naturalistic fallacy," let us look more closely at the idea that any ethical theory requires "empirical assumptions." Even if there are some distinctions to be made between "facts" and "values," the elementary distinction between these terms needs to be conceptually unpacked and elaborated. More complexity is involved than is typically assumed by sociological positivism (Alexander, 1982; Bryant, 1985). Utilizing an evolutionary or biosocial perspective influences social policy decisions even if the traditional Cartesian split between "facts" and "values" is assumed to be valid.

Consider the arguments over eugenics that were common in the United States during the early part of this century (Hofstadter, 1955, pp. 161–204; Degler, 1991, pp. 32–55). It was assumed by many during that period that "positive" steps could be taken genetically to promote racial "fitness" and that the reduction of "undesirable" genetic material was one useful approach. Involuntary sterilization of the genetically "unfit" began in Indiana, which in 1907 became the first state to enact an involuntary sterilization law (Degler, 1991, p. 45). By the 1930s, 12,000 involuntary sterilizations had been carried out in the U.S. on various definitions of "misfits" (Degler, 1991, p. 46). Irrespective of their many other faults, it was soon clear to biologists that empirical facts demonstrated the absolute futility of the sterilization programs. Human beings were simply not biologically constituted in the manner which the sterilization laws assumed. As W.D. Hudson has written, there is clearly a connection between evaluations and factual assumptions (Hudson, 1969, p. 29).

The basic biological difficulty involved in all the sterilization programs is that the carriers of the majority of harmful genetic defects are heterozygous.

This means that the individual involved carries at least two different alleles, or alternative forms of a gene, in the same position. Many genetic deficiencies, however, which result in such conditions as cystic fibrosis are homozygous recessive traits. Thus in a familiar example, the sickle-cell anemia trait only develops in children when it is passed on by both parents (Sutton and Wagner, 1985, p. 321). If the trait is only inherited from one parent, the negative effects of the disease are recessive (Cummings, 1991, pp. 378–380).

Given the elementary assumptions of population genetics, it is possible to calculate the heterozygote frequency in a population which is necessary in order to produce a particular homozygous frequency. The frequency of heterozygous carriers required is much greater than the corresponding homozygous population which manifests observable phenotypic "defects." For example sickle-cell anemia affects approximately 1 in 500 black North Americans (Cummings, 1991, p. 379). In order for this frequency to occur, it requires a heterozygous frequency of 1 in 12.

Cummings gives a simple example with respect to albinism. Assume that it has one chance in 10,000 of occurring. Most people might assume that the corresponding heterozygote frequency must also be quite low, but such is not the case. If 1 in 10,000 people are homozygous for albinism, 1 in 50 people must be heterozygous to produce this result. Why? The chances that two homozygous persons will marry is $1/2500$ ($1/50 \times 1/50$). Because they are heterozygous, according to the basic assumptions of Mendelian genetics, the chance they will produce a homozygous recessive child is $1/4$. The chance that the marriage will produce an albino child is therefore $1/2500 \times 1/4 = 1/10,000$. For the trait to be present in $1/10,000$ people, 1 in 50 must be heterozygous. Similar disparities exist with other seemingly small percentages. The corresponding figure for a 1 in 20,000 chance of developing a recessive trait is that 1 in 71 persons must be heterozygous for that trait (Cummings, 1991, pp. 379–380).

The empirical facts concerning genetic distribution can now be seen as having a major bearing on the question of "sterilization" legislation. It does no "good," even accepting the aims of the legislation, to sterilize homozygous or recognizable "carriers" of a particular trait because the vast majority of those responsible for producing the phenotypic variations are heterozygous carriers. There is no way to determine this population by visual inspection. They appear entirely "normal." There is, in fact, nothing "wrong" with them, except that in combination with a similar individual the resulting children may carry a genetic disorder. Even if involuntary sterilizations had been performed on all "visible" carriers, it would have had very little effect on the extent of inherited genetic differences. Neil Tennant estimates that for many recessive traits "sterilization of all homozygotes would only *halve the frequency of the recessive gene in 500 generations*" (Tennant, 1983, p. 291, emphasis added). The factual relationships in this case preclude by definition the "success" of the attempted programs. Facts have a bearing on ethical decisions.

Both Midgley and Richards assume that people need to justify and give reasons for their ethical choices. They both argue that the assumptions one makes concerning "human nature" influence ethical decisions. When we think we are doing something praiseworthy, we are necessarily assuming something about the particular situation or the people that are influenced by our actions. Sociologists are not, as has been suggested by both Karl Mannheim (1936) and Karl Popper (1963), a kind of "unattached" species of "free-floating" falsificationists. As both Midgley and Richards make clear, our evolutionary and biosocial history make a difference. Richards believes that his position bridges the gap between facts and values. If that is true, his writings are of the utmost importance for sociologists.

B. ROBERT RICHARDS' EVOLUTIONARY ETHICS

Contrary to contemporary specialization in academia, Dr. Robert Richards is professor of history, philosophy, and behavioral science at the University of Chicago. He is also chairman of the Committee on the Conceptual Foundations of Science and director of the Program in History, Philosophy, and Social Studies of Science and Medicine (Callebaut, 1993, p. 435; Richards, 1987). In 1988 he received the Pfizer Prize given by the History of Science Society for *Darwin and the Emergence of Evolutionary Theories of Mind and Behavior* (1987). The award honors the outstanding book in the history of science during the preceding three years (Callebaut, 1993, p. 435). This work also contains Richards' most extensive treatment of evolutionary ethics (Richards, 1987, pp. 595–627).

Richards describes his own approach as "a kind of meta-ethical perspective meant to deal with certain problems in the conceptions of ethics, namely problems related to the naturalistic fallacy" (Richards, quoted in Callebaut, 1993, p. 439). As will become evident, Richards vehemently disagrees with Hume's depiction of an unbridgeable fact/value dichotomy. At the same time, he believes that evolutionary biology is inevitably concerned with the kinds of philosophical problems which have been the subject of much historical debate. He argues that evolutionary biology is "intrinsically historical":

> The practitioners of contemporary evolutionary theory have—perhaps because of the nature of their own science—become terribly interested in both conceptual philosophical problems and historical problems. One only has to mention people like Steve Gould, Richard Lewontin, and Ernst Mayr to recognize that philosophical and historical considerations inform the development of their own views. (Richards, quoted in Callebaut, 1993, p. 77)

According to Richards, evolutionary biologists have a tendency to argue that they are promoting a "Darwinian" point of view. A work such as his prize-winning volume on Darwin may at least help to clarify this particular issue:

> This [appeal to a "patron saint" such as Darwin] goes on all the time in science in one fashion or another. It is a little more obvious, I think, in evolutionary biology. And by the opponents there are attempts to undercut that authority by suggesting that someone advancing a so-called "Darwinian" view would, if he were thinking correctly about the problem, discover that it is not Darwin at all whose case he is moving, but someone like, perhaps, Ernst Haeckel. In this way, historical considerations play a large role in the kinds of disputes and their arbitration that go on in evolutionary biology. That is one of the ways in which historians can play—a rather modest—role in contemporary discussions, if only as referees to point out when one side is playing loose with the evidence.[18] (Richards, quoted in Callebaut, 1993, p. 78)

While Richards has been appropriately honored for his contributions to a Darwinian "dialogue,"[19] it is in his role as a philosopher of science dealing with "problems related to the naturalistic fallacy" which is of special concern to sociologists. As philosopher William Hughes has stated of Richards, "He has a much better understanding of the logic that lies behind the naturalistic fallacy than earlier evolutionary theorists, and his arguments therefore deserve careful consideration" (Hughes, 1986, p. 307). If, as Richards argues, facts in some sense imply particular values, than we should be able to similarly claim that "objective" situations suggest or imply particular courses of action. This is a conclusion which would be of considerable interest to the positivistic tradition in sociology which "draws an unbridgeable distinction between empirical facts and judgments of value" (Rhoads, 1991, p. 37).

Despite all the "critical," "subjective" or "postmodernist" theories available in sociology today, I agree with John Rhoads' estimation that the "positivist model...influences profoundly" the way research is formulated and conducted and that "it is so ingrained in sociological thinking that it is mostly taken for granted" (Rhoads, 1991, p. 37). I suspect that most sociologists would agree with the following description of the "scientific method" by sociobiologist Sarah Blaffer Hrdy:

In spite of its limitations, scientific inquiry as currently practiced, with all of the drawbacks—including reductionist models, underlying assumptions that have been influenced by cultural context, domination of disciplines by males, and so forth, all the things that gave us several generations of male-biased primatology— science with all these drawbacks is better than such unabashedly ideological programs that have become advocated in certain religious as well as in some feminist research programs (such as those advocating "conscious partiality"— the notion that since we can't help being biased, let's be biased in an ideologically correct way). (Hrdy, 1990, p. 136)

In rejecting the "unbridgeable gap" between empirical observations and value judgments, Richards is challenging the basic assumptions of an often "taken-for-granted" scientific positivism. If, as he suggests, the "naturalistic fallacy" is no fallacy, than perhaps the stark dichotomies believed necessary by what Rhoads terms "social theory according to positivism" are avoidable (Rhoads, 1991, pp. 7–37). Perhaps the black and white tones painted by the sociologist as philosophical dualist will dissolve into stippled grays in the spaces made possible by Richards' conceptual moves. The acceptance of what Richards terms his "Revised Theory" would be the death knell for the sociologist as a kind of long-suffering, frustrated positivist manque. If Richards is correct, the frustration was unnecessary because the "problem" was nonexistent and framed in incorrect terms. It is as if one built a better telescope to look into the ocean. The image will always be blurred no matter how precisely the lens was ground.

Richards outlines his "Revised Version" of evolutionary ethics in an appendix to his study of Darwin (1987, pp. 595 – 627), as well as in shorter statements and comments on critics (Richards, 1986b, pp. 337 – 354; 1988, pp. 149 – 168; 1989, pp. 331 – 343).

Richards refers to his theory as a "revised" version because it "augments Darwin's and differs in certain respects from [Edward] Wilson's" (Richards, 1987, p. 603). His aim is "fundamentally logical and conceptual: to demonstrate that an ethics based on presumed facts of biological evolution...can be justified by using those facts and the theory articulating them" (Richards, 1987, p. 603).

Richards wants to develop a theory which is "morally superior" to the "contract altruism" of Edward Wilson (e.g., relying exclusively on kin selection and reciprocal altruism). Richards argues that "RV supposes that a moral sense has evolved in the human group" (1987, p. 603). People have been "selected to provide for the welfare" of our own family members, "aided perhaps by group selection on small communities" (Richards, 1987, p. 603). Richards asks us to accept his version of evolutionary history as given. Assuming its validity, what then follows?

Contrary to the reductionism of Wilson in *Sociobiology* (1975), Richards realizes that people are "cultural animals" whose actions "are interpreted according to the traditions established in the history of particular groups" (1987, p. 604). Richards, in other words, does not reduce a cultural level of analysis to individualistic psychology, as does Wilson in *On Human Nature* (1978). Wilson assumes that "cultural change is the statistical product of large numbers of human beings who cope as well as they can with social existence" (Wilson, 1978, p. 81). Presumably one can, according to this perspective, comprehend such things as the effects of Social Security or a Declaration of War by looking at the "statistical product" of individual psyches. But as Marshall Sahlins has correctly remarked, "the reasons why millions of

Americans fought in World War II...would not account for the occurrence or the nature of that war" (Sahlins, 1976, p. 8). Individuals may have fought because they were scared, angry, aggressive, patriotic, conformist, afraid of jail, hated Germans, followed orders, etc. The causal factors responsible for World War II require emergent levels of analysis which are taken into account in Richards' conceptual analysis.

Following Darwin, Richards argues that our evolutionary history was responsible for the development of a moral sense in *Homo sapiens* and that a human "is ineluctably a moral being" (Richards, 1987, p. 612). This assumption is central to his examination of the "naturalistic fallacy" and it is based on the similar analysis Darwin developed in *The Descent of Man* (1871).

Contrary to the popular notion of an amoral winner-take-all "Social Darwinism," Darwin wrote in *The Descent of Man* that natural selection was responsible for the origin of human moral systems. He argued "that any animal whatever endowed with well-marked social instincts, would inevitably acquire a moral sense or conscience, as soon as its intellectual powers had become well-developed, or nearly as well developed as in man" (Darwin, 1981 [1871], vol. I, pp. 71 – 72). He "did not wish to maintain" that they "would acquire exactly the same moral sense as ours," but an "inward monitor would tell the animal that it would have been better to have followed the one impulse rather than the other" (Darwin, 1981 [1871], vol. I, p. 73). In order to support this position, Darwin posited a natural history of moral development.

Initially, "social instincts" will lead an individual "to take pleasure in the society of its fellows" (Darwin, 1981 [1871], vol. I, p. 72). People are naturally social and gregarious. They "feel a certain amount of sympathy" towards their conspecifics (Darwin, 1981 [1871], vol I, p. 72). According to Darwin, and in line with current thinking about "kin selection" and "reciprocal altruism" (Wilson, 1975, pp. 117 – 121), the "social instincts" are not "extended" to all other members of the same species, but "only to those of the same association" [i.e, genetic relations and everyday companions] (Darwin, 1981 [1871], vol. I, p. 72). The significant point for Darwin, as well as for Richards, is that hominids very early recognized the importance of others. Successful adaptations required other people. The solitary *Australopithecus afarensis* was an easy prey.

Secondly, according to Darwin, our mental powers developed to the point where "images of past actions and motives would be incessantly passing through the brain of each individual" (Darwin, 1981 [1871], vol. I, p. 72). We became gradually able to remember and analyze our actions. We slowly became aware of the conflict between "the enduring and always present social instinct" and other instincts of "short duration" such as hunger (Darwin, 1981 [1871], vol. I, p. 72). In modern terminology, we might say we often show "a lack of judgment" based on Darwin's instincts of "short duration." As a result, Darwin argued that a "feeling of dissatisfaction...inevitably results" (Darwin, 1981 [1871], vol. I, p. 72). We develop a "guilty conscience."

Thirdly, what Darwin calls "common opinion" and "the power of language" comes to express and represent "the wishes of members of the same community" (Darwin, 1981 [1871], vol. I, p. 72). We gradually are able to express our views to others and vice versa. "Public opinion" gradually strengthens the "social instinct" of every group member as each person becomes increasingly aware of the interests of others and the "judgment of the community" (Darwin, 1981 [1871], vol. I, p. 73). As we experience life in groups and grow in our ability to reflect on and understand our actions, we are more likely to take the opinions of others into account.

Darwin recognized, once again in agreement with current sociobiological opinion, that we are more likely to be sympathetic to kin than to strangers and that we often help others with the expectation of future assistance on their part (Darwin, 1981 [1871], vol. I, pp. 81 –82). He writes that as our "reasoning powers" improve, "each man would soon learn from experience that if he aided his fellow-men, he would be aided in return" (Darwin, 1981 [1871], vol. I, p. 163). Given his emphasis on "social virtues" and the importance of "praise and the blame of our fellow-men" on their continued development, Darwin was optimistic about long-range projections of evolutionary trends (Darwin, 1981 [1871], vol. I, p. 164). He remarks that "Looking to future generations, there is no cause to fear that the social instincts will grow weaker, and we may expect that virtuous habits will grow stronger" (Darwin, 1981 [1871], vol. I, p. 104).

The ability to reason and reflect on behavior and the increasing importance of "public opinion" improved the likelihood of people developing "virtuous habits." Contrary to popular images of a violent Darwinian social conflagration, Darwin believed the overall trends in his description of natural selection were in some sense progressive (Richards, 1988, pp. 129–148). In this opinion, he is closer to current ecological perspectives which stress the overall balance of natural processes (Rolston, 1986, 1993; Orr, 1992), as opposed to the random "kill-or-be-killed" images of Tennyson's "nature red in tooth and claw" and its contemporary exponents (Williams, 1988). According to Darwin, "it is apparently a truer and more cheerful view that progress has been much more general that retrogression" (Darwin, 1981 [1871], vol. I, p. 184). After a close textual analysis and comparison of Spencer and Darwin, Richards even suggests that "If we take Darwin whole, we see that his view of progress in evolution does not differ terribly from that of Spencer" (Richards, 1988, p. 146).[20]

"Progress" for Darwin is defined as improvement in general group welfare. He sharply distinguished his version of "good" from utilitarian notions of "happiness" as a guiding moral principle (Richards, 1987, pp. 217 –219). Richards is likewise critical of utilitarianism and argues that his evolutionary explanation is based on a nonconsequentionalist emphasis on the importance of motives. He believes that the human motive of altruism "has been established by community or kin selection" (Richards, 1987, p. 609). For an act to be moral it has to be performed from an altruistic motive and the actor has to intend to act from that motive. Other species may engage in actions with altruistic consequences, but they don't, according to Richards, do so with altruistic intentions.

Richards asks us to assume, as did Darwin, that the "criterion of morality" is the "general good" or the "welfare and survival of the group" (Richards, 1987, p. 600). In accordance with Richards' recognition of more complex levels of analysis, he states that the general or community "good" must be "intelligently applied; choices are not "automatic" but are subject to "improvable reason" (Richards, 1987, p. 612). While human beings are in part constituted by the process of making value judgments—it's part of what we mean by "being human"—the specific choices we make are always affected by differing cultural realities. We all necessarily make moral choices, but we base them on differing criteria. As Richards states, "The claim that man is ineluctably a moral creature means by virtue of specific evolutionary processes, he has the capacity for acting morally" (Richards, 1986, p. 342, emphasis in original). Richards proposes that we assume his evolutionary "Just-So" story is valid. Given that assumption, he believes that his evolutionary ethics escapes the "usual form" of the naturalistic fallacy (Richards, 1987, p. 612).

Richards first notes that one form of the "naturalistic fallacy" is to assume that whatever exists represents "the good." Ernst Haeckel, for example, believed in the racial superiority of the German Volk (Richards, 1987, p. 596; Lerner, 1992, p. 38). The German Volk was, by definition, the "highest" product of evolutionary history. All others could be compared to that "standard" and found wanting. Whatever is—in this case Germany—is right. Naturally, many writers have objected to this kind of "evolutionary ethics" (Lerner, 1992; Degler, 1991).

Darwin's theory, however, and Richards' "Revised Version," do "not specify a particular social arrangement as being best" (Richards, 1987, p. 613). They assume, rather, that people will tend to "enhance the community good," but that "what constitutes an ideal pattern" will change historically and cross-culturally (Richards, 1987, p. 613). Richards argues that the process of making moral choices is a result of evolutionary history, not our specific moral positions. His Revised Version sanctions "acts that, on balance, appear to be conducive to the community good...the criterion of morally approved behavior will remain constant, while the conception of what particular acts fall under the criterion will continue to change" (Richards, 1987, p. 614). Richards' theory does not glorify any specific society or suggest the apotheosis of the status quo. He therefore claims that one form of the "naturalistic fallacy" has been successfully overcome by his version of evolutionary ethics.

"But does," Richards asks, "RV derive ethical norms from evolutionary facts in some way? Unequivocally, yes" (Richards, 1987, p. 614). He claims, however, that "this involves no logically or morally fallacious move" (Richards, 1987, p. 614). All ethical theories, according to Richards, utilize empirical evidence in "framework" assumptions and "internal" assumptions (Richards, 1987, p. 614). Internal questions "concern the logic of the moral principle and the terms of discourse of a particular ethical system" (Richards, 1987, p. 614). That is, if we assume the validity of a certain moral system, how do we specifically determine what it recommends as valid? For example, assuming the concept of a "just war," how does the concept relate to a particular society at a particular point in time? In order to carry out the analysis, certain empirical assumptions about the effects of military actions need to be analyzed. How do military actions impinge on human communities? A sociologist might say one needs to "operationalize" the concept of a "just war.

"Framework" questions also require empirical evidence. Every ethical system makes ontological assumptions about "human nature." Even deontological systems such as Kant's assume that people are capable of understanding and following rules which are ultimately based on empirical considerations (Richards, 1987, p. 615). It does no good to explain the "Categorical Imperative" to, say, a platypus. The fact that this example seems a prima facie absurdity only indicates how many empirical assumptions are taken for granted by even the most "rational" systems of ethics. If every system of ethics uses empirical evidence, a critique of evolutionary ethics for doing the same thing is unwarranted. "Consequently," says Richards, "either the naturalistic fallacy is no fallacy, or no ethical system can be justified" (Richards, 1987, p. 620). As Abraham Edel has argued, our definitions of "good" and "ought" depend on information about the "nature" of human beings (Edel, 1955, p. 78).

According to Richards' evolutionary "information," the evolutionary process "has equipped human beings with a number of social instincts such as the need to protect offspring, to provide for the general well-being of members of the community (including oneself)...and other dispositions that constitute a moral creature" (Richards, 1987, p. 620). Richards wants us to grant him the "supposition" that RV "correctly accounts for all relevant biological facts" (Richards, 1987, p. 620). Given that assumption, Richards advances three "Justifying Arguments" in which he presents his case for negating the arguments of Hume and overcoming the fact/value dichotomy.

Richards bases his First Justifying Argument on Alan Gewirth's discussion of "inference rules" (Gewirth, 1982). An "inference rule" permits "the assertion of the conclusion on the basis of the premises" (Richards, 1987, p. 617). As a "causal" inference rule, Gewirth gives the example "It is lightning, therefore it ought to thunder" (Gewirth, 1982, p. 108). Richards puts this in the language of modern logic: "From 'x causes y' infer 'since x, y ought to occur'" (Richards, 1987, p. 621). One can think of many similar examples such as "It is snowing, therefore it ought to be cold" or "I am in Death Valley, therefore it ought to be hot." According to Richards, this is one way of deriving an "ought" from an "is."

Richards' Second Justifying Argument involves assuming the inference rule that "from a particular sort of structured context, conclude that the activity appropriate to that context ought to occur" (Richards, 1987, p. 623). This is similar to Darwin's comment in *The Descent of Man* that "hounds ought to hunt, pointers to point, and retrievers to retrieve their game" (Darwin, 1981 [1871], vol. I, p. 92). Animals "ought" to do what their evolutionary history predisposes them to do (i.e., pointers to point). According to Richards, the same reasoning should follow for human beings. *Homo sapiens* is a particular species with a unique evolutionary past. Richards contends that:

> *The evidence shows that evolution has, as a matter of fact, constructed human beings to act for the community good; but to act for the community good is what we mean by being moral. Since, therefore, human beings are moral beings—an unavoidable condition produced by evolution—each ought to act for the community good.* (Richards, 1987, pp. 623–624, emphasis in original)

If humans are constituted as moral, they should act "to promote the community good" (Richards, 1987, p. 624). In doing so, we are only doing what in the ultimate, evolutionary sense is analogous to the pointer learning to point. Basing his argument on Darwin's natural history of morality, Richards states that acting morally defines what it means to be human.

Altruism—acting for the community good—is part of the evolutionary dispositions which we "naturally" tend to follow. This is what allows Richards to argue that his theory avoids a total relativism such as the "canonization of Hitler along with Saint Francis" (Richards, 1987, p. 620). If someone challenges his definition of "altruism" as a "moral act," Richards says the best he can do to justify his "framework assumptions" is to ask the reader to "consult" his or her own intuitions and "those commonly of the run of human beings" (Richards, 1987, p. 624). Richards agrees with the idea that "no system can validate its own first principles" but must "move outside the system" in order to avoid tautological reasoning (Richards, 1987, p. 617). One can, nevertheless, rely on "common sense moral judgments" and "intuitively clear cases" (Richards, 1987, p. 617). Richards suggests that we can count on people "acquiescing in the general moral principle of altruism" because "men [sic] are made that way" (Richards, 1986b, p. 345).

Richards' Third Justifying Argument shows that his Revised Version is warranted because it "grounds" other "key strategies" used to construct moral systems (Richards, 1987, p. 626). Most ethical systems are universalistic. Spencer, for example, believed that his notion of "equal freedom" should be acceptable to anyone as "an intuitively valid moral axiom" (Richards, 1987, p. 312), but he provides no justification as to why we might expect ultimate agreement. Richards believes that RV "shows that the pith of every person's nature, the core by which he or she is constituted a social and moral being, has been created according to the same standard" (Richards, 1987, p. 627). It is our common evolutionary history which is responsible for our "capacity for acting morally" (Richards, 1986b, p. 342). The fact that we share common human capabilities is the result of our transcultural evolutionary history. We share common species characteristics including the capacity for moral reasoning which Richards sees as an intrinsic and exceptional characteristic of *Homo sapiens*— the differentia distinguishing humankind from all other species.

Richards' rejection of the "naturalistic fallacy" and his suggestion that evolutionary history presupposes certain moral values has drawn considerable critical commentary (Gewirth, 1986; Hughes, 1986; Trigg, 1986; Thomas, 1986; Cela-Conde, 1986; Williams, 1990). Alan Gewirth attacks Richards for not being specific enough to differentiate what is morally right from what is morally wrong (Gewirth, 1986, pp. 297 –305). If, as Richards admits, "aggressive and murderous impulses" are also a result of the evolutionary process, how do we distinguish between those and the "altruism" which Richards proposes? (Gewirth, 1986, p. 301). Evolution is being used as a generic explanation for what are considered both "moral" and "immoral" actions. Evolution has resulted in individuals who act against the community good. How do we explain their actions? According to Gewirth, the only possibility is to utilize more rationalistic criteria and to recognize that "Both morality and rationality are normative concepts: they involve not merely empirically factual or causal relations but also considerations of *rightness* or *validity*" (Gewirth, 1986, pp. 304 –305, emphasis in original).

Gewirth attacks Richards' "solution" of the naturalistic fallacy from the standpoint of specificity. Even if we could somehow deduce certain moral considerations from evolutionary history, Gewirth argues that Richards' reasoning provides no way to distinguish "moral" from "immoral" actions and is therefore necessarily invalid. Descriptions of evolutionary processes in themselves provide no criteria for solving moral dilemmas. He argues that "The independent operation of human reason is indispensable for explaining and justifying the criteria and operations of morality" (Gewirth, 1986, p. 305).

Patricia Williams presents a forceful critique of Richards on a number of levels (Williams, 1990). She points to logical problems with Richards' claims concerning the naturalistic fallacy. If we examine Richards' claims as logical postulates, we find the following progression:

1. People evolved to have altruistic motives.
2. People evolved to believe altruistic motives are real motives.
3. Altruistic motives are moral motives.
4. To act from moral motives is to act as people ought.
5. People ought to act altruistically. (Williams, 1990, p. 452)

The inconsistency in Richards' argument, according to Williams, is premise (3). The claim that altruistic motives are moral motives "says nothing about biology" (Williams, 1986, p. 452). It is based on external rational or moral criteria which have no direct connection with Richards' evolutionary history. It is "imported illegitimately from a non-biological source" (Williams, 1990, p. 453). Without premise (3), Richards, argument is reduced to "People ought to act altruistically if altruistic motives are moral motives" (Williams, 1990, p. 453). This statement is a conditional "if-then" kind of argument and is not categorical in its implications: if altruistic actions are moral, then we ought to act altruistically. Williams criticizes Richards for claiming more than this.

She also convincingly demonstrates that Richards' use of the term "ought," in his "solution" to the naturalistic fallacy, is ambiguous and depends on a variety of definitional forms. There is the "ought" of natural processes, which is a causal ought, as in Richards' example that thunder ought to follow lightning. Following Gewirth (1982), Williams also argues that there is a hypothetical "ought" in the sense that if we commit ourselves to "structured contexts," then we ought to do what those contexts require. If we are teaching in a university, then we should prepare adequately for our classes. If we live in a democracy, then we should follow democratic procedures. Clearly a causal "ought" and a hypothetical "ought" are two very different things. Williams' argues that Richard's mistake is to confuse the two meanings and assume that a causal statement is the same as a hypothetical statement. Such is not the case. For this reason, says Williams, as well as for a lack of specificity, Richards' "solution" of the naturalistic fallacy is no solution at all.

Richards can also be challenged with respect to the empirical assumptions he asks us to accept. As Roger Trigg argues, aspects of Richards' argument seem "remarkably optimistic" (Trigg, 1986, p. 334). It is by no means self-evident that "every person's nature...must resound to the same moral cord: acting for the common good" (Richards, 1987, p. 627). Much of modern biological theory has reached exactly opposite conclusions (Dawkins, 1989;

Ruse, 1988, pp. 63–70). As Richard Dawkins has argued, "Nothing, it seems, can prevent the march of selfish genes" (Dawkins, 1986, p. 267. Biologist George Williams argues that the "modern concept" of natural selection "can honestly be described as process for maximizing short-sighted selfishness" (Williams, 1988, p. 385).

If, however, everyone is "naturally" moral, those who are not moral must somehow be "different." As Trigg suggests, other than those who have somehow misunderstood the situation—or give in to Darwin's "instincts of short duration"—all other people should be "moral beings." If they continue to act immorally or selfishly, then in some sense they logically must be sub-human (Trigg, 1986, p. 333). Richards, for example, refers to the problem of "psychopaths among us" and suggests that, according to the terms of his analysis, they are "born deformed in spirit" and "are to be regarded as less than moral creatures" (Richards, 1987, p. 627). Similarly, he states that "one who cannot comprehend the soundness of basic moral principles...we regard as hardly a man" (Richards, 1987, p. 618). But if someone is "deformed" and "less than moral" he or she can, perhaps, be treated much differently with impunity. One easily develops the attitudes of a social elite that assumes that its "servants" are a qualitatively different "species."[21]

One of Richards' principal shortcomings is that he has no theory of human needs but wants to avoid what he calls "the moral muck of relativism" (Richards, 1987, p. 618). He states that he is trying to develop an evolutionary perspective *"without the objectionable detour through human needs"* (Richards, 1987, p. 622, emphasis added). Richards relies instead on a deontological ethical theory which stresses the importance of following rules and the importance of the moral agent's intentions. One can give examples, however, of many different and conflicting rules. As Richards himself points out, Inca priests no doubt believed that they were contributing to the peace and harmony of Incan society by killing sacrificial victims (Richards, 1987, p. 615). The inescapable conclusion is that we have to "judge the Inca high priest as a good and moral man for sacrificing virgins" (Richards, 1987, p. 615). As Patricia Williams has argued, even some people at Auschwitz "believed that they were acting for the community good" (Williams, 1990 p. 456). If that is the case, however, Richards' theory cannot distinguish between the morality of his own intuitively clear comparison of Hitler and Saint Francis (Richards, 1987, p. 620). Even assuming the veracity of the evolutionary story told by Richards, his evolutionary ethics is fatally flawed by what anthropologists term a total "cultural relativism." As I will argue in Chapter 4, one needs an explicit transcultural theory of human needs in order to avoid Richards' dilemma.

It is important for sociologists to understand both the strengths and weaknesses of Richards' analysis. His work provides a sophisticated philosophical analysis of the kinds of assumptions surrounding "facts" and "values" which sociology often leaves unexamined. It provides an interdisciplinary "push" towards a critique of our taken-for-granted assumptions. Sociology would benefit from renewed discourse on the "naturalistic fallacy" which includes discussion about the problem of warranted knowledge. Richards' work on evolutionary ethics is a useful beginning.

It is absolutely clear, as Richards states, that empirical evidence is essential for making value judgments. Richards is correct to argue that all ethical theories utilize some conception of the "facts" and, in that sense, the "naturalistic fallacy" is no fallacy. Every sociologist assumes that it is in some sense possible to obtain data. Even the most enthusiastic social constructionist assumes that one may collect data about the process of construction. Following Richard Rorty, a sociologist might argue that "we understand knowledge when we understand the social justification of belief" (Rorty, 1979, p. 170). But there still must be some method of understanding the "social justification." If there were no data, there would be no sociology.

Richards is right to argue that the connections between empirical data and value judgments are more complex than many textbook homilies on "objectivity" suggest. He is wrong in his conflation of the "causal" and the "hypothetical" usage of the term "ought." That someone ought to do something is not isomorphic with a causal sequence such as the example that thunder ought to follow lightning. That a person ought to perform a duty toward others is a moral value judgment. To claim they are identical, as Richards suggests in his "Second Justifying Argument" begs the question. He assumes the "naturalistic fallacy" is no fallacy by equating alternative usages of a multivalent term. As Abraham Edel has observed, "It is true, roughly speaking, that a categorical assertion containing a given term does not follow validly from premises which do not contain that term" (Edel, 1955, p. 75). From the statement "This is a rock" one cannot determine if the proper course of action is to throw it at someone, take the stone home and polish it, or simply leave it alone.

On the other hand, Edel's qualifying phrase "roughly speaking" still allows us space to make relevant distinctions within and around the logical categories of description and prescription. Perhaps it is true that there is no logical way, ultimately, to overcome Hume's strictures about the "naturalistic fallacy." But if the phrase "fact/value" has dualistic qualities, it is a dualism with many connections and areas that overlap. It is more analogous, say, to two jellyfish tangled together in the waves than to a shark and a dolphin warily eyeing each other from a distance.

Richards' discussion would be greatly improved if he would make use of the multiplicity of subtle connections between "facts" and "values." It is obvious that simply choosing an area of research involves some values (i.e., what is considered important enough to justify research). The research process itself, as Jacob Bronowski wrote, assumes that "We ought to act in such a way that what is true can be verified to be so" (Bronowski, 1956, p. 74). Scientific research assumes that one ought to be truthful.

Robert Friedrichs, in his book *A Sociology of Sociology* (1970) provides a number of arguments which Richards could use in his discussion of the naturalistic fallacy. Friedrichs first notes that problem selection is inevitably a reflection of value judgments. He also argues that terminology such as "system" or "equilibrium" is not "value free" (Friedrichs, 1970, pp. 138 – 148). He refers to John Seeley's "inexhaustibility theorem" which states that "the subject matter of something cannot in principle be exhausted if the first description both alters and in any case increases the subject matter to be described" (Seeley, 1963, p. 56). The results of scientific research in themselves become a part of the social matrix. They have an impact. Logically, one cannot know the consequences of the impact before it occurs. How could anyone have "known" the impact of Marx's writings before he was born? It was a gradually emergent, singular, unpredictable occurrence which had enormous social consequences. "Pure" research (i.e., Marx's historical studies of the working class in England) had tremendous "applied" consequences.

The level of significance which is acceptable in research is also a value judgment. Friedrichs notes that psychology tends to "demand more assurance" about significance levels than do sociologists (Friedrichs, 1970, p. 158). Perhaps this is because their experimental designs may involve more practical consequences or they "must accept greater responsibility than a typical sociologist" for their results (Friedrichs, 1970, p. 158). Friedrichs' makes the obvious point that the Manhattan Project required a greater degree of certainty than the latest Harris Poll. The consequences of error in any research influence the degree of certainty required. What is required reflects value judgments external to the "ideal" research design of classic positivism. It is not—a la Comte—that sociologists should become the new clergy. Friedrichs' point is rather that the course of ordinary research inevitably involves choices between various alternatives. Friedrichs' argument is, that while a Comtean sacerdotal sociology would clearly combine "facts" and "values," so too does a rigorously behavioristic sociology when carrying out its most "objective" experiments. The naturalistic fallacy is still a fallacy of sorts, but it has lost some of its bite. All research involves making choices and value judgments.

Richards would also improve his argument if he made use of John Dewey's discussion of "ends-in-view" and the "means-ends continuum" (Hook, 1971 [1939], pp. 127 – 148). Dewey refused to place the "means" of accomplishing a task in an inferior position compared to "ends." We may discover, for example, "that our declared end is such that no available methods or means seem likely to achieve it" (Hook, 1971 [1939], p. 144). In that case the possibility of achieving the "end-in-view" is "causally determined by the physical and social means employed to implement the end-in-view" (Hook, 1971 [1939], p. 144). As Larry Hickman has noted concerning Dewey's analysis: "In production that is fruitful, means and ends cooperate; they receive checks from one another, they undergo alteration and accommodation with respect to one another" (Hickman, 1990, p. 67).

What is seen as an "end" at one time may later be viewed as a means to a further "end." Which term is applied to any particular process is historically contingent. For example, the civil rights movement in the 1960s often sought such specific "ends" as the right to vote (Viorst, 1979). At the time of the "movement," voting rights were clearly viewed as one objective or "end." At a later date, when the possibility of voting was a taken-for-granted activity, it was just as clearly viewed as a means to other "ends." Its function was now seen as instrumental to the achievement of different ends such as political power. The relationship between means and ends is better seen as a continuum than as an absolute dualism.

When a patient voluntarily enters a drug treatment center, his first end-in-view may be to not use alcohol for twenty-four hours. Perhaps he later extends the time frame to one week. At another point he decides he wants to see how much reading he can get done during the time he remains in the treatment center. Perhaps at an even later date he decides to change his attitude towards good nutrition and drastically alters his diet. At each point in his stay at the center he chooses another "end." Ultimately his goal will be to leave the treatment center and resume other activities. All of the ends presuppose the successful completion of his first "end," which was to discontinue drinking. The "ends" expand and earlier ends-in-view are accomplished and taken-for-granted while pursuing later ends-in-view. Dewey's analysis helps to clarify the convoluted relationships between "means" and "ends" or "facts" and "values." Richards would improve his analysis if he incorporated some of the distinctions and terminology utilized by John Dewey.

It would also help Richards to augment his emphasis on "group morality" with a consideration of specific human needs. As Edel has argued, "Cultural forms are...capable of being estimated for their satisfaction of human needs" (Edel, 1955, p. 242). By excluding an "objectionable" detour through human needs (Richards, 1987, p. 622), Richards eliminates an approach that would help him avoid a total cultural relativism. We must also assume, of course, that needs should be met.

Robert Richards presents a detailed and sophisticated defense of evolutionary ethics. Any work which deals with the "naturalistic fallacy" should consider Richards' analysis. While he is ultimately not successful in his attempts to overcome the "fallacy," his analysis enables sociologists to examine the fact/value dichotomy with increased philosophical and conceptual sophistication. He avoids the tautology of assuming that "whatever is, is right." By expunging the concept of "need," however, he ignores an additional sense of the word "ought" which would prove very helpful to the case he is attempting to prove. If it makes sense, as Darwin wrote in *The Descent of Man*, that pointers should point, it also makes sense that human beings should do what they are best suited for. What we are best suited for would, by definition, meet our needs. We now turn to a discussion of human needs.

IV

TOWARD A BIOSOCIAL THEORY OF HUMAN NEEDS

Evolutionary psychologists, as well as many others who advocate a biosocial approach to research and analysis, emphasize the importance of "human needs." Our survival as a species presupposes our ability to respond to the generic needs of infants. Human beings as a species share a number of common needs.[22] Human needs transgress cultural and geographical boundaries. A different evolutionary history would have produced different needs. We share a number of similarities by virtue of our biological commonalities which have been minimized or ignored altogether by much of social science. The lack of recognition is, however, unrelated to the significance of that which is ignored.

The concept of "human needs" is woefully undertheorized within the sociological tradition. Standard reference works such as Timasheff (1957), Bottomore and Nisbet (1978), Collins (1988) and Ritzer (1988) contain no references to "needs" or "human needs" in their subject indexes. This reflects in part a sociological bias against consideration of any "individualistic" traits. Jonathan Turner has noted, for example, that "motivation has not been examined either explicitly or extensively by sociologists in recent decades" (Turner, 1987, p. 26). These theoretical lacunae have had a number of harmful consequences for sociology which will be examined in this chapter. My contention is that the development of an adequate theory of human needs is the key theoretical move necessary for sociology to move beyond the disciplinary myopia and polemics which are increasingly evident to sociologists (Sanderson and Ellis, 1992) and even to the mass media (Kanrowite, 1992).

The concept of "human needs" enables us to begin the necessary integration between disciplines which is a prerequisite to warranted social science inferences. Social science needs to take into account any relevant data. What has been termed "vertical integration" suggests that data within each discipline should be mutually consistent and also consistent with what is known in the natural sciences (Tooby and Cosmides, 1992, pp. 19 –24). Sociologists, for example, should be utilizing the results of current research in evolutionary psychology.

It has been demonstrated by researchers John Tooby and Leda Cosmides (1992) that the basic manner in which we approach and solve cognitive problems is strongly influenced by our evolutionary history. In an interview with William Allman (1994, p. 40), Cosmides argues that "the human mind contains a number of specific mechanisms...for processing information about the social world. One of these mechanisms is a 'cheater detector.'" We find it easier to solve logical problems when they are presented in familiar or "social" terms than if they are presented as problems of abstract logic (Allman, 1994, pp. 29 – 51). Sociologists should seriously consider the possibility that the human brain is by no means a tabula rasa. We need to utilize relevant research from such areas as evolutionary psychology and genetics in order to even begin to adequately develop a social science. There is no good reason for sociology to promote theories which are blatantly contradicted by the latest findings in, say, paleontology or population genetics. At the very least, the data should be taken into account and/or challenged—as opposed to simply being ignored. As Gerhard Lenski has argued, evolutionary ecology is one possible approach to interdisciplinary adequacy (Lenski, 1988). This becomes clear in any sociological analysis of social problems.

A biosocial theory of human needs enables us to move forward in the seemingly endless debates in sociology over social problems and "social constructionism." As Mary Midgley has suggested, any criticism of existing "social customs" must be made "on the grounds that these customs fail to meet real human needs" (Midgley, 1983b, p. 91). The concept of "social problems" *ipso facto* assumes that a particular institutional arrangement is not adequately meeting a specific human need. If there is no "need," there is no "problem." If a theorist has no explicit theory of human needs, she has no way of legitimately arguing that one particular "problem" is more serious or important than any other "problem." As we shall see, much sociological confusion in this area is due to a failure to adequately distinguish between "needs" and "wants." If there are, however, a number of specific human needs, this provides warranted grounds for enumerating whatever are then viewed as social problems. Given the emergence of what Pauline Rosenau (1992) terms "skeptical postmodernists"—those who dispute the possibility of "performativity" for the social science (i.e., Dewey's "warranted knowledge")—this is no small feat.

If human beings, as such, have certain transcultural needs, then it is clear that different cultures and societies vary in how well they provide for those needs. A biosocial approach assumes that specific needs are a result of our evolutionary history as a species. If, like Durkheim, we eliminate by fiat all consideration of biological/evolutionary data, we also eliminate important knowledge about what it means to be a member of *Homo sapiens*. As Cosmides suggests, this applies to both "subjective" as well as more "macro" or "objective" sociological theorizing— a point that seems especially misunderstood within sociology today. A theory of human needs is essential for sociological perspectives. While this has often been an acceptable idea— if only implicitly—in much sociological theorizing, it needs to become much more explicit and commonplace.

Increased awareness of the significance of human needs would enable sociology to begin to answer what Ritzer calls "a central problem in contemporary sociological theory": the "macro-micro link" (Ritzer, 1988, pp. 366 – 384). Human needs provide a "link" between theorizing on the "macro" or "social" level and the individual or "micro" level. While the concept of "human needs" has been traditionally viewed by sociologists as merely an individualistic phenomenon, or even taken-for-granted under the ceteris paribus assumption, I will show here and in the following chapters that this is an erroneous and unnecessarily limiting position.

Much of the contemporary debate concerning human needs is the result of conceptual confusion between the idea of "wants" as opposed to the idea of "needs." Neo-classical economists, for example, assume by their use of "marginal utility" that all "wants" are commensurate and of potentially equal significance. It is useless, they believe, to talk of "needs" because all we can measure are "choices" or "wants." Every "choice," as recorded by a market sale of equal monetary value, is, by definition, "equal." The conceptual difficulty which results is that drugs such as cocaine are of equal "value" to anything else which has the same price (Junker, 1962, pp. 193 – 198; Tool, 1985, pp. 292 – 314).

The orthodox economist is in much the same position as the positivistic sociologist with respect to the determination of social problems. If "wants" are measured by the market, "opinions" are measured by a survey. The only legitimate method of determining social problems is to *ask people what they define as problems* in the manner of the Gallup or Harris Polls. If "wants" are defined by what people purchase in the market, "social problems" are defined by public opinion polls, or, in effect, what people say in the "market." If "intelligence" is what is measured by intelligence tests, social problems are what are measured by opinion "tests."

Given this definition of social problems, "social constructionists" argue that the proper area of investigation for the sociologist qua sociologist is to determine how social problems have come to be "defined" as such. Given this "definition" by the public, social problems are examined by looking at "claims-making activities" or public "complaints" (Spector and Kitsuse, 1977, p. 96). The significance of the claim is not the issue. For the sociologist, as Spector and Kitsuse write, "Social problems should be defined without reference to the numbers of people involved" (Spector and Kitsuse, 1977, p. 39). This logically follows from their argument that they "are not concerned whether or not the imputed condition exists" (Spector and Kitsuse, 1977, p. 76). Every "social problem" has equal epistemological validity. This necessarily follows if one argues that "the existence of the condition itself is irrelevant to and outside our analysis" (Spector and Kitsuse, 1977, p. 76). By this definition, Nazism and flying saucers are both social problems. That is really all the sociologist can say, other than looking at the ways the problems were "socially constructed." The strict constructionist in this case reaches the same conclusion as the skeptical postmodernist: Each "story" is as valid as any other.

One of the reasons sociology arrived at this solipsistic absurdity[23] is its refusal to develop or take seriously a transcultural theory of human needs. As David Braybrooke has argued, *"Just by being asserted and recognized as a need it has normative force"* (Braybrooke, 1987, p. 111, emphasis added). What we are concerned with in discussions of social problems are examining social conditions and processes which do not meet human needs. Given a determinate conception of human needs, it is possible to empirically analyze which social conditions or processes are most deficient in meeting those needs. Social problems are conditions which negatively affect human needs. They are not what sociologists define as social problems, or what the public defines as social problems. They are not merely the processes which determine their public visibility. Social problems are the result of historical processes and current social conditions which fail to meet determinate human needs.

Assume, for example, that one visits rural Colombia, as I did for ten weeks as a college sophomore. If one visits a *finca* or *hacienda* in Colombia, or in other Latin American countries, it is entirely possible that the *campesinos* living in the poorest conditions might tell you they were perfectly "content." This is, admittedly, much less likely today but was certainly a likelihood historically. If, however, the peasant has a life expectancy of 40, lacks adequate nutrition, has no possibility of improving his or her social class, has no chance of formal education, and, in all important aspects, is experiencing a condition the average person in the U.S. might term "feudal," is it reasonable to say no social problems exist? Given a determinate conception of human needs, the answer is clearly negative.

In the Colombian example, obvious human needs are not being met. The fact that the individual *campesino* might not agree with an "outside" analysis does not affect the validity of the analysis. Different social situations produce different "life chances" (Gerth and Mills, 1953, p. 313). Preferences or wants should be freely arrived at and a result of relevant knowledge and experience (Braybrooke, 1989, p. 241). Differing social experiences produce different "wants." Whether or not the Colombian peasant "says" his situation is problematic depends on a complexity of factors which involves much besides the "opinion" survey. As Patricia Hill Collins notes, "Under hegemonic conditions, less powerful groups may define their condition as a social problem, but may choose or be forced to hide their self-definitions from the more powerful groups" (Collins, 1989, p. 87). The advantage of looking at "needs" as opposed to "wants" is that everyone has certain needs that must be met no matter the "local" conditions." This suggests a transcultural means of analyzing social problems. As Braybrooke argues, "People will not have any opportunity to have further preferences heeded if the needs that their biological functioning and survival imply go unmet" (Braybrooke, 1989, p. 199).

Following the analysis of Martha Nussbaum (1992, 1993), a determinate conception of human needs implies that "human life has certain central defining features" (Nussbaum, 1992, p. 205). She calls her position "internalist" to distinguish it from "metaphysical essentialism" (Nussbaum, 1992, pp. 206–207). Her own conception "does not claim to derive from any source external to self-interpretations and self-evaluations of human beings in history" (Nussbaum, 1992, p. 215). She also recognizes that "the hope for a pure unmediated account of our human essence as it is in itself, apart from history and interpretation, is no hope at all but a deep confusion" (Nussbaum, 1992, p. 207). There are, in other words, no "unmediated" categories of "reality construction," a position that agrees with theoretical work in the sociology of knowledge (Berger and Luckmann, 1966).

It is possible, nevertheless, to discuss the "shared conditions of human existence" (Nussbaum, 1993, p. 248). Because these conditions are indeed "shared," it is possible to "criticize local and traditional moralities in the name of a more inclusive account of the circumstances of human life, and the needs for human functioning that these circumstances call forth" (Nussbaum, 1993, p. 250).

Every "social problem" is not simply a matter of "definition" or "social construction." Nor is a "social problem" merely a culturally relative, "local" concern impervious to "outside" critique. As Amitai Etzioni has argued, "Theories which assume autonomous human needs provide an independent basis with which to compare societies to each other, as more or less consonant with basic human needs" (Etzioni, 1968, p. 878).

It is very difficult to carry out the kind of empirical "bracketing" Spector and Kitsuse propose. They state, for example, "We have defined social problem activities as *claims-making, complaints, and demands for the relief and amelioration of offensive conditions*" (Spector and Kitsuse, 1977, p. 96, emphasis added). But why should the conditions be described as "offensive"? We are presumably making no judgments at all about the "imputed" conditions. Clearly, if they do not in some sense "exist," it is difficult to see how they could be labeled "offensive." Even Joseph Gusfield, who is one of sociology's leading social constructionists, has argued that "It is the social problems arena itself that emerges as the object of [constructionist] critique...*the sociologist becomes the critic of the effort of public agencies to make legitimate claims to solve social problems as technical problems*" (Gusfield, 1980, p. 13, emphasis added). If, however, sociologists can judge the legitimacy of the activities of "public agencies," why can't they do the same with other groups?

It is this practical difficulty of sticking to the "strict constructionist" perspective which Steve Woolgar and Dorothy Pawluch refer to as "ontological gerrymandering" (Woolgar and Pawluch, 1985). Strict constructionists, in other words, demonstrate the same kinds of shortcomings they see in those they criticize. Why should sociologists consistently ignore empirical considerations? Incredibly, Spector and Kitsuse argue at one point that they are not suggesting that objective conditions are not "real":

Does this mean that we maintain that such conditions do not exist, or that the *sociologist or any other scientist* should not attempt to document their existence and study their causes?   Not at all. Whatever the factual basis of the various conditions imputed to exist, the claims-making and responding activities themselves are the subject matter of the sociology of social problems. (Spector and Kitsuse, 1977, p. 78, emphasis added)

This can only mean that it is "acceptable" for the sociologist as a "scientist" to examine "objective conditions" but not the sociologist who is only interested in examining social problems.   This is, at the very least, a very confused position. It is a kind of "territorial gerrymandering" which makes little sense. It suggests a highly dubious distinction between "sociologists" who as "scientists" are allowed to study the "factual basis" of social problems, but who are not, by definition, "really" dealing with "the subject matter of the sociology of social problems" which is only "claims-making and responding activities themselves." But surely this intellectual Scholasticism is the result of an arid and artificial attempt to deny recognition of the fact that social problems involve determinate needs of human beings. Social problems, for example, adversely affect human health.

Jaber Gubrium argues in "For a Cautious Naturalism" that his "constructionist work" on Alzheimer's "is linked to related, nonpublic neurophysiological, cognitive, and behavioral facts in a complex way" (Gubrium, 1993, p. 59). Alzheimer's disease, therefore, is clearly related to some kind of "objective facts," but its social meanings and definitions vary historically. This is very different from Spector and Kitsuse who argue that "We would go farther and insist that the very characterization of a condition as physical, genetic, or physiological is *part of the definition of the condition*, and not, analytically speaking, a characteristic of the objective condition itself" (Spector and Kitsuse, 1977, p. 47, emphasis in original). At this point, the social constructionist argument is almost unintelligible. A person doesn't in some sense have syphilis until its "meaning" is "socially constructed"? Obviously people might react to the disease in completely different fashions with major differences in social interaction as a result. The same is true of Alzheimer's.   This doesn't mean that syphilis or Alzheimer's is totally "emergent" or "socially constructed."

Martha Nussbaum's perspective is diametrically opposed to the social constructionist approach of Spector and Kitsuse.   These two conflicting perspectives illuminate the importance of a theory of human needs and clearly demonstrate where it impacts on sociological theory. One of the reasons for the degree of controversy we see today within the "constructionist field" (Miller and Holstein, 1993), is that there are difficulties and ambiguities in both "objective" and "subjective" arguments. This is related in part to the lack of a determinate theory of human needs in each approach.

In a view contrary to Nussbaum's, Armand Mauss criticizes the "objectivist" approach of D. Stanley Eitzen for suggesting that there are certain "universals" or an "ideal social life against which *actual* social conditions can be compared" (Mauss, 1989, p. 22, emphasis in original). Eitzen had argued:

> that there is an objective reality to social problems. There are structures that induce material or psychic suffering for certain segments of the population...there are structures that prevent certain societal participants from developing and realizing their full human potential. (Eitzen, 1984, p. 10)

According to Mauss it is "apparent" that there are no such objective, transcultural standards (Mauss, 1989, p. 22). He quotes Spector and Kitsuse who affirm that "there are no such universals across times and cultures" (Mauss, 1989, p. 22). What is lacking in this entire discussion, however, is any recognition that this is an empirical question or any recognition of the fact that a great many people outside the discipline of sociology have been investigating this specific topic (Ruse and Wilson, 1986; Brown, 1991; Callebaut, 1993). Edward Wilson, for example, argues that it is because of the kind of cross-cultural universals that Mauss rejects that people, ultimately, will not tolerate slavery. It is in some sense, therefore, "unnatural" (Wilson, 1978, pp. 80 –81). Mary Midgley in *Beast and Man* (1978) presents a variety of similar arguments. What is astounding to anyone familiar with evolutionary and biosocial research is the lack of awareness within sociology that these data are significant for the kinds of questions being debated in the area of social problems.

If there are social "structures that induce material or psychic suffering," it is because they are not meeting specific human needs. Eitzen, although using an "objective" approach, says nothing about any such needs. Mauss says that it is "apparent" that no such "universals" exist "across times and cultures" because social systems exhibit so much variation. Presumably the variation produces different needs and values, but Mauss has nothing specific to say on this topic.   Without a mutual discourse on human needs there is no way to advance beyond the conflicting polemics of both authors. But should social science come down to who can shout the loudest? I think not, even though this is the logical result of total epistemological skepticism. Absolute cultural relativism implies that "the criterion of truth will derive from one's contingent position of social authority" (Nussbaum, 1992, p. 209). Totally skeptical postmodernists might consider that this argument is explicitly made by Robert Bork in his recent work *The Tempting of America* (1990). Given complete epistemological skepticism, there is no principled way, claims Bork, to distinguish between the pain caused him by his knowledge of abortions and the actions of a torturer (Bork, 1990, p. 258). The best we can do is follow the wishes of the majority as expressed in a popular vote. If the majority now wishes to abolish legal abortions, there is no reason why they shouldn't. As Nussbaum writes, "*Caveat deconstructor*" (Nussbaum, 1992, p. 221).

If, however, we assume that the pragmatic tradition in philosophy has even partial validity—a limitation its own assumptions would certainly suggest—it is reasonable to believe that some kinds of knowledge and information are more pragmatically warranted than others: In a particular situation, some knowledge works better, and this is true transculturally. The airplanes we fly from culture to culture utilize the same technological principles no matter the country of origin. The principles they embody are pragmatically demonstrated every time they successfully depart. As Dewey wrote, "knowing is not the act of an outside spectator, but of a *participator inside the natural and social scene*" (Dewey, 1929, p. 196, emphasis added). A simple "clash of opinions" is the only possible result when "general ideas are not capable of being continuously checked and revised by observation" (Dewey, 1989 [1939], p. 91). Pragmatically warranted knowledge "resides in the consequences of directed action" (Dewey, 1929, p. 196). Epistemology is a process. Even Jeffrey Stout, who is highly critical of Dewey's term "warranted knowledge," writes that we justify our knowledge by "reasons" and "evidence" and "the experience and wisdom which we've accumulated so far" (Stout, 1988a, p. 29). Dewey would certainly agree that all knowledge is tentative and affected by its historical and social context (Campbell, 1992, 1995).[24]

Spector and Kitsuse assume that their case for social constructionism is strengthened by the argument that "The notion that social problems are a kind of *condition* must be abandoned in favor of them as a kind of *activity*" (Spector and Kitsuse, 1977, p. 73, emphasis in original). Clearly this is a false binary. In the philosophy of Dewey, problems are seen as *activities* of various durations.   The problem of a child not receiving adequate nutrition is obviously a condition which is the result of varying temporal dimensions in specific situations.   Urban deterioration is a process which has occurred over time. If a situation is defined as problematic due to the prevalence of certain childhood diseases, this, quite clearly, is not a synchronic development.

Social problems are the result of diachronic processes producing contemporary conditions which fail to meet specific human needs. Defining a "social problem" is not, therefore, simply a matter of personal inclination. As Nussbaum argues, "It is that gap between basic (potential) humanness and its full realization that exerts a claim on society and government" (Nussbaum, 1992, p. 228). But how do we begin to establish what "potential humanness" might represent? How, in other words, do we begin to develop a determinate theory of needs?

We might first observe that the notion of "potential" need not involve a completely non-empirical orientation. When discussing a loss of potential one need not postulate a totally metaphysical rendering of the *elan vital*. A loss of potential refers to certain determinate needs which are not being met by any particular society.   The determination of transcultural human needs depends on our species-specific evolutionary history which has resulted in the particular abilities, traits and needs generic to *Homo sapiens* (Barkow, Cosmides, Tooby, 1992). The only way to investigate which needs are being met is to implicitly or explicitly assume human beings *as such* require certain kinds of need satisfaction. Our biosocial evolutionary history has resulted in specific needs which need to be met by any member of our own species. As Donald Symons has noted, "Eucalyptus leaves are tasty to koalas but not to human beings because the two species have different feeding adaptations" (Symons, 1992, p. 142). How, however, do we know what kinds of needs are specific to human beings?

One way of looking at the question of human needs is by attempting to determine what is "natural" in the sense of "in accord with our genetically determined biochemistry and physiology" (Eaton, Shostak and Konner, 1988, p. 88). A tremendous amount of research has been carried out on the ecology, health and diets of both contemporary hunter/gatherers and our Paleolithic ancestors (Diamond, 1992; Johanson, Johanson and Edgar, 1994; Willis, 1989). As Eaton, Shostak and Konner observe, "Before about 10,000 years ago there were no farmers" (Eaton, Shostak and Konner, 1988, p. 24).

Human beings existed for 100,000 generations as hunters and gatherers, but only about 500 generations have utilized agriculture and approximately 10 generations have experienced the industrial revolution (Eaton, Shostak and Konner, 1988, p. 26)). As Diamond notes, "Hunter-gatherers practiced the most successful and long-persistent life style in the career of our species" (Diamond, 1992, p. 190). Our genetic endowment, in other words, is the result of adaptations to an environment that was massively different from what we experience in an age of computers: "That the vast majority of our genes are ancient in origin means that nearly all our biochemistry and physiology are fine-tuned to conditions of life that existed before 10,000 years ago" (Eaton, Shostak and Konner, 1988, p. 39).

The importance of this approach for a determinate conception of human needs revolves around what Eaton, Shostak and Konner have termed "the discordance hypothesis." Given the rapid pace of cultural evolution and the gradual effects of genetic evolution, "an inevitable discordance exists between the world we live in today and the world our genes 'think' we live in still" (Eaton, Shostak and Konner, 1988, p. 43). As Alexandra Maryanski recently observed, "the shift from food foraging to a sedentary lifestyle without a corresponding shift in human biology is likely to have skewed the direct historical relation between behavior and adaptation" (Maryanski, 1994, p. 381). This has resulted in what have been termed 'degenerative diseases' (Burkitt, 1979, pp. 17 – 18) or "diseases of civilization" (Eaton, Shostak and Konner, 1988, pp. 46 – 68) "which cause 75 percent of the deaths in industrial societies" (Eaton, Shostak and Konner, 1988, p. 43). Contemporary hunter/gatherer societies , which are closer to Paleolithic living conditions, demonstrate greatly different epidemiological patterns. This suggests that the "discordance hypothesis" has considerable validity (Konner, 1990, pp. 39 – 46).

Average serum cholesterol values of contemporary hunters and gatherers are extremely low compared to levels in the United States. Various groups examined by Eaton, Shostak and Konner recorded average cholesterol levels between 106 and 141, compared with a U.S. average of 210 (Eaton, Shostak and Konner, 1988, p. 114). Diseases such as diabetes, coronary heart disease, lung diseases, various kinds of cancers, osteoporosis, hearing loss, dental caries, alcohol-related diseases, hypertension, and obesity are all concentrated in industrial societies and are clearly related to the diet and health practices of the West (Burkitt, 1979, pp. 25 – 31; Eaton, Shostak and Konner, 1988, pp. 38 – 68).

The level of fat consumption in the United States—the percentage of total calories provided by fat—"is unprecedented in human evolutionary experience" (Eaton, Shostak and Konner, 1988, p. 111). Paleontological evidence concerning Paleolithic nutrition practices suggests that the percentage of total fat intake was one-half the current U.S. consumption in the Late Paleolithic (Eaton, Shostak and Konner, 1988, p. 84). Protein consumption was about triple our current rates. People consumed very little sugar and alcohol, no tobacco expect in Australia, about one-quarter the sodium, five to ten times the nonnutrient fiber, and approximately twice the calcium of current rates (Eaton, Shostak and Konner, 1988, p. 86). In providing a determinate conception of human needs, it is helpful to recognize that:

> Our genes were selected to operate within the most ancient human spectrum of experience.... Following a diet comparable to the one that humans were genetically adapted to should postpone, mitigate, and in many cases prevent altogether, a host of diseases that debilitate us— diseases almost unknown among recent hunters and gatherers. (Eaton, Shostak and Konner, 1986, p. 87)[25]

Another approach to the question of human needs is provided by the philosophical and conceptual analysis of Martha Nussbaum (1992) and David Braybrooke (1987). Nussbaum notes that in spite of the obvious cultural diversity between various societies, "we do recognize others as humans across many divisions of time and place" (Nussbaum, 1992, p. 215). Whatever else is the case, we are usually aware of when we are dealing with a human being and when we are not.

Second, according to Nussbaum, we have "a broadly shared general consensus about the features whose absence means *the end of a human form of life*" (Nusbaum, 1992, p. 215, emphasis added). Likewise the addition of nonhuman abilities such as immortality or unlimited power lead to our recognition of what is particular to *Homo sapiens*. If we look, for example, at human mythologies and stories, we often find accounts of what it might be to become other than human. All human beings "live all our lives in bodies of a certain sort" (Nussbaum, 1992, p. 217). We all knowingly face the inevitability of death. An immortal sentient being would, by definition, not be human. A being who occupied another corporal form would, by definition, not be human. As members of the species *Homo sapiens*, Nussbaum argues (1992, pp. 216 – 220) that each of us minimally needs the following:

1. A need to satisfy hunger and thirst. The need for sustenance. "If we discovered someone who really did not experience hunger or thirst at all," it would be reasonable to conclude that this was a different kind of being.

2. A need for shelter. All humans need to "find refuge from the cold...the sun, from rain, wind, snow and frost."

3. A need for extended and adequate care as infants. Our prolonged period of infant dependency produces species-specific needs and requirements.

4. A need for affiliation with other human beings. We live "for and with others" and would regard a life devoid of friendship and social interaction as seriously deficient.

5. A need for play and humor. "Laughter and play" are often our "first modes" of "mutual recognition." The "inability to play or laugh" is "a sign of deep disturbance in an individual child." Laughter is a species-specific characteristic.

6. A need to utilize "practical reason." We need to take part "in the planning and managing of our own lives." We need to have input and choice concerning our daily activities.

7. A need for sexual activity. While "less urgent" than hunger or thirst, in the sense that it is possible to live longer without its satisfaction, it is one of our strongest evolutionary traits.

In addition, Braybrooke suggests "The need (beyond what is covered under the proceeding needs) for whatever is indispensable to preserving the body intact in important respects" (Braybrooke, 1987, p. 36). We will include this as (8) and add it to our list above.

This list of basic needs is similar to what Braybrooke terms "course-of life" needs, which he defines as needs which are "indispensable to mind or body in performing...the roles of parent, householder, worker, and citizen" (Braybrooke, 1987, pp. 32 -38 and p. 48). For both Nussbaum and Braybooke, their lists provide a starting point for examining the question of what particular needs are generic to humans as such. As Braybrooke notes, once basic needs have been outlined, it is then possible to develop "minimum standards of provision" (Braybrooke, 1987, pp. 38 -47). At that point, determining whether needs have been met or not is a matter of empirical inquiry. Determination involves "observing the condition" of the members of the "reference population" (Braybrooke, 1989, p. 39). The development of a bioevolutionary theory of human needs is the key to moving beyond debates over "social constructionism." If human beings, as a species, have determinate needs, we are able make empirical judgments concerning which social arrangements and conditions are doing more or less to adequately meet those needs. Transcultural comparisons need not inevitably be based on pure subjectivism.

What Nussbaum terms her "thick value conception" of "basic human functional capabilities" is based upon her initial list of needs (Nussbaum, 1992, p. 222). That is, given her determinate conception of human needs, the implications as far as what people should experience logically follows. She argues that the generic human "capability to function" should be the "goal of legislation and public planning" and should include the following (Nussbaum, 1992, pp. 221 -222):

1. Being able to live to the end of a complete human life, as far as possible; not dying prematurely, or before one's life is so reduced as to not be worth living.

2. Being able to have good health; to be adequately nourished; to have adequate shelter; having opportunities for sexual satisfaction.

3. Being able to live for and with others, to recognize and show concern for other human beings, to engage in various forms of familial and social interaction.

4. Being able to laugh, to play, to enjoy recreational activities.

5. Being able to live one's own life and nobody else's; being able to live one's own life in one's very own surroundings and context.

According to Nussbaum, these functional capabilities are constitutive of what it means to be human in a meaningful sense. They are derived from needs which are basic to all members of *Homo sapiens*. They are not contingent upon particular circumstances. They are categorical and generic to humankind.

As C. B. Megone has noted, one may make a distinction between an "instrumental" and a "categorical" need (Megone, 1992, pp. 14 – 27). For example, I might say "I need to fly to California to see my daughter." In this case, because my daughter is in California—and given various time constraints which would preclude any alternative method of transportation— I can accurately state that, if I am going to see her, then I need to fly there, as there are no available alternatives. The flight is a "means" to what Dewey would call an "end-in-view": a wish to visit my daughter. The "need" is relative to the specific context and limiting conditions of my particular desire. It is contingent. If I am going to see her at all, then I need to take an airplane because it is the only way possible, given my circumstances, for me to make the trip.

Megone suggests that there is another basic type of need which exists "in virtue of the nature of human beings" (Megone, 1992, p. 22). That is, for a human being, there are certain needs which need to be met because "in the absence of these a human being is not able to be a good member of its kind" (Megone, 1992, p. 22). A "categorical need," is such that "the fulfillment of the need, is constitutive of the thing (a human being) developing as the kind of thing that it is (as a human being)" (Megone, 1992, p. 23). Human beings have a categorical need for food and shelter simply in order to live. Adequate levels of nutrition are presupposed by what it means to be human. They are not, therefore, instrumental in the sense of my flight to California. The satisfaction of this categorical need is intrinsically valuable because all other human activities require this as an antecedent condition.

A need for adequate nutrition, shelter, companionship, sexual activity, and practical reason are constitutive of *Homo sapiens* as a species. They are the result of our species-specific evolutionary history. If these particular needs are not in some sense adequately met, those affected will not develop the possibilities which they embody simply as a member of a specific species.

Contrary to much sociological opinion, as Cosmides and Tooby assert: "Evolved structure does not constrain; it creates or enables" (Tooby and Cosmides, 1992, p. 39). Each species' "evolved structure" is, however, evolutionarily distinct. The particular "structures," which define our species characteristics, enable all *Homo sapiens* to make use of abilities which are generic to each of us. Our common features require that we also have common "categorical needs." Evident commonalities allow the use of transcultural standards in the determination of social problems. The use of categorical needs also provide a more realistic possibility of measurement (e.g., required minimum calories per day, required minimum standard of living) as opposed to the seemingly more sophisticated reliance on "marginal utility." As Braybrooke observes, "the fact remains that no one has drawn up anything like a full schedule of even a single person's utilities" (Braybrooke, 1987, p. 172).

It is important to recognize that categorical needs or course-of-life needs do not depend on personal desires or preferences. People need adequate nutrition whether they recognize that need or not. People need to exercise whether they like exercise or not. People need companions and meaningful relationships whether they recognize their necessity or not. The theoretical orientation of "biocriticism" or "biocritique," which I will develop in the next chapter, assumes that determinate human needs are an empirical possibility. I agree with Braybrooke that "It is course-of-life needs that are crucial to assessing social policy" (Braybrooke, 1989, p. 32). The link between "macro" and "micro" analyses are our transcultural, species-specific human needs and evolutionary characteristics. They need to be made explicit and taken into account.

There are significant problems and areas of practical concern with the position that I am advancing. If one assumes that there are important theoretical and empirical distinctions between "needs" and "wants," it is clear that in many situations a specific individual may not recognize his or her own "authentic" needs. My example of the Colombian *campesino*, for example, implied that an outside observer was more likely to understand the "real" needs of the peasant than the peasant himself. Clearly this suggests the possibility that the outside observer is in possession of "The Truth" which needs to be provided to the ignorant and benighted peasant. We are close to the logic which seems to indicate that only the "Revolutionary Vanguard" understands the situation "correctly" or without "false consciousness."

If I know what is best for you, but you—for various reasons—are unaware of the same necessities, perhaps, in Rousseau's famous phrase, you should be "forced to be free" (Russell, 1945, p. 697). The practical reason why humankind should concentrate on "wants" as opposed to "needs" is that each person presumably determines his or her own wants individually. In a market economy, for example, purchases are explicit expression of "wants." They represent, according to laissez faire assumptions, the most democratic method possible to measure those "wants." Any presumption that it is possible to make a valid or coherent distinction between "needs" and "wants" runs the risk of developing totalitarian political implications. The "ideal type" of this situation is the distant bureaucrat who informs the "locals" what is "best" for them. The normal reaction is to tell the bureaucrat to go to hell.

The difficulties inherent in the distinction between "needs" and "wants" or "preferences" should not be minimized. There is a kind of authoritarian logic to any presumption of "false consciousness" on the part of another individual. If I am absolutely certain of "The Truth," in the sense, for example, of the Pope speaking *ex cathedra*, then I am likely to feel justified in forcing you to do whatever is necessary to "save your soul." One sees a first step toward the kind of "logic" utilized by the Catholic Inquisition. As Jeffrey Stout has noted, "What made the creation of liberal institutions necessary, in large part, was the manifest failure of religious groups to establish rational agreement on their competing detailed visions of the good" (Stout, 1988a, p. 212). Many different religions are, of course, absolutely certain of their own definitions of "the good." Unfortunately their definitions are mutually contradictory. Something of the same problem is inherent in any discussion of "needs" which distinguishes between "needs" and "wants."

As C. Wright Mills wrote:

If we take the simple democratic view that what men [sic] are interested in is all that concerns us, then we are accepting the values that have been inculcated, often accidentally and often deliberately by vested interests. These values are often the only ones men have had any chance to develop. They are unconsciously acquired habits rather than choices.

If we take the dogmatic view that what is to men's interests, whether they are interested in it or not, is all that need concern us morally,

then we run the risk of violating democratic values. We *may become*
manipulators or coercers, or both, rather than persuaders. (Mills,
1959, p. 194, emphasis in original)

Mills himself suggests one possible approach to this dilemma which is to
persuade as opposed to manipulate or coerce. Sociologists have not always
recognized the difference. One of the chief virtues of works like Foucault's
Discipline and Punish (1979) is a demonstration of the myraid techniques of
social control by social institutions. What Foucault terms "the gentle way in
punishment" is a classic analysis of "enlightened" social control by "modern"
professionals (Foucault, 1979, pp. 104 – 131). Along with "institutional"
methods of social control, social science developed its own specialized "insider"
jargon which has continued uninterrupted into the era of postmodernism and
critical theory.

If we are going to try to convince another person of her needs, it is clear
she has to first of all understand what we are talking about. As we will make
clear in the discussion of biocritique, it is absolutely essential that one
understand the language of "the other" in order for any egalitarian dialogue
to occur. Anyone in a position to make specific policy recommendations
which may run counter to the expressed wishes of any group, needs to speak
the language of the group to which the policy measures apply.

One of the major faults of critical theory has been a tendency to theorize
in an absolutely opaque vocabulary which is only comprehensible to a "select"
group. The same criticism applies to much of the current writings of
postmodernists. (One thinks, for example, of the extreme difficulty of
understanding Adorno or Derrida.) Postmodernists argue that we need to
rely on "local standards" for making moral judgments but express their ideas
in ways that almost no "local" person could possibly comprehend.

As Ashley and Orenstein note in their discussion of "interpretative theory":

To test the accuracy of interpretive theory, it is necessary to refer to
human practice. Interpretive theory fails to receive corroboration
when there is a disappointment of expectation within a context of
communicative interaction. For instance, one's knowledge of a
foreign language can be tested by seeing whether it is possible to give
orders successfully in that language and to have such orders obeyed

by the actions one intended to produce through speech. (Ashley and Orenstein, 1990, p. 50)

From Dewey's perspective, the intended actions which were a result of the orders given provide a pragmatic warrant for assuming that one was able to express what was intended. In my own experiences in Colombia, it was clear that every conversation in Spanish provided immediate feedback concerning any "expectation within a context of communicative interaction." Employing a second language produces a constant experiment in "interpretive theory." It also suggests one possible approach towards transcending the kind of dualistic needs/wants dilemma outlined by Mills. It is essential that both parties to any dialogue speak the same language.

It is still possible, of course, that differences will remain after the most extensive and mutually comprehensible dialogue. In that case, all one can practically do is abide by the results of political democracy. In a democracy, people by definition have the option of ignoring their needs and engaging in activities that are personally harmful. People should be allowed to follow their own preferences and make mistakes. It is entirely possible that someone might recognize his or her "real" needs and still choose to follow another path. Speaking the same language, however, at least allows the possibility for Mills's "persuasion," as opposed to "coercion," to occur. It is a necessary, if not sufficient, condition for egalitarian dialogue.

The stipulation of mutual comprehensibility has important implications for sociological theory. Contrary to the arcane "insider" vocabulary of much postmodernist analysis (Rosenau, 1992, pp. xi-xiv), the theory of human needs which I am proposing is continually subject to, and should be modified by, what Alfred Schutz called "the postulate of adequacy."

Each term in a scientific model of human action must be constructed in such a way that a human act performed within the life-world by an individual actor in the way indicated by the typical construct would be understandable for the actor himself as well as for his fellow-men in terms of common-sense interpretation of everyday life. Compliance with this postulate warrants the consistency of the constructs of the social scientist with the constructs of common-sense experience of the social reality. (Schutz, 1962, p. 44)

A discussion of human needs should be potentially comprehensible to any individual whether acting in a manner in compliance or contrary to his or her postulated needs. Assuming the prerequisite of a common language, the "other" should be able to understand what you are talking about. The result of following the "postulate of adequacy" is a kind of theoretical and practical modesty. Social scientists are likely to be critical of this formulation because it implies that most disciplinary jargon is methodologically unwarranted. It suggests that, as a practical matter, introductory sociology students should be able to understand any instructor's theories. Any theory should make sense in terms of "common-sense interpretations of everyday life." Given adequate levels of nutrition, education, income, and freedom of choice—Braybrooke's "needs freely arrived at" (Braybrooke, 1987, p. 241)—the differences expressed between the "wants" of the "other" and the "needs" postulated by a particular theory should decrease, assuming the theory is pragmatically warranted, logically consistent, and meets Schutz's "postulate of adequacy."

A second method of dealing with the problem of what might be termed an "Inquisition Complex" is to adopt a position of epistemological humility. It is important to recognize at all times that *one's viewpoint is necessarily a reflection of one's own history, culture and personal experiences*. Knowledge is a process which continually produces new information. As Tooby and Cosmides write:

> Given the fact that we are almost entirely ignorant of the computational specifics of the hundreds of thousands of mechanisms which comprise the human mind, it is far beyond the present competence of anyone living to say what are and are not achievable outcomes for human beings. (Tooby and Cosmides, 1992, p. 40)

It should also be noted that one may adopt this position of modesty when postulating any cross-cultural, generic human needs. A theory of human needs is always open to revision in the light of new experience and information. The possibility of shared, transcultural human needs does not imply any kind of rigid "essentialism." Our knowledge of human evolutionary history, for example, is continually changing (Willis, 1989; Johanson, Johanson and Edgar, 1994). In proposing that sociologists take into account our evolutionary history, I am not arguing that human evolution has produced completely known and invariant human needs. It is entirely possible that different human needs, in the sense described earlier, are still to be determined. The most important implication of the earlier discussion is that, based on the best available data, it is possible in principle to make a determination of transcultural human needs. Any individual, simply as a member of *Homo sapiens*, shares the postulated needs.

We may encounter alternative human capabilities and necessities based on additional information. Contrary to the suggestion that any description of human needs is necessarily ethnocentric and culturally biased, it is entirely possible that encounters with other cultures will demonstrate shortcomings in our own identification of needs. The theories which we advance are, of course, necessarily influenced by our own cultural and historical contexts (Phillips, 1986, pp. 41–49). As Derek Phillips has argued, "there is no place to stand outside our beliefs and our language" (Phillips, 1986, p. 44). Every theory contains its own biases and assumptions. As Tooby and Cosmides observe:

> This is because the world itself provides no framework that can decide among the infinite number of potential category dimensions, the infinite number of relations, and the infinite number of potential hypotheses that could be used to analyze it. (Tooby and Cosmides 1992, p. 106)

The ability to falsify a proposition is not, by itself, a useful or practical research strategy insofar as the number of possible empirical generalizations is infinite (Tooby and Cosmides, 1992, p. 76). One of the principal functions of theory is to narrow the range of possibilities and suggest where to look. The possibility of empirical refutation is not *ipso facto* helpful for research unless it is embedded in a specific theoretical context.

On the other hand, "our theories have an oddly reciprocal relationship between language and nature.... There is sometimes feedback from nature, and theoretical accounts are adjusted accordingly" (Phillips, 1986, p. 44). We are able to develop a pragmatically warranted system of knowledge, even though the "feedback" is "never totally free of theoretical influences" (Phillips, 1986, p. 44). Every time we turn on the ignition and the car starts, we are justified in assuming that the knowledge used to construct the car was adequate for its functioning.[26]

There is no reason why theories in the social sciences cannot make similar kinds of pragmatically warranted assumptions and statements. But our assumptions and statements as sociologists are more likely to be pragmatically warranted if they take into account information available from disciplines outside sociology. A theory of human needs, for example, should include any relevant information concerning needs from such areas as evolutionary psychology, biology, endocrinology, genetics, or physical anthropology. If one is going to assume as did Marx, for example, that under conditions of "primitive communism" more egalitarian social arrangements obtained than in industrial societies, clearly information from any discipline relevant to that assertion should be considered (Symons, 1992, p. 152; Barkow, Cosmides and Tooby, 1992, pp. 3 – 15). Only a myopic and misguided sense of disciplinary proprietorship suggests otherwise. As C. Wright Mills accurately noted in 1959, we need to expand "the sociological imagination" (Mills, 1959). Only the crudest kinds of sociological prejudices exclude "nonsociological" data from "sociological" explanations of human behavior.

Consider the typical discussion of "probability sampling" in light of the data available from paleoanthropology and evolutionary psychology. The usual discussion of "sample designs" points to the advantages of the "random" sample, as opposed to "purposive" or "convenience samples" (Nachmias and Nachmias, 1981, pp. 429 – 441). The language used and the implicit judgments made imply that only "random" samples provide "scientific" data because "only probability sampling makes possible representative sampling designs" (Nachmias and Nachmias, 1981, p. 429). This is a taken-for-granted assumption of what Tooby and Cosmides refer to as the "standard social science model" (Tooby and Cosmides, 1992, pp. 31 – 34). Sociological "domain assumptions" (Goulder, 1970, pp. 31 – 35) devalue any information which is not a product of standard random sampling techniques. A reflexive sociology, however, needs to recognize that it is merely a metaphysical assumption to presume that differences between human beings *preclude by definition* any meaningful data from a nonrepresentative sample or even a "sample" of one.

Suppose, as the most recent data available to evolutionary psychologists indicate, that much of interest to social science is generic to *Homo sapiens* (Barkow, Cosmides and Tooby, 1992; Brown, 1991). What that means is that a sample of one may provide data and information which is of transcultural significance if we know where to look and consider the data relevant. One must take into account data which analyze what Tooby and Cosmides refer to "a clearly recognizable species-typical architecture" (Tooby and Cosmides, 1992, p. 80). For example, there are now large amounts of data on "the perceptual organization of colors" (Shepard, 1992, pp. 495 –532; Durham, 1991, pp. 213 –223), the significance of language mechanisms and vocalizations (Fernald, 1992, pp. 391 –428; Pinker and Bloom, 1992, pp. 451 –493), or "evolved responses to landscapes" (Orians, 1980; Orians and Heerwagen, 1992, pp. 555 –579). All of this information is of interest to evolutionary psychologists because it is believed that our evolutionary history has resulted in particular kinds of responses which are species-specific. The "discordance hypothesis" is based on a similar perspective.

"Sociological explanations often implicitly assume that all our important characteristics are a result of cultural development and we may safely ignore individual psychology and biology" (Tooby and Cosmides, 1992, p. 32). Human variations, as expressed in cultural differences, are the relevant causal variables. A single individual, therefore, provides very little "useful" data. Whatever "needs" are specific to a single individual are, by sociological fiat, unimportant. But what if our evolutionary past has resulted in biosocial adaptations which are generic to our species? If that is the case, a researcher should be aware of transcultural biological and psychological similarities, not simply cultural differences. The only way to obtain particular kinds of data is to begin on the individual level. In his description of a *sui generis* methodology exclusive to sociology, Durkheim was profoundly mistaken.

It should be obvious that "a universal evolved psychology will produce variable manifest behavior given different environmental conditions" (Tooby and Cosmides, 1992, p. 46). This has resulted in the sociological emphasis on cultural differences. In this case, however, one individual, no matter how great the cultural variation between different societies, may still provide a great deal of useful data. Because sociology dismisses the logic behind this argument, it misconstrues or ignores relevant data from other disciplines.

Consider the incredible elation described by Donald Johanson during his group's discovery of "Lucy" in 1974 (Johanson and Edey, 1981, pp. 13 –24). This single, small *Austraolpithecus afarensis* skeleton is almost certainly the most famous fossil of all time. Why should one small three and one-half feet tall skeleton produce such astounding jubilation? "Oh, Jesus we've got it. We've got the Whole Thing!" yelled Johanson's assistant Tom Gray (Johanson and Edey, 1981, p. 17). Johanson's description of the resulting scene at his camp is a classic description of the emotion which accompanies scientific discovery:

> The camp was rocking with excitement. That first night we never went to bed at all. We talked and talked. We drank beer after beer. There was a tape recorder in the camp, and a tape of the Beatles song "Lucy in the Sky with Diamonds" went belting out into the night sky, and was played at full volume over and over again out of sheer exuberance. At some point during that unforgettable evening—I no longer remember exactly when—the new fossil picked up the name of Lucy. (Johanson and Edey, 1981, p. 18)

One can picture the reaction of *Sociolicus archtypicalus* to the same find: "Oh throw the damn thing away" said Emile. "After all, there's only one."

An unfair comparison? But why should paleontologists be able to obtain so much data from one fossil compared to sociology's trained incompetence with a single living individual? The facile response is "Sociology deals with groups, paleontology with individual remains." Why, however, should sociologists ignore relevant data from all other disciplines simply because it is obtained on an individualistic basis? Other than a kind of traditionalistic dogmatism and superstition, I see no reason for making such an arbitrary and artificial distinction. A naturalistic perspective suggests we proceed otherwise. In this case, it also agrees with much current postmodernist thought in rejecting binaries such as "nature/nurture."

Conceptual and empirical analysis of human needs is in a pivotal position to close the distance between research on "individual" and research on "group" phenomena. "Needs," according to Braybrooke, are "founded on persistent features of human biology and psychology" (Braybrooke, 1987, p. 244). He also argues that needs "can be ascribed with presumptive universality to human beings regardless of differences in cultures and circumstances" (Braybrooke, 1987, p. 244). On the one hand, it is clearly the individual who experiences the kinds of needs Braybrooke and Nussbaum believe are constitutive of *Homo sapiens*. We begin once again with Dennis Wrong's observation that "in the beginning there is the body" (Wrong, 1961, p. 191). According to current perspectives in sociology, this is obviously a "micro" perspective. We are looking at separate individuals.

Let us assume, however, that these "separate" individuals all have similar needs, as much current research in a variety of disciplines implies. As Tooby and Cosmides propose, let us define the psychological mechanisms of *Homo sapiens* as "domain-specific inferential systems" (Tooby and Cosmides, 1992, p. 92). This is contrary to traditional assumptions in sociology which have viewed a general *capacity* for culture as the only relevant evolutionary factor. Sociologists have placed great emphasis on "learning" as a context-free, generalized socialization mechanism. As Leslie White observes, "the sociology of human beings...is a function of this external suprabiological, supraorganic tradition called culture" (White, 1973, p. 10). The problem for White's line of reasoning, however, is that it is completely contradicted by current findings in areas other than sociology:

> Results out of cognitive psychology, evolutionary biology, artificial intelligence, developmental psychology, linguistics, and philosophy converge on the same conclusion: A psychological architecture that consisted of nothing but equipotential, general-purpose, content-independent or content-free mechanisms could not successfully perform the tasks the human mind is known to perform or solve the adaptive problems humans evolved to solve—from seeing, to learning a language, to recognizing an emotional expression...to the many disparate activities aggregated under the term "learning culture." (Tooby and Cosmides, 1992, p. 34)

By more adequately investigating and theorizing human needs, sociologists would be able to understand and interpret information from these diverse areas. Sociology traditionally ignores the kinds of findings listed by Tooby and Cosmides because they are defined as "psychological" or "biological." If one assumes that sociology, by disciplinary stipulation, only deals with emergent or group phenomena, there is simply no way to use these kind of data. The single most important result of my proposed sociological reexamination of human needs is that it potentially broadens sociology's "domain-specific inferential systems" and increases the possible utility of information collected in other disciplines. We have to reintroduce the idea of the individual into sociology not simply as a "correction" to a "macro" orientation, but *in order to make sense of what has happened in other disciplines*. Discussion of "human needs" invites an expanded sociological discourse which includes previously neglected participants.

To the extent that similar needs are species-specific, the familiar distinction between "micro" and "macro" is even more tenuous. Specific needs are individualistic qualities, but they are shared by the members of particular groups. In that sense, they are also "group" phenomena. This is not to deny, however, the importance of "emergent" characteristics in any social situation. Anyone, for example, subject to an unpopular military draft should have no difficulty accepting the pragmatic significance of institutional phenomena. In my discussion of Edward O. Wilson, I previously pointed out the distinction between an institutional explanation of the causes of war and analyses of the motivations of individual soldiers. Individual soldiers fight for various reasons which have very little to do with the political and economic decisions which precipitated a specific conflict, although it would be foolish to ignore psychological characteristics of the powerful.

The emphasis placed on the importance of the individual in this chapter in no way minimizes the significance of "macro" or institutional processes. Sociologists need to take seriously, however, the commonly expressed truism that institutions presuppose the necessity of individual actors. From the standpoint of evolutionary psychology, "The claim that some phenomena are 'socially constructed' only means that the social environment provided some of the inputs used by the psychological mechanisms of the individuals involved" (Tooby and Cosmides, 1992, p. 117). This is the opposite of a sociological perspective which presupposes the unique significance of cultural levels of explanation. By making use of an analysis of "human needs," we can more usefully interpret research which begins at the individual level. As we shall see in the following chapter, an emphasis on needs also suggests a more "critical" orientation than simple preoccupation with "wants." According to Braybrooke, "Far better to say, in defense of progressive taxation, that the poor find it difficult to cover their basic needs, while the rich can indulge in the most frivolous preferences" (Braybrooke, 1987, p. 173). A biocritical perspective presupposes determinate human needs.

V

TOWARD A BIOCRITICAL PERSPECTIVE

A. INTRODUCTION

The development of a biocritical perspective begins with the observation that human beings share a common evolutionary history. An adequate recognition of our evolutionary past suggests several things with respect to our fellow human beings:

1. We all evolved from an original African context.

2. We are all members of the same species and genetically we all have a great deal in common.

3. All our distinctive species-specific characteristics developed as a result of our evolutionary history. What we value in our fellow human beings is ultimately a result of the same evolutionary process.

4. Because of our similar evolutionary history, the great majority of human beings share similar neural-biological characteristics and common ontogenetic development. We begin life with similar "hard-wiring" and go through similar stages of growth.

5. Due ultimately to our biological similarities, we share common and distinctive physiological and psychological needs.

It is clear from paleoanthropological evidence that we are all of African descent (Willis, 1989; Leakey, 1981; Johanson, Johanson and Edgar, 1994). The fact that we are "North Americans" is the chance result of evolutionary history and migrations. While a number of controversies exist with respect to the processes and manner in which this evolution occurred (Dawkins, 1986, pp. 223–318; Ruse, 1988, pp. 31–42), the origin of humankind in Africa and our subsequent evolutionary development are not in dispute. As Richard Dawkins argues, Darwinism is the only available empirical theory which adequately accounts for contemporary data (Dawkins, 1986, p. x).

We came from the same place. The stochastic evolutionary mechanisms of mutation, natural selection, gene flow, and genetic drift are responsible for the phenotypical variations between human groups which we see today (Cummings, 1988, pp. 386 –413; Sutton and Wagner, 1985, pp. 290 –411). The variation in phenotypes among *Homo sapiens* is a principal source of the lack of recognition of commonalities among contemporary populations.

Most of the genetic variation which occurs among humans is variation within populations as opposed to variation among populations. Biologist Michael Cummings estimates that genetic differences between what are viewed as "racial groups" accounts for 7% of all human genetic diversity. The remaining 93% is a result of variation within each "racial" group (Cummings, 1988, p. 404).

There are several specific genetic differences between various human groupings. Genetic polymorphisms exist with respect to such things as lactose tolerance and blood groups which have been well-documented cross-culturally (Sutton and Wagner, 1985, pp. 398–405). If, however, the overwhelming majority of genetic variations among human beings occur within groups which have traditionally been defined as racially distinct, it is clear that we have much more in common biologically than a cursory inspection of phenotypical variation reveals. We see the differences but don't understand the similarities which a biocritical perspective suggests are the evolutionary background of our common needs.

It is unreasonable to assume that natural selection has operated in the development of all other species and has not affected humankind. It is only our own anthropocentric hubris which allows us to view our own evolutionary history as *sui generis* (Callebaut, 1993). In Jared Diamond's phrase, we are "the third chimpanzee" and this makes a difference both in our perceptions and in our needs (Diamond, 1992). By not recognizing our evolutionary history, we distort our social development and construct the kind of artificial dualism which Durkheim proclaimed as the essence of the sociological method (1966 [1895]). As Timothy Crippen has argued, "discussions of and efforts to explain human cultural behavior are incomplete to the degree that they ignore the complex influences of genes, hormones, neurotransmitters, and experience on brain ontogeny and phylogeny" (Crippen 1992, pp. 390 –391).

We are of nature and in nature. As Mary Midgley has observed, "We are not just rather like animals; we are animals" (Midgley, 1978, p. xiii, emphasis in original). Certainly the differences between humans and other animals are striking and important. As we have seen in Chapter 1, however, ethological investigations have narrowed the previously accepted "qualitative" distinctions between *Homo sapiens* and other species. With respect to the evolutionary history which we have shared with other species, the term "the human animal" is redundant. As William Gray has noted, "We are here for the same reason that tigers and whales and starfish are here—because of our adaptive fitness to our biological circumstances" (Grey, 1987, p. 479).

Human beings are not some kind of disembodied spiritual wraiths—a "ghost in the machine" on Emile Durkheim's "culturological" stage. Once again, we note that "in the beginning there is the body." Sociology needs to literally re-member the discipline (i.e., remake it today while also recalling an evolutionary perspective). Sociology needs to develop an approach to theory which incorporates an epistemological and evolutionary naturalism. What we value as human beings is ultimately dependent on our evolutionary history. If all biological considerations are excluded by definition from sociological analysis, we unnecessarily distort and limit our understandings of social behavior. Other than academic "tradition" (i.e., an automatic defense of academic "turf"), there is no justifiable reason to not make use of whatever kinds of data help to explain the problem at hand.

From the standpoint of the biocritical perspective I am developing, a major problem in contemporary social science is not the difference between accepting a "hard" or "soft" version of genetic influence, but rather the nearly total lack of recognition that evolutionary processes have any significance at all (Sanderson and Ellis, 1992, pp. 32 – 33). The theoretical difficulty for sociologists is that all of the human characteristics which we value are ultimately the result of natural evolutionary processes. As Franz Wuketits has written:

> The human mind is a systems property of the human brain; it depends on the specific arrangement of nerve cells. Thus, "mental life" in humans can only be understood by studying its neuro-biological basis. This means that organic evolution was the precondition to the development or evolution of psychic and spiritual (mental) phenomena: Cognitive behavior in animals and humans is a result of evolutionary processes. (Wuketits, 1988, p. 457)

This means, of course, that all the dualities established by sociologists to distinguish their field—nature/culture, mind/body, human/animal deny the evolutionary history which was involved in the very qualities which we now define as distinctly "human." All of our philosophy, science, technology and art was ultimately made possible by the same evolutionary forces which produced all other earthly biota. In this respect, we are certainly not unique.

In his recognition of this commonality, Edward Wilson's sociobiological orientation is accurate and warranted. Nature, as Richard Dawkins has cogently argued, is "the blind watchmaker" (Dawkins, 1986). Evolutionary epistemologist Henry Plotkin, in his recent book *Darwin Machines and the Nature of Knowledge* (1994, p. xiv), summarizes the significance of evolutionary literature:

> We simply will not understand human rationality and intelligence, or human communication and culture, until we understand how these seemingly unnatural attributes are deeply rooted in human biology. They are...the special adaptations that make us special. What is unarguable is that they are the products of human evolution.... There really are no substantive alternative ways of understanding our extraordinary capacity for knowledge.

Assuming for the moment that the above statements constitute "warranted knowledge" in John Dewey's sense of the term (Dewey, 1929), what implications do they suggest for sociological theory and analysis? What I term "biocritique" builds on knowledge of our common evolutionary history. It is primarily a different way of looking at data by taking into account information which is normally neglected or considered sociologically insignificant. Because they are presumably cross-cultural "constants" sociologists tend to assume that biological or psychological factors may be ignored in the explanation of social behavior: They have the "same" influence in all cultures; so we may safely ignore their effects.

The utterly fallacious nature of this assumption is made clear by looking at statements which are logically similar to the biological *ceteris paribus* assumption: "If language is a constant in all cultures, we may safely ignore its effects on human actions." Or "The use of fire is a cross-cultural constant, so we may ignore its influence on human behavior." Because something is a transcultural constant does not mean that it has no significance for human actions. As Tooby and Cosmides observe, "a universal evolved psychology will produce variable manifest behavior given different environmental conditions" (Tooby and Cosmides, 1992, p. 46). This statement obviously does not indicate that human psychological characteristics are inconsequential for understanding human actions or that "You can't explain a variable with a constant." Evolutionary and environmental factors interact over time. What the resulting effects are is an empirical question.

Because we inevitably misperceive what we don't understand or simply ignore, sociologists who only focus on cultural differences can't accept the plausibility of transcultural common interests and necessities. Richard Dawkins terms this "The Argument from Personal Incredulity." He discusses the comment by a bishop to the effect that "camouflage...is not always easily explicable" in Darwinian terms. The bishop wondered why the polar bear needs to be colored white if it is so "dominant." Dawkins points out that "predators also benefit from being concealed from their prey" (Dawkins, 1986, pp. 38-39). He suggests that the bishop's argument might be "translated" as follows:

> I personally, off the top of my head sitting in my study, never having visited the Arctic, never having seen a polar bear in the wild, and having been educated in classical literature and theology, have not so far managed to think of why polar bears might benefit from being white. (p. 38)

Sociologists who reject out of hand the possibility of cross-cultural commonalities might keep the "Argument from Personal Incredulity" in mind. Because the biocritical perspective stresses the importance of cross-cultural similarities, it is contrary to the current postmodern "turn" toward "local knowledge" and particularism (Seidman, 1991; 1994). Contemporary fashion, however, is surely a poor reason for the rejection of theoretical concepts. Biocritique suggests that we need to look at our common interests and evolutionary history (Brown, 1991).

Sociologists are taught to examine human differences. When we analyze different groups, classes, races, sexes or cultures we "naturally" are concerned with the different things we see. We look at culture cross-culturally and see distinctive family patterns, customs, and religions. We expect to see differences and we find them everywhere. Languages are obviously different. Sexual customs are very different. Taken-for-granted attitudes and non-verbal communication vary and lead to much cross-cultural confusion (Hall, 1959). What Alfred Schutz called "recipe knowledge"—our "typifications" of everyday life—seemingly have very little transcultural validity (Schutz, 1964, pp. 95–96). People don't act as we expect them to act. What stands out are all the variations in what are normally the nonproblematic assumptions of our own cultural "microcosm." Our recipe-knowledge literally tells us when it is "normal" to eat, but in Spain, we try to adjust to a 10:00 p.m. dinner. Spanish folkways concerning the "proper" mealtime are certainly different from ours.

It is true, nevertheless, that people in Spain do eat dinner. Sociology has made much of the first fact and ignored the second. A biocritical approach to sociological theory assumes the importance of cross-cultural similarities, as well as the differences, in customs which every traveler experiences. A new way of looking at sociological data is both warranted and desirable. The work of Wilson, Richards, Braybrooke, Midgley and Nussbaum suggests unexamined possibilities for improving sociological theories and data. As philosopher Holmes Rolston III has argued, we shape our values "in significant measure in accord with our notion of the kind of universe that we live in" (Rolston, 1986, p. 27). I am proposing that sociological attitudes concerning the extent of cultural differences distort our perceptions of human similarities. When we encounter what postmodernists term "the other," (Boyne, 1990), we see the cultural differences, but not the biological similarities. That is, after all, exactly what we have been taught to see. But suppose an emphasis on our shared evolutionary history had stressed our biological commonalities.

In June 1994 my wife and I stayed for a time with a Mexican family in Cuernavaca. By the third day of our visit, the señora was telling us about her family, about her niece who was having trouble at work, and showing us pictures from family albums. She described the pleasures of Mexican cooking and complained about the strange ways of the "younger generation." She and her husband both worried about their finances, their drinking water, and their health. They told us about a relative who had gone to live in the U.S. and asked us about our own city and living conditions. Their concerns were obviously very similar to those of many families in the United States. Given the translation from Spanish to English, we could have easily been listening to a family in the United States. These kinds of experiences simply wouldn't be possible without profound transcultural human commonalities and similarities. As Tooby and Cosmides note, "The best refutation of cultural relativity is the activity of anthropologists themselves, who could not understand or live within other human groups unless the inhabitants of those groups shared assumptions that were, in fact, very similar to those of the ethnographer" (Tooby and Cosmides, 1992, p. 92).

In order to comprehend the similarities, however, it is necessary to share a common language. In the United States, less than 1% of our total student population studies Chinese, Russian, Spanish, Hindi or Arabic—languages spoken by three-fourths of the world's population (Ferrante, 1992, p. 6). There is no reason to assume that sociology or sociologists are immune to this kind of linguistic know-nothingism. The lack of any understanding of language and the role it plays in influencing our perceptions of other cultures limits our comprehension of cross-cultural similarities.   One of the reasons an evolutionary perspective seems so strange to sociologists is that we are a nation of monoglots. A person who speaks a different language is, by definition, "the other."   Anything defined by the dominant hegemonic perspective as "the other" is considered "strange" or "different" (Rajchman, 1985, pp. 43–76). How can we expect to look for transcultural commonalities when differences are presupposed by the very terms of our linguistic "nondiscourse"? Of course we see "differences" everywhere we look. If you can't talk to someone, they certainly are "different."

Along with being monoglots, we are what might be termed "lenguacentric." That is, we assume that knowledge or information about any other language is unnecessary and that English represents a kind of "chosen" language. Given the predominance of spoken English, there is very little in our everyday experiences to suggest otherwise. As a result, our common experience is also "monoaudible": We normally only hear one language. This has had significant effects on our theories and taken-for-granted assumptions. In a monoaudible culture, one is almost never personally exposed to another language. If one hardly ever hears another language, on the rare occasions that this does occur it will naturally seem extremely "strange" or "different." Someone who uses another language within the cultural context of the United States is very clearly labeled "the other" (Macedo, 1994, pp. 91 –135). The "reasoning" involved appears to be something like this: "I speak English. Everyone I normally see and hear speaks English. Anyone who doesn't speak English is, at the very least, a little "strange" and more likely, a bit stupid or mentally deficient." I.Q., in other words, is positively correlated with non-accented English.

A nation of monoglots necessarily generates a kind of auditory auto-da-fe. The Linguistic Inquisition speaks with a single voice. Why can't the ungrateful imbecile learn English? Nietzsche and Max Scheler wrote about the significance of "resentment" as an influence on behavior (Remmling, 1967, pp. 32 –39, 172 –176). One could construct a "hostility index" and chart the degree of antipathy of English-speakers to spoken Spanish. Why should we have to learn their language? There are, I think, a number of good reasons which are related to the development of a biocritical perspective.

Learning another language makes clear, on an experiential basis, the contingency of one's own language. What I call "house" can just as easily be designated *la casa* by the Spanish speaker. If I had grown up in Spain I would, in fact, call it that. Children everywhere learn the language of their own cultures and "are fluent speakers of complex grammatical sentences by the age of three, *without benefit of formal instruction*" (Pinker and Bloom, 1992, p. 451, emphasis added). The generalized ability to learn a language is a result of our evolutionary history (Pinker and Bloom, 1992, pp. 452 –493). The specific language we learn is obviously dependent on our culture.

If my language is totally arbitrary, then perhaps the same can be said about my clothing or my food. This reasoning may lead to a more flexible kind of mentality and less of a tendency to label the merely different as "the other." It becomes clear that beneath the ethnographic differences there are common human concerns. By understanding another person's language, I am more likely to understand and recognize her personhood. Until the language barrier is breached, it's easy to assume an unbridgeable gulf between "us" and "them." As George Herbert Mead noted:

> A person learns a new language and...puts himself into the attitude of those that make use of that language. He cannot read its literature, cannot converse with those that belong to that community, without taking on its peculiar attitudes. He becomes in that sense a different individual. You cannot convey a language as pure abstraction; you inevitably in some way convey also the life that lies behind it. And this result builds itself into relationship with the organized attitudes of the individual who gets this language and inevitably brings about a readjustment of views. (Mead, 1962 [1934]), p. 283)

In my own experiences visiting Mexico, working in Colombia and also studying in Spain, the importance of the Spanish language cannot be overestimated. The everyday reality of using a different language was an experiment in participant-observation which experientially demonstrated to me the interaction of language and my perceptions of cross-cultural similarities and differences.

Once "the others," for example, in Mexico, realize that you understand their language, the sort of "faceless cipher" stare and mutual lack of comprehension that tourists often assume is "natural" drastically change. Cab drivers turn into veritable "street poets" with opinions on all topics. The "natural" attitude in Mexico is, in fact, more outgoing and gregarious than is the case in the U.S. One is *supposed* to say "good morning" or "good afternoon" or "good evening" to everyone. Failure to do so may be considered insulting (Gandy, 1990, p. 23). In similar situations in the U.S., an unsolicited greeting might be considered "strange."

A common language opens up the possibility of a phenomenological sharing of everyday life. The "other" takes you into account because you speak the same language and then *acts in such a way as to make you aware of common concerns*. Failure to speak the same language results in a self-fulfilling prophecy of mutual misunderstandings and accentuation of "differences." Without the common linguistic framing of the interaction, there is no possibility of "opening up" towards the other and no possibility of authentic friendship. "Friendship" might be defined as two or more people developing a mutual, taken-for-granted trust. With a common language, such trust is potentially available. Without it, we are likely as the archetypal "tourist" to find blank stares and mutual incomprehension.

Because we don't understand the "other's" language, we don't understand what she or he is trying to do or say. Because we don't understand the language, we don't understand the different cultural situation. Because we don't understand the different cultural situation, we don't perceive the similarity of cross-cultural activities, needs, and concerns. Because we misperceive what we don't understand, we can't accept the plausibility of transcultural necessities and common interests. We are all members of the same species. When we actually see each other we should recognize our overwhelming similarities as a species. We all begin life with many of the same human needs.

B. THE LOGIC OF BIOCRITIQUE

A "biocritical" approach to sociological theory assumes that the biosocial perspectives we have been examining have demonstrated the plausibility of species-specific human characteristics and needs. By taking our evolutionary history into account, we accentuate and make visible the transcultural needs and common developments of *Homo sapiens* as a distinct species. The discussion in previous chapters has, I believe, established the plausibility of determinate human needs.

Let us take as our "ideal type" the short list provided by Nussbaum in Chapter Four. Human beings, as such, have a need to satisfy hunger and thirst, a need for shelter, a need for extended and adequate care as infants, a need for affiliation with other human beings, a need for play and humor, a need for sexual activity, and a need to make use of "practical reason" (Nussbaum, 1992, pp. 216 –220). It is possible that this list should be extended, but let us assume it minimally describes human needs. Other efforts to provide policy recommendations have produced very similar lists (Braybrooke, 1987, pp. 32–47). Nussbaum's list reflects the kinds of transcultural similarities which are often ignored by "cultural relativists" (Geertz, 1973). It is difficult to argue that any of Nussbaum's categories should be excluded. Even if differences persist, however, the possibility of such a list is more important than its specific provisions.

A biocritical analysis assumes that we do, in fact, know a considerable amount about human needs. It assumes that our needs are ultimately the result of our specific evolutionary history. It takes information about needs from any discipline which seems relevant. In the establishment of cross-cultural human needs, it utilizes research done in evolutionary biology, neurophysiology, psychology, sociobiology, physical anthropology, genetics, and any other areas which are germane to the problem at hand. It assumes that it is possible to generate a list of basic "course-of-life" needs, although each list will vary somewhat over time. It takes as axiomatic and self-evident that human needs should be adequately met by supportive social institutions.

Sociology in general has posited the cultural relativity of all "value judgments." Durkheim, for example, assumed that the morality of a society was simply a function of its particular social organization: "History has established...each society has in the main a morality suited to it" (Durkheim,

1953 [1924], p. 56). Perhaps the most famous proponent of "coexisting and equally valid patterns of life" was Ruth Benedict (1934, p. 240). Sociology, according to this perspective, has nothing to add to ethical discussions. As Randall Collins puts it, "ethics is always an area of the ultimately arbitrary" (Collins, 1975, p. 547). Even Jeffrey Alexander, who is well known for his critique of "positivism" (Alexander, 1982), has written that "The question of moral rationality must be argued on a deeper plane, and we must be prepared to accept certain inevitable differences of opinion" (Alexander, 1981, p. 286). As Stephen Seidman argues, "The values of the community of which the critic is a part stands as the 'ultimate' realm of moral appeal" (Seidman, 1991, p. 143). Sociological opinion has generally proposed the cultural relativity of all value judgments. In the realm of ethics, the sociological Owl of Minerva is grounded and flightless.

A biocritical approach suggests that at least short flights of critical reason are possible. It observes that some social institutions or cultures are better than others at adequately meeting specific human needs. Not every society is as effective as every other in the satisfaction of a particular need. The extent of variation is an empirical question which may be investigated in the same manner as any other research problem. In the United States, for example, heart disease is the leading cause of death and is responsible for 34% of the total mortality among the fifteen leading causes of death (United States Department of Health and Public Services, 1993, p. 11). Different countries have different rates of mortality resulting from different diseases. Those which have lower rates than others are doing a better job of meeting needs in particular areas. Research can be conducted on needs in the same fashion as all other social science research.

It may be possible to utilize official documents or census data. With proper qualifications and interpretation, it may be possible to use various kinds of survey data. Perhaps above all else we need to observe behavior and use various methods of participant observation. The important theoretical point is that it is possible to make meaningful comparisons between cultures with respect to the satisfaction of human needs. We are capable of providing reasons why certain countries do a better job of meeting human needs than others. This capability is what allows us to make comparative judgments about social institutions in Nazi Germany, Stalinist Russia, Cuba, or Sweden. Hitler's "Final Solution" was fundamentally wrong because it was obviously the direct antithesis of the satisfaction of transcultural human needs which is at the theoretical base of biocritique.

To use Hans Gerth's and C. Wright Mills' phrase, different countries do better or worse jobs of giving people various "life chances." These are defined as "factual probabilities of the class structure" and might include:

> Everything from the chance to stay alive during the first year after birth to the chance to view fine art, the chance to remain healthy and grow tall, and if sick to get well again quickly, the chance to avoid becoming a juvenile delinquent—and very crucially, the chance to complete an intermediate or higher educational grade. (Gerth and Mills, 1953, p. 313)

Biocritique suggests that we can make intelligent choices in the realm of values. Assuming a common evolutionary history which has produced common human needs, it is clear that some societies are better able than others to meet those needs. As Etzioni has argued, determinate human needs provide an "independent basis with which to compare societies with each other" (Etzioni, 1968, p. 878). As Derek Phillips has suggested, a consistent moral and cultural relativism presents a host of theoretical and practical problems (Phillips, 1986).

If we assume that every culture has values which are "proper" for its own peoples, which "local values" do we accept? There are, after all, going to be differences of opinion in any community. Furthermore, as Phillips asks, does the mere fact of a presumed "consensus" in Stalinist Russia or Cuba or Sweden mean that all three countries "have the same identical moral status?" (Phillips, 1986, p. 21). Phillips gives the example of the value judgment "Hitler's 'Final Solution' to the so-called 'Jewish Question' was wrong" (Phillips, 1986, p. 40). He notes that it is much easier to reach agreement on this statement among social scientists than it is to reach agreement about presumably "scientific" statements. This suggests that relying exclusively on "local standards" or "internal criteria" is not an adequate solution to ethical conflict or differences. It is difficult to know what to do when the indigenous populations disagree.

What are required to make intelligent value judgments, according to Phillips, are relevant data and clearly reasoned and comprehensible arguments (Phillips, 1986, p. 40). He argues that the "rational justifiability" of a value judgment is in principle the same as the "rational justifiability" of an empirical statement. Phillips bases this conclusion on the ethical theorizing of Alan Gewirth (Phillips, 1986, pp. 85 – 115).

Briefly, Gewirth argues that the two "categorical" features of human action are its intentional and voluntary nature. The fact that action occurs at all shows that the actor considers it worthwhile.[27] Because each actor feels he has a right as a human being to "freedom and well-being" in the pursuit of his own goals, he must, by the principle of "universalizability" extend the same right to others. If he did not, "he would be in the position of asserting that being a prospective purposive agent both *is and is not* a sufficient condition for having the generic rights" [i.e., to freedom and well-being as the necessary precondition for human action] (Phillips, 1986, p. 96, emphasis in original). Gewirth presents a logical justification of Kant's categorical imperative (Gewirth, 1978). We should, logically, treat others as we expect to be treated ourselves.

While Gewrith and Phillips present an interesting discussion of the question of cultural relativity, they weaken their position by the exclusion of all biological and evolutionary data. If the only requirements of human action are its "voluntary" and "free" nature, it would seem that the most blatant laissez faire Social Darwinism would be one logically desirable environment. It is clear that Gewirth does not personally view that environment as culturally desirable. Nevertheless, it is difficult to see how the ideal system of conservative theorists such as Milton Friedman (1962) could be legitimately rejected by Gewirth. He develops no specific theory of human needs and, therefore, has no logical way of critiquing any particular social arrangements as long as people define them as "voluntary" or "free."

Biocritique is a "critical" perspective because it assumes that there is always some gap between "what is" and "what could be" under different conditions. Perfection is a nonexistent virtue. All discussions of "social problems" involve some estimation of a loss of potential. Adolescent suicide or leukemia is viewed as particularly tragic due to the presumed loss of potential resulting from premature death. "She could have accomplished so much more" is a common refrain. She could have loved more, or seen more, or done any number of things. The fact that everyone feels this way at times does not detract from the general argument. It only indicates that none of us believes that we accomplish all that we could.

In making comparative evaluations, as well as making an "internal" critique of one's own culture, biocritical analysis looks at how well each group is meeting basic human needs. It develops empirical indicators to measure the effectiveness of each society in meeting its people's needs. While recognizing the futility of "utopian" critique, it utilizes as a basis of comparison the standards and social practices in whatever cultures or societies appear to be doing the best contemporary job of meeting human needs. It bases its criticism, ultimately, on the fact that each of us could learn the language and culture of any other group as the result of our basic biological and species similarities.

In its critical analysis, biocritique takes note of the implications of the fact that any nongenetically damaged human being can learn the language and culture of any society. Thus the "life chances" which are theoretically potentially available to any individual are the life chances which obtain in that country which is doing the best job of meeting human needs. Irrespective of the situation in which any individual finds herself, it is a realistic assumption to conclude that she could have developed in the cultures which provide optimal satisfaction of human needs. Biocitique suggests that a theoretically adequate estimation of a person's loss of potential or life chances would compare her situation with the average situation in the country *which best meets human needs*. To use a simple example, if "Country X" has an average life expectancy of 53 and "Country Y" has an average life expectancy of 78, the average loss of "life chances" comparing Country X to Country Y is twenty-five years.

Because of basic species similarities, it is clear that the average person in Country X could have been raised in, accepted, and utilized the resources of Country Y. There is no special reason why she did not do so expect for the fact of historical and evolutionary contingency. We are where we are as the result of chance factors in our evolutionary and historical background. There are no "essential" differences between the people in Country X compared to Country Y which preclude in principle a completely different cultural development for both peoples. Obviously a person in Country Y is also capable of being socialized in Country X and losing the advantages, on the average, which are enjoyed by her former fellow citizens. Newscasts of famine and epidemics in Africa seem particularly tragic because we in the West realize how different life might have been for the stricken individuals with the kind of education, medical care and nutrition which many of us take for granted. As suggested earlier, "consciousness of kind" increases in emergency situations.

If we are able to learn and absorb any culture into which we are born and in which we develop, we all, by definition, could absorb whatever extant culture best meets our generic human needs. Ralph Burhoe has coined the phrase "cultural kin" to refer to a shared coevolutionary process of cultural/genetic adaptation (Burhoe, 1988, p. 423). Biocritique proposes that we all have the potential of becoming cultural kin because we all have the potential to learn each other's language and absorb each other's culture. A child from China raised by Canadian parents naturally learns Canadian culture. The child from Canada raised in China becomes Chinese.

This potential cultural equality depends on and is ultimately made possible by biological similarity. Because we are all *Homo sapiens*, we all can learn whatever "recipe" knowledge we encounter. Our cultural background is best seen as an accident of birth. One does not choose one's parents. Our common biological development allows for the possibility of us all becoming "cultural kin." Biocritique takes the theoretical implications of our shared commonalities and makes them explicit. It valorizes and discloses the awareness of our genotypical similarities which has been overwhelmed as a result of our phenotypic and cultural dissimilarities. It suggests that we re-member that we are indeed all brothers and sisters "under the skin." What we define as "the other" are our own genetic reflections. We "see" others through our own specific linguistic and culturally distorted lenses and don't realize that we are always looking into mirrors. The indistinct images we dimly perceive are of ourselves.

If we attempt to provide a warranted justification for making value judgments, we need to take this potential cultural equality into account. If we are able to learn any culture, we all could, by definition, absorb whatever culture best meets our needs. If we determined, by using explicit criteria designed to measure the effectiveness of need satisfaction, that Denmark was the country which best met those needs, it is obvious that we all could learn Danish as a common language. The fact that this is possible at all indicates our shared biosocial transcultural commonality. No human beings are reproductively isolated from any others and anyone could potentially share the same culture at birth.

Assuming that the satisfaction of human needs is a desideratum, biocritique makes explicit what was often only implied in classical "critical theory." It was not usually clear in the writings of critical theorists such as Horkheimer and Adorno why they were critical or on what criteria they were basing their critiques and justifying their value judgments (Horkheimer, 1947, 1972; Horkheimer and Adorno, 1972; Kellner, 1989). Derek Phillips has argued that the same lack of clarity concerning "the moral element in social theory" exists in the work of Habermas (Phillips, 1986, p. 83).

It does no good to argue that one should not make value judgments because social science should be "objective." As Michael Polanyi has stated, "if we decided to examine the universe objectively in the sense of paying equal attention to portions of equal mass, that would result in a lifetime preoccupation with interstellar dust" (Polanyi, 1962, p. 3). Simply by choosing a research topic, we imply that we think that this subject is important and worth discussing. Beginning with W. V. O. Quine's brilliant analysis of "Two Dogmas of Empiricism" (1961, pp. 20 – 46), it has been clearly demonstrated that a simplistic "fact/value" dichotomy simply won't do. A biocritical approach realizes the complexity surrounding this issue and makes its theory of valuation explicit.[28]

As the earlier discussion of Donna Haraway's work *Primate Visions* (1989) indicated, the conceptual categories and "domain assumptions" that we bring to our research inevitably affect our work. Japanese primatologists made assumptions that were different from their North American counterparts and reached different conclusions (Haraway, 1989, pp. 244 – 258). Among North American scientists, gender was a factor which strongly influenced orientation towards primate research and the types of questions which were pursued (Haraway, 1989, pp. 279 – 367). Men and women "saw" their research subjects quite differently and concentrated on different aspects of primate behavior. Male primatologists tend not to recognize bias when their analyses are centered around the male sex (i.e., "man the hunter"). When females write about females, however, the resulting "distortions" seem self-evident to many male colleagues. But all analysis is selective.

As Michael Polanyi has made clear, it doesn't help to make an antiquated and erroneous distinction between "pure" and "applied" science. Even "pure" science disguises a hidden desire for social control. Polanyi nicely captures the Faustian dimension of science in his discussion of "intellectual passions":

Heuristic passion seeks no personal possession. It sets out not to conquer, but to enrich the world. Yet such a move is also an attack.

It raises a claim and makes a tremendous demand on other men for it asks that its gift to humanity be accepted by all. In order to be satisfied, our intellectual passions must find a response. This universal intent creates a tension; we suffer when a vision of reality to which we have been committed ourselves is contemptuously ignored by others. For a general unbelief imperils our own convictions by evoking an echo in us. *Our vision must conquer or die.* (Polanyi, 1962, p. 150, emphasis added)

It may only be a "theory," but an author is going to do his or her best to make converts. "How can other people be so blind to what is so obvious to me?" is certainly a common academic question. People have a strong tendency to define "rationality" as any shared opinion. Intellectual disagreements can be very frustrating:

To the extent to which a discoverer has committed himself to a new vision of reality, he has separated himself from others who still think on the old lines. His persuasive passion spurs him now to cross the gap by converting everybody to his way of seeing things. (Polanyi, 1962, p. 150)

Polanyi gives us a glimpse as to why Thomas Kuhn's "scientific revolutions" (1970) are always so acrimonious. Scientists' subjective commitments are always involved and always at risk. The "subjective" and the "objective" are convoluted and combined. The reaction of the participants to the discovery of "Lucy" is a classic example of the emotion of science (Johanson and Edey, 1981, pp. 13–24). While I believe that John Dewey demonstrated that knowledge may be differentially warranted (Dewey, 1920, 1929), it is nevertheless true that no knowledge is "complete." We do the best we can with the information available.

Given that some evaluation is implied in any sociological description, how should we proceed? Looking at Durkheim, Weber, Collins and Alexander, we have seen that sociology has generally assumed that all value judgments are relative to the situation which is being described. Logically, according to this view, one simply can't make justified criticisms of any social practice. Presumably a "biocritical" approach would be a contradiction in terms. But surely this puts sociologists in a classic "double bind": One cannot avoid making value judgments while doing research but one should not make value judgments because there are no justifiable criteria on which they can be based. Suppose, however, that this assumption is fundamentally mistaken. It is, after all, very difficult to justify a strict culturally relative view of the Nazis.

A biocritical perspective assumes that human beings have generic human needs. David Braybrooke terms these "course-of-life" needs (Braybrooke, 1987, pp. 32–38). Human beings have course-of-life needs for such things as food and water, exercise and companionship. Assuming that the satisfaction of human needs is a desirable state allows for the possibility of meaningful comparisons concerning how well different cultures meet these needs. As we have seen in the analysis of Robert Richard's evolutionary ethics, evolution and natural selection do not, by themselves, provide objective value criteria for value judgments. The key theoretical move necessary is the development of an empirical description of transcultural human needs. Given the warranted assertability of such needs, it is then possible to make comparisons dealing with the question of the adequacy of social arrangements in meeting particular needs. Cross-cultural comparisons may be made using objective criteria, such as comparative standards of health and human welfare, which avoid an absolute cultural relativism.

Knowledge is best viewed as an unceasing process or activity. It is entirely possible that human beings have capacities which are as yet unrecognized. It is also clear that needs are based on a coevolutionary process. What are seen as needs will vary depending on our knowledge. The genetic discoveries of the last several decades have altered the conceptions of human needs of even the most orthodox Darwinist. Dawkins, for example, argues (1986, 1989) that our basic human need is the maximum propagation of our genetic inheritance (i.e., the "selfish gene").

While philosophers like Mary Midgley (1979) have argued that the idea of a "selfish gene" is a category mistake—one cannot legitimately apply a term that implies human volition to an entity that exhibits no consciousness—it is nevertheless true that Dawkins and others have introduced a new "need" into our scientific and moral discourse (i.e., the "maximization" principle or maximum genetic reproduction). Other needs may be described or understood only at a future date. This does not exclude the possibility of utilizing the kind of naturalistic analysis of needs provided by Braybrooke, Midgley, and others as a pragmatic but revisable model of human necessities. We have some idea of what kinds of conditions satisfy our needs. In actuality, we know a considerable amount about this topic, but the narrowness of our disciplinary vision has prevented us from realizing the extent of our understanding. While all description implies some kinds of evaluation, one useful way of helping to recognize some of our own biases is to broaden the base of acceptable information.

Sociology, for example, has almost completely ignored the findings of researchers in the areas of human ecology and environmental studies. In his studies of "habitat selection," for example, Gordon Orians has argued that the kinds of habitats and environments *Homo sapiens* select for occupation show significant cross-cultural similarities. People generally respond positively to "open savannah environments with scattered trees and abundant grass, while they reacted negatively to treeless plains, especially if they were flat" (Orians, 1980, p. 61). Furthermore, "valleys of modest size" have attracted humans "for ages" and the attraction of water "is also very familiar" (Orians, 1980, p. 61).

Orians argues that people have definite preferences for particular kinds of habitats and that these preferences show a great deal of historical and cross-cultural stability (Orians and Heerwagen, 1992, pp. 555–579). We seem to prefer a savannah-like environment of open spaces, vegetation, trees, and a view of the water. Orians makes the observation that the real estate market is an obvious indicator of habitat preference. In his hometown of Seattle:

> Views of waterfronts enter into appraisals of real estate in all parts of the county but the manner in which they do is very complex. Real estate agents in Seattle have an unofficial complex classification of views, ranging from "pigeon-hole views" that permit a small section of the mountains to be seen, to "sweeping views" which can encompass the entire Olympic Mountains or an extensive stretch of the Cascade Mountains. The more extensive the view, the greater the increment to the value of the property. If a view of Puget Sound or Lake Washington is also included in the foreground, the value of the property is even greater. (Orians, 1980, p. 62)

It is a fundamental assumption of evolutionary theory that certain kinds of environments are more conducive to survival than others. Clearly a source of water was a prerequisite for our survival. Perhaps the open savannah was a more promising environment than an arid or treeless climate. Possibly the risk of being attacked in a dense forest was greater than on the open savannah on which one could observe approaching dangers for some distance.

The possibility exists that we possess generalized predispositions favoring certain environmental conditions which increased the chances of our survival in the past. We are, as a result, aesthetically attracted to particular living conditions. The existence of predispositonal habitat preferences would be no more surprising than the well-established cross-cultural similarities in color classification (Durham, 1991, pp. 211–223).

Given the necessary resources and geographical flexibility, people tend to select certain environments and habitats over others. In Michigan, for example, it is difficult to understand the phenomenal growth of places like Traverse City without assuming some differential attractions. I am not suggesting that we all have a need to go "back to nature" or live in the woods like ersatz Thoreaus. As Stephen Jay Gould has written, however, "We really must make room for nature in our hearts" (Gould, 1991, p. 14). Holmes Rolston's notion of a "microrural environment" is useful in this regard. He defines it as "an urban garden, a city park, an avenue of trees with squirrels and rabbits, a suburban fence row with cardinals and mockingbirds, a creekside path to school" (Rolston, 1986, p. 42). The kind of naturalistic integration of human and habitat practiced by Frank Lloyd Wright in the designs of his homes Taliesin and Taliesin West may serve as an ideal type for an optimal human/environmental relationship. If, as we say, "money talks," it speaks in a loud voice with little variation about our choice of living spaces. We do not randomly seek environments in which to live. Not all campsites are equally attractive or beneficial.

Biocritique proposes that sociologists expand the range of what is considered relevant or significant data. If our moral and intellectual faculties are the result of our common evolutionary history, it is clear that we need to improve our understanding of that process. We need to understand the causal relationships that produced our current genotype. We need to better understand how the brain works and how it influences our perception and attitudes (Restak, 1984, 1991; Wills, 1993). We need to understand the genetic and behavioral similarities between other species and ourselves. A biocritical analysis should take into account what is being learned in the area of human ecology. Human beings are not "blank slates" able to adjust to any environment with equal efficiency.

Biocritique suggests that it makes a great deal of difference how we look at our fellow human beings. A major change in perception is overdue and should be based, ultimately, on the biological and evolutionary considerations which we have been discussing. A black person and a white person looking at each other in the United States cannot, of course, ignore their distinctive colors. But they should also be aware of their shared species-specific characteristics.

Biocritique recognizes the possibility, as Bill McKibben has argued, that in spite of all the technological advances in communication, we also suffer from "an age of missing information" (McKibben, 1992). In the age of television sound bites, "vital knowledge that humans have always possessed about who we are and where we live seems beyond our reach" (McKibben, 1992, p. 9). We can only "want" what we know about or personally experience. Much of the information what indicates "who we are" has been ignored by contemporary sociology. Awareness of who we are presupposes an understanding of our evolutionary history. Awareness of human similarities requires experiential activities, such as authentic cross-cultural communication, which are not a part of standard sociological instruction. An awareness of the necessity and importance of the need for human companionship assumes that one belongs to groups in which it is possible to socialize. Biocritique takes for granted the desirability of increasing our "cultural kin." As Robert Richards has stated, we may someday come to see that our "kind" "reaches to all individuals having a common biological nature" (Richards, 1989, p. 341).

We are all the same species living in the same hotel, but some of us begin life in the penthouse. A biocritical approach recognizes that human needs are more likely to be met in first class than in steerage. It is ludicrous to assume that all the differences involved between the two classifications are nonexistent, or that the only important questions for sociology are why the different areas of the hotel or the boat were constructed in the first place.

VI

A RE-READING OF THE COMMUNITARIAN PERSPECTIVE:
A CASE STUDY IN THE USE OF BIOCRITIQUE

A. THE LOGIC OF COMMUNITARIANISM

Since the publication of the bestselling *Habits of the Heart* by Robert Bellah and his co-authors in 1985, the interest in what has been termed the "communitarian" approach or "communitarianism" has steadily increased. A recent White House conference on "ways to rebuild the American character" emphasized the communitarian perspective. Sociologist Amitai Etzioni, a leader of the "Communitarian Movement," said that national leaders can

> act without fear that attempts to shore up our values, responsibilities, institutions and communities will cause us to charge into a dark tunnel of moralism and authoritarianism that leads to a church-dominated state or right-wing world. (Etzioni, quoted in Powell, 1994, p. A7)

Etzioni has outlined his position in detail in a volume entitled *The Spirit of Community* (1993). The book contains a "communitarian platform" (pp. 251–267) and a summary of communitarian positions on the family, school, institutions, and politics. Along with Bellah's work, Etzioni's volume provides a clear and comprehensive summary of the communitarian approach. While the social criticism of Bellah, Etzioni and other communitarians is a valuable contribution to political debate, I will demonstrate in this chapter that its theoretical approach is fundamentally flawed by its lack of attention to our evolutionary past and biosocial present. The biocritical perspective allows for a "re-reading" or deconstruction of communitarian discourse. It opens the communitarian field to alternative interpretations. It accentuates the aporias or gaps in communitarian narratives and suggests the re-presentation of alternative narratives.

Alasdair MacIntyre, whose book *After Virtue* (1984) provides a philosophical foundation for communitarianism, argues that "man [sic] is in his actions and practice, as well as in his fictions, essentially a story-telling animal" (MacIntyre, 1984, p. 216). A biocritical perspective assumes the same. We need to take seriously and understand the ways stories were told in the past (Pfeiffer, 1982). We need to understand what John Pfeiffer has termed the "hidden images" of our own "creative explosion" (Pfeiffer, 1982, pp. 1–18). Just as others have done in the past, today we need to expand the range and type of the stories we tell. The interstices of communitarian space may be successfully occupied by biocritical narratives. My reading of the communitarian approach is critical but not destructive. In any re-reading or "intervention"[29] one looks to preserve the strongest arguments encountered, not only to expose the weakest links. As Dewey believed, the objective should be enhanced co-existence, not mutual extermination. Conflicting narratives often have more in common than appearances suggest. Given a different perspective, supposed dualisms often dissolve.

The communitarian perspective is fundamentally a critique of "liberalism" (MacIntyre, 1984). Bellah and other communitarians believe that "It is precisely the persistence of nonliberal practices that makes our society viable at all" (Bellah, 1988, p. 271). As they argue in *Habits of the Heart*, "modern individualism seems to be producing a way of life that is neither individually nor socially viable" (p. 144). According to Bellah, "it is only the presence of practices rooted in older traditions [the older 'civic' and 'biblical' traditions] that makes our society possible at all" (Bellah, 1988, p. 274).

"Liberalism," according to these authors, valorizes only the pursuit of egoistic self-interest. There is no sense of "a common allegiance to and a common pursuit" of shared activities (MacIntyre, 1984, p. 156). In a legal system based on individualistic conceptions of "rights," "there seems to be no rational way of securing moral agreement" (MacIntyre, 1984, p. 6). In a completely Hobbesian world of egoistic conflict, the best we can hope for "is the construction of local forms of community within which civility and the intellectual and moral life can be sustained through the new dark ages which are already upon us" (MacIntyre, 1984, p. 263). The rational "self-interest" of liberalism allows for no common interest. Individual "rationality" results in social catastrophe. We seem to have nothing in common. We have no sense of "community." The only people who seem happy are "a motley party of defenders of liberal individualism—some of them utilitarians, some Kantians" (MacIntyre, 1984, p. 260).

According to Bellah, "A *community* is a group of people who live in a common territory, have a common history and shared values, participate in various activities, and have a high degree of solidarity" (Phillips, 1993, p. 14, emphasis in original). Living together creates much greater solidarity than joining voluntary organizations and associations. People who share a "common tradition" and a shared conception of the "public good" will experience a better life than those who do not (Bellah, et al., 1985, pp. 251 –252). Without social solidarity, "Progress...seems less compelling when it appears that it may be progress into the abyss" (Bellah, et al., 1985, p. 277).

Bellah criticizes what he terms "Welfare Liberals" for their belief that "the purpose of government is to give individuals the means to pursue their private ends" (Bellah et al., 1985, p. 265). Egoistic self-interest does not provide adequate grounding for social solidarity. We need instead "a more explicit understanding of what we have in common" (Bellah, et al., 1985, p. 287). Given such a self-understanding, "the differences between us that remain would be less threatening" (Bellah, et al., p. 287).

Communitarians are critical of the procedural emphasis of liberalism, which they claim "cannot support a coherent and effective political system" (Bellah, et al., 1985, p. 287). Concentrating only on individual rights and entitlements produces social chaos and "free-riders" who take advantage of the "system" but contribute nothing in return. "Rights," as Etzioni argues, "presume responsibilities" (Etzioni, 1993, pp. 9 –11). Bellah et al. complain that defining "freedom" as "freedom from the demands of others provides no vocabulary in which...Americans can address common conceptions of the ends of a good life or ways to coordinate cooperative action with others" (Bellah, et al., 1985, p. 24).

Habits of the Heart, as its authors state, "is, explicitly and implicitly, a detailed reading of, and commentary on, Tocqueville, the predecessor who has influenced us most profoundly" (Bellah, et al., 1985, p. 306). They argue that "Tocqueville's sense of American society as a whole...has never been equaled.... Nor has anyone ever better pointed out the moral and political meaning of the American experiment" (Bellah, et al., p. 298). Certainly Tocqueville's comments on such topics as "the three races that inhabit the United States" are brilliant and should be consulted in the original by anyone interested in U.S. history (Tocqueville, 1969 [1835], pp. 316 –407). Bellah's own work is meant to be an updated analysis on the "moral and political meaning" of contemporary liberalism.

In *Democracy in America*, Tocqueville referred to "*moeurs* [mores] in the strict sense which might be called the habits of the heart" (Tocqueville, 1969 [1835], vol. I, p. 287).[30] He was particularly interested, as is Bellah, in the social consequences of religion. Tocqueville argued that "men cannot do without dogmatic beliefs, and...religious dogmas seem to me the most desirable of all" (Tocqueville, 1969 [1840], vol. II, p. 442). He called "a passion for well-being" the "mother of all desires" in the United States and believed the function of religion was to "purify, control and restrain that excessive and exclusive taste for well-being which men acquire in times of equality" (Tocqueville, 1969 [1840], vol. II, p. 464). Bellah and other communitarians believe that religion should still serve similar purposes (Bellah et al., 1985, pp. 219 – 249).

A reading of Tocqueville suggests concerns very similar to what Bellah and other communitarians are critical of today. (Remarkably, for the time, Tocqueville believed that the "two great nations in the world" were the United States and Russia [Tocqueville, 1969 {1835}, vol. I, p. 412]). His vision of the future United States suggests a kind of communitarian ideal:

Therefore, the time must come when there will be in North America one hundred and fifty million people all equal one to the other, belonging to the same family, having the same point of departure, the same civilization, language, religion, habits, and mores, and among whom thought will circulate in similar forms and with like nuances. All else is doubtful, but that is sure. (Tocqueville, 1969 [1835], vol. I, p. 412)

While Bellah and Etzioni would argue that the communitarian perspective does not imply that "thought will circulate in similar forms," numerous references to "older civic and biblical traditions," as well as the positive valorization of Tocqueville, imply exactly that (Bellah et al., 1985, p. 144). In a response to his critics Bellah chides Fredric Jameson for his use of a postmodernist/Marxist discourse (Jameson, 1988). Bellah suggests that "intellectuals who cannot speak an American tongue have small audiences" and that if Marxism is ever "*to be an effective public voice in America, it will have to learn to speak American*" (Bellah, 1988, p. 282, emphasis added).

The unstated implication is "My language—Love it or leave it." But the point is that *there is no single "American" language*. There is an English language which is always evolving and is vastly different from what was spoken in, say, England in 1776. There are American citizens who have different linguistic experiences and backgrounds. If my background is Latin American, there is a very real sense in which, even if my spoken English is "perfect," I don't speak the "same" language as Tocqueville's Anglo-Americans (Shorris, 1992). The same is true if I am bilingual as opposed to monolingual. There is no one "American." As Derek Phillips has observed, "the pursuit of community often has very negative consequences for those who are to be excluded from membership" (Phillips, 1993, p. 163).

Vincent Harding finds *Habits of the Heart* "fundamentally and sadly flawed" because of its exclusive "white, middle-class" focus, and his complaint is clearly justified (Harding, 1988, pp. 67–83). One obtains a much different perspective from books like Walt Harrington's "journey into black America" (Harrington, 1992). As Harding observes, "Do my nonwhite students mistake the work when they say 'I just don't see myself there'?" (Harding, 1988, p. 78). I think not. They are simply not present. Neither are any Latinos.

There are, nevertheless, many attractive features to the communitarian critique. People are justifiably concerned with many of the critical issues raised by communitarian discourse. As Bellah accurately observes, "There is a widespread feeling that the promise of the modern era is slipping away from us" (Bellah, et al., 1985, p. 277). Surveys find "a national mood of disillusionment and self-absorption" (Lawrence, 1994, p. A1). It seems that we increasingly have less and less in common. Crime and corruption are believed omnipresent. Everyone is only "out to make a buck." *The New York Times* notes that "Anger and Cynicism Well Up in Voters as Hope Gives Way" (Berke, 1994, p. A1 and A9). People believe that the United States is "losing its moral roots" and, in a significant sense, "the system is broken" (Berke, 1994, p. A9). The recent Republican electoral landslide can be interpreted in these terms.

Perhaps MacIntyre's perception of a new "dark ages" is correct. Certainly the condition of many cities suggests as much (Wilson, 1987). It's blacks vs. whites, affluent vs. poor, suburbs vs. inner-cities, "us" vs. "them." There is "no moral common ground" and everyone is locked into a "language of individual self-interest" (Bellah, et al., 1985, pp. 141, 175). We no longer can control "the destructive consequences of the pursuit of economic success" (Bellah, et al., 1985, p. 199). Americans are so preoccupied with their individual "rights" that they "are deprived of a language genuinely able to mediate among self, society, the natural world, and ultimate reality" (Bellah, et al., 1985, p. 237). We are lost in the land of "Me," but need to think about "Us."

In a key passage in *Democracy in America*, Tocqueville indicates the heart of the communitarian complaint against the rights-based, procedural ethics of liberalism:

> If the lights ever go out, they will fade little by little, as if of their own accord. Confining ourselves to practice, we may lose sight of basic principles, and when these have been entirely forgotten, we may apply the methods derived from them badly; we might be left without the capacity to invent new methods, and only able to make a clumsy and an unintelligent use of wise procedures no longer understood. (Tocqueville, 1969 [1840], vol. II, p. 464)

Bellah, MacIntyre, Etzioni and other communitarians argue that we have lost all knowledge of the "virtues" or any conception of the "good." We are the bureaucrats in Max Weber's *Zweckrational* or "rationally purposeful" machines. We have no way to arrive at ends. We can only rationally argue over the means to arrive at a "given" end (Ashley and Orenstein, 1990, pp. 271–274). We have no communal methods to agree on "value-rational" actions: "goals or ends that are defined in terms of subjectively meaningful values" (Ashley and Orenstein, 1990, p. 273). As Bellah observes, "we have put our own good, as individuals...ahead of the common good" (Bellah, et al., 1985, p. 285).

Our narcissistic language, "the language of individualism, the primary American language of self-understanding, limits the ways in which people think" (Bellah, et al., 1985, p. 290). We cannot conceive of a common good in the language of individual rights and rational egoism. According to the communitarians, "the language of individualism" nullifies the possibility of communal projects. One way in which this occurs is by the individualistic obliteration of the distinction between "internal" and "external" practices.

According to MacIntyre, a "'practice' involves standards of excellence and obedience to rules as well as the achievement of goods" (MacIntyre, 1984, p. 190). His more formal definition is:

By a "practice" I am going to mean any coherent and complex form of socially established cooperative human activity through which goods internal to that form of activity are realized in the course of trying to achieve those standards of excellence which are appropriate to, and partially definitive of, that form of activity, with the result that human powers to achieve excellence, and human conceptions of the ends and goods involved, are systematically extended. (MacIntyre, 1984, p. 187)

One example that MacIntyre uses is the game of chess. Certain kinds of "goods" are specific to the game itself: analytical skill, concentration, competitive intensity. They can "only be identified and recognized by the experience of participating in the practice in question" (MacIntyre, 1984, pp. 188–189). In order to "achieve these standards of excellence," one must learn to play the game. One can easily extend the notion of "internal" standards to other activities: writing, physics, baseball, painting. Each activity demands certain kinds of skills specific to that activity.

There are also "goods externally and contingently attached to chess-playing and other practices by the accidents of social circumstances...such goods as prestige, status and money" (MacIntyre, 1984, p. 188). These "external" goods "are always some individual's property and possession...characteristically they are such that the more someone has of them, the less there is for other people" (MacIntyre, 1984, p. 190). External goods, as defined by MacIntyre, are a zero-sum game. My reward is your loss. In the case of "internal" goods, the opposite is the case: The whole is greater than the sum of its parts.

Someone else learning how to play chess does not reduce the intrinsic rewards which I have received in learning to play myself. We are both better off for our efforts. If I learn the skills that are necessary to write a good book, my skills are not decreased by the similar efforts of others. It may be that other books sell more copies, but, in MacIntryre's terms, total sales are extrinsic rewards and have no necessary relationship to the skills necessary to produce the book. In a sense no longer familiar to many "rational" capitalists, I am better off no matter how my book sells. The quality of the book has no relationship to its quantity of sales or profits. What categorizes a book as "good" or "bad" are other kinds of standards internal to the tradition in which the book was written.

MacIntyre's complaint, echoed by Bellah and others, is that modern "rights-based" liberalism increasingly only recognizes extrinsic standards and assumes that all practices are commensurable and subject to an identical pecuniary calculus. All that is important, under this assumption, is necessarily part of a gigantic zero-sum game. Whatever I achieve lessens the chances of your achievement. Communitarians argue that this is not a particularly likely method of building social solidarity. They accurately note that this kind of "hedonistic calculus" excludes by definition many activities that human beings throughout history have considered particularly meaningful.

I spent several summers working as a camp counselor. Whatever good I did as an archery counselor—whatever proficiency I achieved—did not somehow detract from anyone else's work. Increasing the level of individual achievement improved the camp as a whole. There was no necessary conflict between individual excellence and group goals: Each presupposed and included the other. The same was true of the friendships which developed— and MacIntryre would certainly include "friendship" under his notion of a "practice." Friendship, as Ronald Sharp has argued, is a "gift exchange" which increases the "wealth" of both individuals (Sharp, 1986, pp. 82 – 117). Both people gain.

To continue the logic used by Martha Nussbaum in her discussion of human needs, it is difficult to imagine a human existence with no friends. Contemporary liberalism, according to MacIntyre and Bellah, reduces everything to "market" relationships and ignores the profound differences between "internal" and "external" rewards. The authors of *Habits of the Heart* make a good case for their argument that much contemporary cynicism and disillusionment are a result of the widespread belief that *politicians and other "leaders" perceive no distinctions whatsoever between these two kinds of rewards*.

To summarize the communitarian arguments and criticisms:

1. There is no way in our culture to "secure moral agreement." There is a fundamental conflict between an individualistic and a communal orientation.

2. This conflict is reflected in the liberal emphasis on individual "rights" or entitlements and the communitarian emphasis on the "common good."

3. The result of excessive individualism is a total lack of concern with other people and social necessities, whereas what is desperately needed is a new emphasis on what we share and have in common.

4. Our individualistic philosophy and discourse do not allow us to understand or adequately deal with what we have in common.

5. This can only be accomplished by a new emphasis on the classic "biblical and republican" traditions (Bellah and MacIntyre), or through a neoprogressive communitarian social movement (Etzioni).

B. THE COMMUNITARIAN LOSS OF MEMORY

One of the concepts Bellah et al. develop in *Habits of the Heart* is the idea of "communities of memory." "Communities," in their sense of the term, "have a history—in an important sense they are constituted by their past" (Bellah, et al., 1985, p. 153). A "genuine community of memory" will tell and preserve stories to each other. The common stories "carry a context of meaning that can allow us to connect our aspirations for ourselves and those closest to us with the aspirations of a larger whole" (Bellah, et al., 1985, p. 153). When they ignore or forget their history, communities degenerate into what Bellah terms a "lifestyle enclave," which "celebrates the narcissism of similarity" instead of the "interdependence of public and private life" (Bellah, et al., 1985, p. 72). Those who have no historical memories have no authentic communities.

It is particularly off-putting and also ironic, given the communitarian emphasis on "memory" and shared history, that the authors of *Habits of the Heart* ignore the writings of the "progressive" communitarian critics such as John Dewey, Randolph Bourne, Van Wyck Brooks, Waldo Frank and Lewis Mumford. They also ignore more recent commentaries such as Robert Nisbet's well-known volume *The Quest for Community* (1953) which advances many of the same communitarian themes. There are others in the "communitarian tradition" besides Tocqueville. As historian Christopher Lasch has written:

> In the twentieth century, the communitarian tradition was present as an undercurrent in prewar progressivism, as interpreted by writers like Josiah Royce, Jane Addams, Mary Parker Follet, and Randolph Bourne; and it was carried on in late years by John Collier, Waldo Frank, Lewis Mumford, and Paul Goodman. (Lasch, 1988, p. 175)

In his incisive volume *Beloved Community*, historian Casey Nelson Blake suggests that:

> The need for...a living tradition of critical thought becomes especially evident in the light of the current crisis of American liberalism, which in the 1980s received its most searching analysis in the works of philosopher Alasdair MacIntyre and the group of social scientists working under the direction of Robert Bellah. MacIntyre's *After Virtue* and the Bellah group's *Habits of the Heart* reiterate themes that occupied thinkers like John Dewey and the Young Americans [Bourne et al.] at the start of this century, although neither book acknowledges the existence of these precursors. (Blake, 1990, p. 298)

As Blake observes, a "viable usable past...would free present-day criticism from the endless rediscovery of past positions" (Blake, 1990, p. 298). The similarity of concerns between Bourne, Mumford, Dewey, Brooks, Frank and Bellah and MacIntyre is remarkable. In one of his most famous essays Bourne spoke of his "future social goals in which all can participate, the good life of personality[31] lived in the environment of the Beloved Community.... It must be a future America, on which all can unite" (Bourne, 1977, p. 264). In a passage that could have been written by MacIntyre or Bellah, Bourne deplores the "cheapness" of American life and the "hordes of men and women without a spiritual country, cultural outlaws without taste, without standards" (Bourne, 1977, p. 254). Speaking of "the American community," Bourne writes:

> The influences at the fringe, however, are centrifugal, anarchical. They make for detached fragments of peoples. Those who come to find liberty achieve only license. They become the flotsam and jetsam of American life, the downward undertow of our civilization with its leering cheapness and falseness of taste and spiritual outlook, the absence of mind and sincere feeling which we see in our slovenly towns, our vapid moving pictures, our popular novels, and the vacuous faces of the crowds on the city streets. (Bourne, 1977, p. 255)

Bourne, in contrast to MacIntyre and Bellah, blamed a conformist Anglo-Saxon mediocrity for the forced "denationalization" of new immigrants and the resulting "falseness of taste." But his conception of "democracy" could also have been taken from Etzioni's 1993 communitarian handbook:

> If freedom means the right to do pretty much as one pleases, so long as one does not interfere with others, the immigrant has found freedom.... But if freedom means a democratic cooperation in determining the ideals and purposes and industrial and social institutions of a country, then the immigrant has not been free. (Bourne, 1977, p. 252)

MacIntrye and Bellah would certainly agree with Bourne that "The modern radical opposes the present social system not because it does not give him his 'rights,' but because it warps and stunts the potentialities of society and human nature" (Bourne, 1977, p. 246). They would similarly agree with other progressive critics such as Lewis Mumford's critique of "the eclipse of the notion of the common good" (Blake, 1990, p. 211), or Van Wyck Brooks's desire to "reestablish the organic unity of preindustrial cultures on a modern, democratic basis" (Blake, 1990, p. 99). Brooks's famous distinction between "highbrow" and "lowbrow" culture, which he published in 1915, is very similar to MacIntyre's and Bellah's critique:

> In everything one finds this frank acceptance of twin values which are not expected to have anything in common: on the one hand a quite unclouded, quite unhypocritical assumption of transcendent theory ("high ideals"); and on the other a simultaneous acceptance of catchpenny realities. Between university ethics and business ethics...between good government and Tammany...there is no community, no genial middle ground. (Brooks, 1915, p. 7)

The value of this kind of historical analysis is to avoid "the endless rediscovery of past positions." Bourne, Brooks, and Mumford were all engaged in a critique of the "culture of individualism." If a contemporary author is trying to develop a communitarian "community of memory," why not also look at the results and problems of similar positions taken in the past? As Blake observes, "The current discussion about culture and democratic renewal arrives at the same critical impasse Mumford reached more than a half-century ago" (Blake, 1990, p. 301). Mumford "never fully addressed the

ways in which power reproduces itself through language" and neither do
Bellah or MacIntyre (Blake, 1990, p. 301).

Will the development of a new vocabulary in itself lead to the
development of a communitarian ethos?   Communitarianism requires
development of political alternatives to liberal capitalism. How are we going
to do that? Bourne, Brooks and Mumford were all somewhat vague on the
relationship between cultural criticism and political and economic reform.
Bellah et al. write that "The question, then, is whether the older civic and
biblical traditions have the capacity to reformulate themselves while
simultaneously remaining faithful to their deepest insights" (Bellah, et al.,
1985, p. 144). Even if they did, however, have the capability "to reformulate
themselves," what would that mean?   What are the social forms of
communitarian integration which are being proposed?   Is it enough to
produce a "communitarian" vocabulary as opposed to the language of
"utilitarian individualism"? As John Patrick Diggins has argued:

> Why does it follow that theories about human nature are to be
> replaced by narratives about human life? Cannot the turn toward
> narration be regarded as another temporary product of history rather
> than a final description of the human condition? The poststructuralist
> prides himself on seeing history and contingency where others
> supposedly see theory and necessity. And seeing all language
> constructions as indeterminate productions, the neo-pragmatist wants
> us to appreciate how things can be changed by being redescribed.
> But the spectacle of power and evil may not be contingent and instead
> defy the philosopher who assumes that reality, known only as
> interpreted, can be reinterpreted to suit political purposes.
> Experimenting with vocabularies can do little to change determinate
> phenomena that exist independently of language. (Diggins, 1994, p.
> 481)

It is, of course, possible to argue that no phenomena exist "independently
of language." On the other hand, Blake in his critique of Bourne, Brooks and
Mumford suggests that *no language exists independently of political power*.
Language is not independent of "determinate phenomena" and cannot be

adequately understood apart from those phenomena. The relationships are interactive and reciprocal.

Diggins' argument at least raises the possibility that MacIntyre and Bellah "invoke a new civic language that lacks any political content" (Blake, 1990, p. 300). Sections of *Habits of the Heart* do sound like apolitical banalities delivered by a team of Mannheim's "free-floating" intellectuals in communitarian drag. *Habits of the Heart* was based on a series of extended, or what Bellah et al. term "active," interviews (Bellah, et al., 1985, p. 305). The problem, as Joseph Gusfield notes, is that "cases are held up through the book almost as abstract models of such types as utilitarian individualism and republican tradition" (Gusfield, 1986, p. 9). The lack of any detailed sense of concrete political and economic realities is exactly the same problem which plagued the earlier communitarian writers. Surely their works deserve attention from contemporary communitarians stressing "communities of memory."[32]

C. A BIOCRITICAL RE-READING OF THE COMMUNITARIAN PERSPECTIVE

Communitarians believe that there is a fundamental conflict between an "individualistic" and a "communal" perspective. Our "rugged individualism" causes us to devalue the "common good." As political theorist Michael Walzer has written:

> We cannot sit together and tell comprehensible stories, and we recognize ourselves in the stories we read only when these are fragmented narratives, without plots, the literary equivalent of atonal music and nonrepresentational art. (Walzer, 1990, p. 9)

Our fragmented, liberal, individualistic, rights-oriented society means that we lack any concern for other people or knowledge of what we have in common. Our individualistic vocabularies do not provide the necessary prerequisites for a discussion of the "public good." They are lacking in what might be termed communal "enabling mechanisms." In the solitary world of Hobbes and Locke, the individual is all. For the authors of *Habits of the*

Heart, the only way "forward" is through a remaking and reestablishment of the more communalistic republican and biblical traditions in American life. As Bellah writes: "With a more explicit understanding of what we have in common...the differences between us that remain would be less threatening" (Bellah et al., 1985, p. 287).

A biocritical approach to communitarianism suggests that Bellah, MacIntyre and other communitarians are mistaken in their analyses in several important respects. They present a series of false alternatives: the "individual" vs. "society"; "rights" vs. the "common good"; the present "dark ages" vs. a "communitarian" past. As Jeffrey Stout has argued, "The problem with most communitarian criticism of liberal society...is its implicitly utopian character" (Stout, 1988b, p. 137). Bellah et al. provide perceptive social criticism and intimations of a "communitarian" alternative, but "if imagined utopias are to generate more than terminal wistfulness, we will need also to *imagine how to achieve them by acceptable means*" (Stout, 1988b, p. 137, emphasis added). It is not merely a question of "rights" against the "community good." Consider what Walzer (1990, pp. 11 – 12) terms the "Four Mobilities":

1. "Geographic mobility." Americans change their residences more often than any other people in history.

2. "Social mobility." Children find themselves in different locations and "tell different stories" from their parents.

3. "Marital mobility." Rates of separation and divorce are higher than they have ever been.

4. "Political mobility." Independent voters "stand outside all political organizations." They make for a "volatile electorate" where party loyalty means less and less.

It is clear that excessive movement in these areas affects communities in various ways. Bellah and MacIntyre are right to point out the negative effects of what might be called our hypertrophic migratory patterns. Families are split apart. Children sometimes never see their parents. Etzioni notes that 14.4% of those 65 and older lived alone in 1950. In 1990 the figure was 31% (Etzioni, 1993, pp. 120 – 121). Older people, as well as everyone else, suffer the effects of social isolation. Why bother to make real friendships when the next move is only a year away?

The problem for the communitarians is to provide acceptable alternatives to the "four mobilities." Surely almost no one in the United States would today tolerate any restrictions on geographic, social, or marital freedom of choice. In spite of the current totally negative view of politics, most people don't want to abolish Congress or eliminate the possibility of representative institutions. One could, of course, add other "mobilities" to Walzer's list: the freedom to attend a particular school, the freedom to travel to other countries, the freedom to read a particular book. The "liberal" rights that communitarians devalue *allow for the possibility of numerous freedoms that Americans consider essential*. How, then, are more "communitarian" objectives going to be promoted?

Part of the reason the communitarians' discourse often seems so vapid and unrealistic is due to the unavoidable conclusion that their objectives require such fundamental and politically unacceptable changes. At times we all want to tell the boss to go to hell, leave town, and start over somewhere else. Communitarians in general ignore an entire tradition in American literature, exemplified by such works as *Catch-22* or *Tropic of Cancer*, which brilliantly analyze the conflicts between authentic personal autonomy and excess "social integration." Communitarians would be helped by a sense of humor.

Communitarians would also be helped by more flexibility and willingness to consider alternative perspectives. Assuming, for the moment, the accuracy of the communitarian critique and the desirability of communitarian reforms, one can still seriously doubt the effectiveness of the proposed remedies. Bellah et al. suggest that "Indeed it may be only in terms of those older traditions [biblical and republican] that the deeper meaning of our individualism and the aspirations it embodies can be salvaged at all" (Bellah, et al., 1985, p. 141). Fredric Jameson, in a commentary on *Habits of the Heart*, argues that this particular phrase "rings like an admission of failure if not an anticipation of defeat" (Jameson, 1988, p. 107). His reading of a kind of defeatist tone in *Habits of the Heart* is both perceptive and accurate.

We have ample historical evidence—certainly from our own history—that a religious orientation need not advance the communitarian objectives proposed by Bellah and MacIntyre. It has often been tried and found wanting. As Bellah et al. note:

The ideas Americans have traditionally used to give shape and direction to their most generous impulses no longer suffice to give guidance in controlling the destructive consequences of the pursuit of economic success. (Bellah, et al., 1985, p. 199, emphasis added)

If, in fact, "the ideas Americans have traditionally used"—in the form of religious or republican themes—do not now "give guidance" to our actions, perhaps it is time to look for different ideas, perspectives, and approaches.

In *The Mode of Information* (1990), Mark Poster effectively demonstrates that every new method of transmitting information profoundly affects our social networks.   Computer technology, databases, T.V., global communications, the "information superhighway" all have an impact on our lives.   The entire emphasis on the "postmodern" is a recognition of the differences between our current forms of social organization and what existed earlier in our history. The problems we face today are not the same as those faced by our colonial politicians and theologians, or somewhat later by Abraham Lincoln.   If the sociology of knowledge has any validity, it demonstrates that one cannot artificially "graft" a 17th- or 18th-century *Weltanschauung* onto completely changed material and intellectual landscapes. Our "communities of memory" include science and intellectual history. Knowledge, as Dewey argued, is a process of social change which produces social consequences—like the "information superhighway." It is not easy to travel newly constructed roads back to the *status quo ante*.

A biocritical perspective proposes that communitarians are looking at the wrong kinds of information. Contemporary communitarians face the same difficulties which earlier writers like Bourne and Brooks were unable to overcome in their discourse. This indicates the necessity for new information, new approaches and new stories.   One place to begin is with the most contemporary and warranted information on our own bioevolutionary past.

Communitarians argue that there is no way in our culture "to secure moral agreement" and that there is a fundamental conflict between an "individualistic" and a "communal" perspective. Biocritique suggests that they are mistaken in both these claims. The social consequences of our "language of individualism"[33] depend on what is being said. Suppose we seriously took into account our biological similarities and transcultural human needs. A biocritical discourse notes individual differences, but also foregrounds what we have in common. It is true that each of us has individual needs, but these needs are remarkably similar. The "language [sic] of individualism" is transformed by a recognition of how similar each individual is with respect to "course-of-life" needs. The work of Alan Gewirth, for example (1978), clearly demonstrates that an "individualistic" perspective may develop "communitarian" aims.

In *After Virtue*, MacIntyre completely rejects the moral claims of Gewirth. Gewirth, as indicated in the previous chapter, argues that every human being requires a certain amount of "freedom" and "well-being" to carry out any project. I must logically insist that I require that basic minimum if I am to accomplish anything at all. As MacIntyre observes, it also necessarily follows that "if I claim a right in virtue of my possession of certain characteristics, then I am logically committed to holding that anyone else with the same characteristics also possesses that right" (MacIntyre, 1984, p. 67). Therefore, claims Gewirth, we all have the same generic "right" to "freedom" and "well-being."

MacIntyre holds, however, that Gewirth's discussion of "rights" depends on a specific historical context and that "such types of social institution or practice have not existed universally in human societies" (MacIntyre, 1984, p. 67). That is, certain cultures exist or have existed in which the modern conception of "rights" simply wasn't or isn't present. Practices and "sets of rules" regarding "rights" "are in no way universal features of the human condition" and "always have a highly specific and socially local character" (MacIntyre, 1984, p. 67). It is incorrect to assume that everyone else shares the "same characteristic" of having "rights" in the sense that the term is used in the United States. Gewirth's argument is therefore invalid because his discussion of "rights" lacks universality. We are not logically committed to holding that everyone should possess a minimum standard of freedom and well-being because not everyone possesses "rights."

MacIntyre is, of course, correct in his historical analysis of the concept of "rights." But he is mistaken in his assumption that "rights" are the only relevant and "universal features of the human condition" which should be considered. MacIntyre's entire argument and critique of Gewirth depends on this point. Logically, he must concede that other "universal features" of our particular species would validate Gewirth's approach. A biocritical approach which emphasizes transcultural human similarities and shared needs furnishes the criteria that MacIntrye says are lacking in Gewirth's analysis. It follows that all members of *Homo sapiens* are entitled to the freedom and well-being that Gewirth advocates.

Assuming the above reasoning is correct, it follows that communitarian complaints about the presumed moral "dark ages" which must result from any individualistic orientation are misplaced. It makes a great deal of difference how we frame and contexualize our "individualistic" perspectives and understandings. Sociologists and anthropologists have developed what might be termed a "difference optic" which filters out transcultural human characteristics. The transcultural theory of human needs outlined in Chapter Four suggests that nearly total elimination of cross-cultural similarities and needs from social science discourse results in a profound disciplinary myopia. Positioning "individualism" within the framework of transcultural human needs allows for the potential development of more social options than communitarian critiques of "utilitarian individualism" recognize. There is no necessary logical conflict between individual human needs and the "public good."

Bellah and his co-authors view an "individualistic" and a "communal" orientation as inevitably conflicting:

The extent to which many Americans can understand the workings of our economic and social organization is limited by the capacity of their chief moral language to make sense of human interaction. The limit set by individualism is clear: events that escape the control of individual choice and will cannot coherently be encompassed in a moral calculation. (Bellah, et al., 1985, p. 204)

It is simply untrue, however, that a perspective which begins with the individual does not allow us to understand what we have in common. A biocritical emphasis on *what we share as individuals* is more likely to lead to a renewed emphasis on the construction of "public goods" than is a nostalgic longing for an idealized "communitarian" past.[34] Biocritique begins with the individual as a living, breathing member of a particular species. It does not "reduce" social behavior to individual psychology, but maintains that individual psychology needs to be taken into account in the explanation of social behavior. One begins with the biologically concrete. Taking that level of analysis into account, we can then move "outward" and look at group dynamics, institutions, and cultural configurations. The individual per se seems to vanish in much sociological analysis, but people are always present in any social situation.   All social theories make implicit psychological assumptions.   Social scientists, therefore, need to understand and utilize information from other disciplines which relates to those assumptions. The "limits set by individualism" depend entirely on the nature of the individualism which is being proposed.

The kinds of information which we should take into account in any description of human similarities have only been available for a brief period of time. This has considerable significance for what sociologists may now view as "irresovable" disciplinary conflicts.   Our images of what constitutes humankind are likely to change in the future as rapidly as they have in the past.   Assuming that no further changes in perspective will occur is an egotistical absurdity. Suppose that each grade school in the United States emphasized the potential cultural equality and biological similarities of every member of *Homo sapiens*. Even in a period of conservative ascendancy, this would seem to be a politically feasible goal. Suppose we actually taught students about the latest developments in evolutionary psychology, sociobiology, genetics, and paleontology. Suppose, as Laurel Richardson advocates, that social scientists actually became effective "teacher-facilitators" as opposed to pontificating "philosopher-kings" (Richardson, 1991, p. 177).

Imagine what might happen if people actually believed that cultural diversity depends on species commonalities. If we were another species none of us would have the ability to interpret culture *in any* human fashion. It is more important that humans as a species paint, than it is what we paint. It is more significant, in terms of species characteristics, that human beings live in families—as opposed to the specific type of family. It has been of more consequence for human evolution that most human beings seek religious experiences than it is what kind of religion they seek. It is more significant in terms of human commonalities that human beings need shelter to survive as opposed to the particular kind of shelter. It is far more significant for a biosocial perspective that *people need other people*, as opposed to which specific people are believed important.

If we tell our children only that they are essentially different from children in other human groups, it is no surprise that they come to accept their putative differences as self-evident truths. Almost no one is presenting the kinds of interdisciplinary information now available which accentuate common evolutionary history and biological similarities. In the social sciences, what

Tooby and Cosmides call "'intellectual isolationism'...has only become more extreme with time" (Tooby and Cosmides, 1992, p. 22). We need to look at "the other" and realize that we are looking at ourselves.

Changes in what Mark Poster terms "the mode of information" (1990) and what other writers have referred to as "globalization" (Robertson, 1992) have helped to extend our "consciousness of kind." Our communication networks and data banks have become more extensive and universal. As media critics such as Neil Postman suggest (1992), the information received may be incredibly distorted and biased. The fact that "global" information is available at all, however, is a new factor which influences our perceptions. For example, the first Palestinian-Israeli peace agreement clearly "humanized" the Palestinian representatives such as Hanan Ashrawi in a way that had not occurred in the United States in the past. Given the opportunity for media dialogue and representation, the "demonized other" becomes the comprehensible and rational diplomat.

In his examination of sociobiology, philosopher Peter Singer argues that "Our feelings of benevolence and sympathy are more easily aroused by specific human beings than by a large group in which no individuals stand out" (Singer, 1981, p. 157). Once the Palestinians stand out as individual people similar to ourselves, our perceptions drastically change. Part of the difficulty with the communitarian perspective is that individuals simply disappear. This also suggests that an individualistic orientation which emphasizes individual similarities, contrary to Bellah et al., is likely to produce a more effective political response to social problems than a more communitarian discourse.

What Giddings called "consciousness of kind" increases in emergency situations. We are willing to make sacrifices for earthquake victims. We are willing to send money to fight starvation in Africa. We are prepared to make sacrifices in wartime and help "the other," even if it results in increased risk to ourselves. We "unthinkingly" jump into a lake to rescue a swimmer in trouble. We willingly send relief supplies to people in Florida whose houses have been destroyed by hurricanes. In crisis situations, the degree of similarity to the victims is increasingly recognized. We see them as people who share similar course-of-life needs. We understand that disasters are capricious and could affect us all.

A biocritical perspective proposes that, as we come to understand our human commonalities, we should increasingly view many of the problems described by communitarians as *emergency situations* for similar members of a common species. Given our common human needs, what is increasingly viewed as "normal" is glaringly and undeniably harmful and unacceptable. Given a determinate description of human needs, it is clear that the kinds of conditions writers like Jonathan Kozol have described in great detail are utter emergencies. In *Savage Inequalities* (1991) Kozol presents overwhelming evidence of the everyday crises of urban life. The series of personal narratives he presents is exceptionally persuasive in increasing readers' "consciousness of kind." The voices of individual children are overwhelmingly "present" or "represented" and allowed to speak for themselves. Reading *Savage Inequalities* is an effective way to identify what is lacking in much communitarian discourse.   Communitarian "problems" are often abstract generalities. Biocritical analysis begins with concrete particulars. A special report in *The Washington Post* which investigates poverty in Washington, D.C. by examining its effects on three generations of one family is an example of this type of analysis (Dash, 1994). We see that "normal" experiences of specific individuals result in everyday emergencies. Needs are specific, concretized, identifiable, and unmet. We are able to recognize human commonalities.

In *The Truly Disadvantaged*, William Julius Wilson argues that effective programs for social reform require "the support and commitment of a broad constituency" (Wilson, 1987, p. 120). His orientation is "communitarian" in that he wants programs "in which the more advantaged groups of all races can positively relate" (Wilson, 1987, p. 120). He notes that "the question of reform is a political one" and believes that people increasingly resent programs targeted at particular groups (Wilson, 1987, p. 124). Wilson argues that the possibilities for reform are greater with programs believed to be directed towards the general welfare, as compared to those seen as only benefiting a particular group.[35]

On the other hand, writers like Harold Cruse have cogently maintained that blacks in American society will improve their opportunities only by emphasizing race-specific policies (Cruse, 1987). A biocritical perspective notes that this communitarian/separatist argument is another false dichotomy. To the extent that we recognize species commonalities, the "inevitable" dualism disappears or is marginalized. The more we recognize what we have in common, the easier we are able to imagine ourselves in the "other's" position.

The commonalities we share are the result of our biological and evolutionary history. We share common needs. We share similar neural-biological characteristics and stages of development. We can learn any language. We can share any culture. We have a great deal of genetic commonality. We are all members of the species *Homo sapiens*. We need to develop new stories to tell these things to each other.

We cannot, contrary to Bellah and MacIntyre, share the same religion. We never will. As Jeffrey Stout maintains, the "liberal" institutions disliked by communitarians were in part the result of "the manifest failure of religious groups to establish rational agreement on their competing detailed visions of the good" (Stout, 1988a, p. 212). We cannot, as communitarians suggest, renew 19th-century "republican" traditions in what is to some extent a "postmodern" society (see note 34). The "relations of production," the new "modes of information," the "globalization" of communications and changing ethnic and linguistic relationships all point in the same direction: One cannot base new social forms on what took place in ancient Greece or colonial America. The new narratives we will develop will be based on a constantly evolving understanding of our own past evolution and biosocial commonalities.

In his critique of sociobiology, Peter Singer argues that human reason plays an independent role in the theories and practices we develop. "Reason," he suggests, "is inherently expansionist. It seeks universal application" (Singer, 1981, p. 99). This leads toward what Singer terms an "expanding circle." The use of "reason" results in a bias toward the equal treatment of equals, or what he terms "the principle of impartial consideration of interests" (Singer, 1981, p. 109). This is in some ways similar to the argument concerning "freedom and well-being" of Gewirth. If something is appropriate for me, it is reasonable to suppose that it is proper for a similar being in a similar situation.

Gradually those in the "expanding circle" perceived that Native Americans, blacks, women, Latinos, and Africans were similarly "human." In spite of the racism, sexism, and xenophobia of American society, it is increasingly difficult to argue that anyone *in principle* should be excluded from the opportunities that are available to anyone else. This has been a major achievement of the movement toward individual rights which so exercises communitarians. Contrary to their analyses, an "individualistic" perspective—an expanding circle—has been responsible for the increase in individual "life chances" which communitarians in the United States often take for granted. It will also take a renewed emphasis on individual commonalities to expand that circle in the future. Only in its expansion will we move towards the kinds of human relationships which communitarians from Bourne to Bellah have proposed.

D. EQUAL AND TOGETHER: A BIOCRITICAL REVERIE

Looking out from the observation deck of the starship *Biocommunity* at the rapidly receding image of Earth, Education Specialist Julie Humana was lost in thought. Because this was her twenty-third flight for the United Federation of Planets, she was used to the changes in perspective which came from terrestrial "decentering." She thought of all the other species she had encountered. She knew, of course, that her own species was the result of uniquely shared experiences and a common evolutionary past. Like all humans nowadays, she knew this in a sense that was constitutive of her entire being. Beginning at her primary school, she had gradually come to understand and appreciate the shared needs and characteristics of *Homo sapiens*. She could still remember Madame Diderot in Kindergarten saying— "We are all human beings. *Nous sommes tous les etres humains*. Remember that. Remember to remember." Señor Marquez had said the same thing the next year—in Spanish naturally—"*Somos todos seres humanos*." By her third year, Julie Humana knew three languages.

Her teachers had carefully explained the evolutionary history of humankind. They pointed out to her that a realistic comprehension of genetics had not developed until the 1950s. It had taken much longer to absorb the conceptual and philosophical implications of the new knowledge. The early experiments in DNA hybridization had been one factor. People gradually realized how similar they were to different species, and, by comparison, to each other. Cultural ethnocentrism decreased as people recognized and removed their self-centered blinders. People reacted as Thomas Huxley had so long ago when he finally comprehended Darwin's theory: "How extremely stupid not to have thought of that."

Thinking back on her family's long association with space exploration, she was astounded by the magnitude of the changes in her lifetime. Alterations in self-images had occurred almost as swiftly as the transformations in technology which made possible her career. Peoples' ideas had changed as rapidly as computer technology had changed everyday activities. Just as everyone recognized changes in information processing, people everywhere began to take into account the new information which was being processed. The differences were as great as before and after the time of Copernicus, Galileo, and Newton. Warranted knowledge altered what we saw when we looked at each other. What had been called "the end of history" was now understood as a total chimera.

Today people applied the same "consciousness of kind" to other species as well as our own. It was increasingly difficult to imagine the time before the "veil of ignorance" had been at least partially lifted. Julie knew that the curtain would never be completely removed. The length of the stage always seemed to increase just as the curtain was nearing the end. In fact, there was never any end in sight. While she knew some things her grandmother had not been aware of, her own grandchildren would be in a similar position years from now.

Some of the pre-Federation thinkers and philosophers had understood the changed circumstances and new ways of thinking. In her own area of education, one of her favorites had been Johnny Do. His importance was increasingly recognized. He had seen and understood many of the new possibilities and had tried his best to share that knowledge with others. He knew there was no going back.

Others of the "pre-spacers"—as those between the "post-modernists" and the "Federationists" are labeled today—had not been so prescient. Bob Bella and Al MacTire were two of the "communalists" who had advocated the return of the *status quo ante*. They looked to ancient Greece and the Middle Ages as "exemplars" for contemporary societies. As Johnny Do recognized, however, it was impossible to re-create old ideologies in totally changed circumstances. One had to look in directions which took into account new information. Knowledge and the evaluation of knowledge are connected in a complex web of interrelationships. The evaluations we make depend on what we know.

Julie had several hours before her shift began. Gradually the daydreams became dreams and the dreams became her reality. She saw her classrooms and the people she had taught. Even Afari Olduvai, the Commander of *Biocommunity*, had been one of her students. Julie was proud of her work. She knew she had made a difference in how her students came to understand their common history. She knew that her teaching partner Stephen, as well as all the other members of the crew, shared a living tradition of exploration. They also shared— as equal members of the same species— a variety of

common characteristics which were ultimately the accidental result of our
African origins. But what an astonishing result!

VII

SUMMARY AND CONCLUSIONS

Human beings have a number of things in common. We share a variety of "species-typical" characteristics. We all move through similar ontogenetic stages of development. Contrary to the contemporary "interventions" of skeptical postmodernists, it is unnecessary to restrict sociology to isolated concerns or "local knowledge. It is possible to make transcultural generalizations.[36] Our cultural myopia with respect to other languages is one of the factors which inhibits the recognition of any commonalities. Our well-deserved reputation in the United States as world-class language dolts ensures our misapprehension of the cross-cultural "other." Emergency situations, on the other hand, provide graphic counter examples of "consciousness of kind."

Durkheim's exclusion of biology and psychology from a sociology *sui generis* should be repudiated. Human evolution has resulted in certain species-specific characteristics which enable us to interact with each other. As Tooby and Cosmides observe, we could not "connect" with other people or with the environment at all "without the presence of mechanisms designed to create the connection" (Tooby and Cosmides, 1992, p. 38). Every human social interaction is the result of both individual "mechanisms" and differing environmental contexts. Sociologists who claim individual behavior is merely the result of cultural "socialization" presuppose the existence of unidentified "mechanisms" which allow the socialization to occur in the first place.

A sociologist developing a biosocial perspective may feel like the apocryphal student who suddenly realizes she has been writing "prose" all her life. The significance of our bioevolutionary history should have been obvious long ago, but the most difficult things to reflexively understand are what we take for granted. All sociological discussions of behavior inevitably contain implicit and often underdeveloped psychological assumptions. The mere possibility of a common discourse presupposes various psychological and "individualistic" capabilities.

I have argued throughout this book that any information which helps in the explanation and interpretation of human behavior should be utilized by sociologists. Some of the principal shortcomings of sociology today are the result of the fact that our major conceptual schemata were formulated in the 19th century by Weber, Durkheim, and Marx. Sociology as a discipline developed long before the avalanche of new information now being provided by work in paleoanthropology, genetics, sociobiology, ethology, linguistics, and evolutionary psychology. Each of these areas has data which affect the understanding and interpretation of human actions. There are no good reasons to ignore these kinds of data. As I have maintained elsewhere, the result of our sociological isolationism is a kind of disciplinary hermitage: the sociologist as Robinson Crusoe on an uninhabited and barren island— intellectually "pure" but alone and forgotten, or simply ignored (Neuhaus, 1995).

Durkheim's claim that sociology should by definition eliminate the consideration of all biological and psychological information is intellectually absurd. On the most elementary level, it is clear that the possible identification of a gene responsible for dyslexia or a gene which may help to unclog arteries would have massive social consequences.[37] The kinds of information which lead to these claims were simply not available until recently. Why should sociology be content with an "explanation" for human behavior which is often analogous to previously "learned" commentaries on phlogiston?

I have shown that there are two principal reasons behind much of the sociological rejection of biosocial arguments: Many sociologists believe that any consideration of "biological" data inevitably produces conservative or reactionary political positions. Second, sociologists often exclude analysis of specific "individuals" by disciplinary fiat. In the communitarian analysis of Bellah, MacIntyre and Etzioni, the two positions intersect and overlap. Communitarians advance the notion that any concentration on "the individual" results in the acceptance or promotion of a rapacious, self-centered, Hobbesian ideology. A preoccupation with individual "rights" leads straight to cut-throat consumerism or socially irresponsible "careerism." Wal-Mart and "insider trading" are the unavoidable outcomes.

Neither of these assumptions has any validity. There is no relationship between the use of evolutionary or biological data and a specific political position. The contrary sociological assumption that biology= predetermination=political conservatism/elitism/prejudice/racism has done much to limit our understanding of human actions. Any perspective which stresses the significance of species-specific characteristics and transcultural similarities *ipso facto* decreases invidious distinctions made between peoples. One is less likely to discriminate against a mirror image. The "other" gradually becomes "one of us." There are no valid "political" reasons why sociologists should reject the use of biological or evolutionary data.

Current ethological and genetic information suggests that human beings are more closely related to other species than was previously assumed. Why should sociologists presuppose that the kinds of explanations available for all other species have absolutely no importance for *Homo sapiens*? Behaviors are the result of interactions between "species-specific architectures" and fluctuating environmental conditions. The common sociological assumption that any mention of genetics assures an unchangeable social situation is fundamentally mistaken. Like all other animals, we are influenced by traits and characteristics which are the result of our evolutionary past. The fact that we ignore their effects unnecessarily distorts sociological analyses. It doesn't make a great deal of sense, for example, to write about "the vanishing adolescent" and ignore sex.

The political implications of an evolutionary perspective need not provide troglodytic succor for politicians like Oliver North. Ardent conservatives, for example, often maintain that capitalism and the accumulation of personal wealth are justified and "natural" due to the violent competition evident throughout our evolutionary history. Any attempt to temper capitalistic competition presumably "goes against human nature." The "selfish gene" produces embryonic capitalists.

The problem for this kind pseudo-sophisticated blather is a massive inconsistency in time frames. As Donald Symons has argued, a human activity is only an evolutionary adaptation if it resulted in greater reproductive success for ancestral populations (Symons, 1992, pp. 146–148). Evolution takes time. For example, the "discordance hypothesis" which I discussed in Chapter Four assumes that there are contradictions between the nutritional requirements of our Paleolithic ancestors and our contemporary diets. That is, certain nutritional practices in the Paleolithic resulted in improved chances of reproductive success for the populations which used them. Our current high-fat, fast-food, sugar-loaded diet is not appropriate for the human genotype which evolved throughout prehistory.

Capitalism is a relatively recent human activity. Whatever the significance of evolutionary competition, it is clear that capitalism is not a "natural" adaptation of our genetic inheritance because *the conditions of capitalism did not obtain during our evolutionary development*. The "human needs" which I previously examined are "natural" in the sense of having helped at some point to increase our evolutionary survival. One cannot claim that the "market" is the natural result of our evolutionary heritage when it has only been active for about two hundred years. The kinds of skills necessary to survive in the African savannah do not easily translate to an age of computer technology. A commodities trader is not simply a high-tech version of *Homo habilis*. There was no stock exchange at Olduvai. Bioevolutionary reasoning does not inevitably result in ideological justification of the status quo. A biocritical perspective reaches the opposite conclusion: Biological analysis is less likely to result in a reification of the status quo than is cultural ethnocentrism.

To summarize my findings and conclusions:

1. Contemporary work in ethology and other disciplines points to the close relationships between *Homo sapiens* and other forms of life.

2. It is unreasonable to assume that evolutionary processes have affected all species other than humans, but not *Homo sapiens*.

3. It is therefore logical to conclude that genetic inheritance plays some part in human actions and behavior—that behavior is always the result of combining genotypical and environmental factors.

4. Sociologists attempt to meaningfully interpret behavior.

5. When interpreting behavior, we should make use of all available knowledge.

6. Sociologists who exclude evolutionary or biological data are not making use of all available knowledge.

The results of work in other disciplines affects sociology and should not be excluded from sociological analyses. This is as true for sociology as it is for all other academic disciplines. For example, the famous experiments of Harry Harlow with cloth "mothers" for rhesus monkeys (Haraway, 1989, pp. 231 – 243) conclusively demonstrated that behaviorist assumptions about "mothering" were incorrect. The attraction between mother and child is not simply a matter of "reinforcement" due to feeding schedules. A baby monkey is not merely a "blank slate" subject to the "laws" of operant conditioning. What happens in one discipline does and should have an impact on theories and research in others. Sociology is not exempt from the general processes of intellectual history.

7. The evolutionary history of all other species has resulted in species-specific characteristics and needs.

8. It is reasonable to assume that human beings have certain shared transcultural human needs which are a result of our common evolutionary history and species characteristics.

9. Particular societies do better than others in meeting specific human needs. This can be determined empirically in the same manner as any other social science research.

10. Social problems are the result of failures to meet human needs. The society that best meets human needs has, by definition, the least serious social problems.

11. Due ultimately to our species-specific characteristics, any "normal" human infant can learn any existing language and culture. A child born in the poorest country is as capable of learning the culture of the richest country as a child born in the richest country.

12. People who share common characteristics and needs should be treated in a similar fashion.

13. Every deprived child in the poorest country deserves at least as many opportunities or "life-chances" as an affluent child in the richest country.

A poor child from Haiti brought to the United States as an infant becomes an American. If she is raised in a wealthy family, she potentially encounters the same opportunities as any other member of that family. Her needs are met to the same extent.[38] Thus the standards available in the most adequate country provide an empirical warrant for comparing the opportunities available for any specific individual in his or her own society. Biocritique avoids a utopian conception of "human potential" and suggests that we look at what we have already accomplished. A critical sociology is warranted to the extent that social conditions limit the "life-chances" of any individual in any specific situation. Different groups are better than others in meeting particular human needs. They can be meaningfully compared and evaluated.

It is precisely the emphasis on the individual which allows for valid cross-cultural comparisons. Contrary to the entire communitarian approach, it is our transcultural commonalities as individuals which point to the possibility of effectively reducing the domain of the "other." It seems clear today that we reject out of hand the possibility of social equality. Of course different societies can't be "equal." This notion is dismissed as a completely utopian fantasy. It is much easier, however, to understand and accept the fact that a starving child anywhere in the world could have had very different "life-chances" in a more affluent environment. The child *would be capable of taking advantage of a changed situation due to the common characteristics she shares with any other child*—characteristics which cannot be understood or appreciated without taking evolutionary and biological information into account.

14. An emphasis on an "individualistic" level of analysis need not result in "the new dark ages" proposed by communitarians.

15. We are more likely to recognize our commonalities when we understand what we share as individuals.

16. An emphasis on shared transcultural human characteristics is likely to reduce cultural ethnocentrism, prejudice, and racism.

17. The use of biosocial and evolutionary data has no intrinsic connection to conservatism or satisfaction with the status quo.

18. The evolutionary process does not, in itself, provide a justification for an "evolutionary ethics."

19. It is necessary, *contra* Richards, to add a determinate conception of human needs to evolutionary accounts in order to provide reasonable grounds for a critical sociology.

20. Assuming the satisfaction of human needs as a desideratum, it is possible to make provisionally-warranted value judgments concerning which social and institutional arrangements best meet those needs.

21. Therefore, a complete reliance on "local standards" is unnecessary and counter-productive when analyzing social problems.

Sociology is not in the "hopeless situation" suggested by contemporary prophets of doom. The kinds of information which should lead to a more integrated social science are beginning to be absorbed and taken into account by various disciplines. Evolutionary psychology, genetics, physiology, ecology, and paleoanthropology are all moving toward a new understanding of *Homo sapiens*. It is self-deluding in the extreme to assume that the kinds of information available to 19th-century sociologists are entirely adequate for understanding contemporary human behavior. It is also self-deluding to assume that the perspectives of Durkheim, Marx, and Weber are the best we will ever have.

As Dewey believed, knowledge is a process. We see that easily enough with other peoples and historical periods, but simply can't accept the same limitations on our own perspectives. The fact that our knowledge is, at best, provisional should supply a necessary degree of modesty. The fact that others will in different times and places understand more than we do also supplies a modest degree of hope. A sociology which deals only with cultural differences unnecessarily limits our vision. As David Hollinger argues in *Postethnic America* (1995), "There are contexts in which even species-centered discourse might be critically and cautiously renewed" (p. 109). In an era of "ethnic cleansing" and rising xenophobic nationalism, it is useful to emphasize what we all share: our common biosocial characteristics and evolutionary history as members of *Homo sapiens*.

In her recent study of "collected memories," Janelle Wilson (1995) argues that the pessimistic attitudes her respondents display toward the future "suggest a major historic change in the way Americans conceptualize past, present, and future" (p. 87). One informant stated that people today are "aliens!" "They're not people anymore, they're not humans" (Wilson, p. 87). A biocritical sociology re-presents an alternative viewpoint and valorizes and clarifies our transcultural human commonalities. The "ethnocentrism" decried by sociologists is cultural: Our common traits are the biological and evolutionary result of our membership in a single species. Our shared human needs and characteristics suggest that much which seemingly divides us is illusory or trivial. This further implies that contemporary images of "aliens" are historically contingent and subject to reformulation. A biocritical sociology begins with that understanding.

NOTES

1.　Dewey's argument in 1920 suggests that many contemporary postmodernist positions do not represent quite the decisive break with modernity that their adherents assume (Berman, 1982; Jameson, 1991; Rosenau, 1992).　Randolph Bourne (1964) used the term post-modernism in his brilliant essay "Trans-National America" first published in 1916 (p. 110).

2.　Irving Louis Horowitz, for example, has somehow convinced himself that Regis Debray, the 1960s French revolutionary theorist, and Lynden LaRouche (!) provide good ideal types for what is happening in all of academia, especially in sociology (Horowitz, 1993, pp. 52–73).　He argues that in the very fine work of Stephen Pfohl "the Bohemian ideology takes on the hard edge of totalitarian adventures," whatever that means (p. 48).　With a similar degree of *ad hominem* attacks, Michael Faia (1993) argues that the "me" generation is "merely the latest manifestation of the counterculture" (p. 11), which of course, proves its complete venality.　Horowitz and Faia no longer seem to believe that sociology is about anything, at least as currently practiced.　Disciplinary pessimism is unnecessary and is ultimately a self-fulfilling prophecy.　Diatribes such as the works of Horowitz and Faia assume a generational and disciplinary Cartesian split:　Only my generation and my perspective have any chance of discovering the truth.　Anyone familiar with the works of John Dewey should recognize the shortcomings of such self-serving polemics.　One thinks of Schopenhauer preaching pessimism, asceticism, and resignation, but always being sure to eat in the best restaurants (Russell, 1945, p. 758).　Strangely enough, philosophy did not end with the publication of his *The World as Will and Idea* in 1818.　It is the ultimate conceit to assume that other people will not experience new things and develop new ideas.　We pay lip service to the idea that the acquisition of knowledge is never complete, but we don't seriously consider its implications.

3.　Variables measured included anthropometric variables such as height and weight, electroencephalographic or brainwave measures, psycho-physiologic variables including blood pressure and heart rate, tests of information processing ability, various tests of mental ability, personality tests, psychological interest exams and social attitudes (Bouchard et al., 1990, p.

226). Note the range of responses tested and the kinds of data gathered which are ignored by most sociologists. One of the principal arguments of this book is that a biosocial approach allows sociologists to see the utility of these kinds of data.

4. Wilson, for example, claimed in 1977 that the "critical response to human sociobiology took me by surprise" and that the reactions "of many social scientists were also initially stronger than some of my colleagues and I had expected" (p. xiii). Given the title and contents of his concluding chapter—"Man: From Sociobiology to Sociology"—these comments seem somewhat disingenuous or at least naive. Wilson also writes that "income in a society is distributed to the benefit of the class that controls the government. In the United States, this is of course the middle class" (Wilson, 1978, p. 169, emphasis added). On the contrary, as Philip Mattera argues in *Prosperity Lost*, the idea of an all-encompassing middle class is an ideological construction which has little relationship to family incomes (Mattera, 1990, pp. 9–12). Wilson's comment in this case does seem to reflect a certain political and economic naivete.

5. Part of the problem is simple ignorance. For example, a content analysis by Richard Means of sociological textbooks published between 1930 and 1966 showed that only eight texts out of 112 "suggested in any sense that biological factors are important data for sociologists" (Means, 1967, p. 202). One can't adequately criticize what one refuses to examine. It is interesting, for example, that the first edition of George Ritzer's influential text on sociological theory (1983) contains a detailed discussion of sociobiology and biographical notes on E. O. Wilson (Ritzer, 1983, pp. 401–406), but a more recent volume on contemporary theory (1988) omits the subject entirely. Presumably Ritzer believes the topic is no longer of any interest to sociologists or that we are all adequately informed on the topic.

On the other hand, even anthropologists, all of whom receive, one would presume, some training in physical anthropology, are sharply divided on the relevance of sociobiology for their discipline. Looking at the key concepts of sociobiology as presented by Wilson and others, a survey by Leonard Lieberman showed that animal behaviorists and biological anthropologists are much more receptive to sociobiological reasoning than cultural anthropologists (Lieberman, 1989). For example, 82% of the animal behaviorists agreed that kin selection is a useful topic for future research. The figure for the cultural anthropologists was 35%. A similar comparison for reciprocal altruism was

77% vs. 29% and for gene-culture coevolution 70% vs. 46% (Lieberman, 1989, p. 678).

6. Wilson, of course, uses the signifier "man" to refer to humankind in general. While this was standard practice during the time he was writing *Sociobiology*, it indicates a certain lack of concern and awareness with respect to feminist issues—whether or not it was intended as such by Wilson. See the discussion in Lerner (1992, pp. 127–139).

7. Brent Berlin and Paul Kay are anthropologists who have carried out a number of cross-cultural experiments on the perception and classification of colors. They originally expected to find each culture distinguishing colors in a unique manner. They ultimately found a number of cross-cultural similarities in the way different cultures produced color schemes. They argued that "there appears to be a fixed sequence of evolutionary stages through which a language must pass as its basic color vocabulary increases" (Durham, 1991, p. 218). That is, as the color scheme increases in complexity, the development of color schemes show cross-cultural similarities. See the discussion in Durham (1991, pp. 213–223).

8. There are several authors who have offered specific studies of the influence of what Wilson terms epigenetic rules. Two of the best volumes are *The Tangled Wing* (1982) by Melvin Konner and *Coevolution* (1991) by William Durham. Durham, for example, demonstrates that it is impossible to adequately understand the epidemiology of sickle-cell anemia in West Africa without taking into account both genetic and cultural factors (Durham, 1991, pp. 102–153).

9. A great deal of controversy was generated by the publication of *Sociobiology* when Wilson declared that altruism was "the central theoretical problem of sociobiology" (Wilson, 1975, p. 3). That is, how can something which by (sociobiological) definition "reduces personal fitness" evolve by natural selection? By the time Wilson and Lumsden wrote *Promethean Fire*, they declared that the concepts and empirical studies of kin selection and reciprocal altruism have largely solved the altruism problem and that "the central problem was now the relation between genetic evolution and cultural evolution" (Lumsden & Wilson, 1983, p. 49). This is an important difference in emphasis which, I believe, has gone unrecognized in many critiques of Wilson.

10. On the other hand, it would appear that Wilson's understanding of

philosophy at the time he wrote *Sociobiology* was not completely first-rate. Looking at Wilson's brief discussion of Rawls and Kant in that work, philosopher Mary Midgley writes: "A certain numbness strikes me when I find that Wilson seems to think Kant was an Intuitionist (which is roughly equivalent to calling Darwin a champion of the Genesis creation story) and also to equate Intuitionism with Social Contract ethics" (Midgley, 1978, p. 175). What is even more significant, I think, is that Wilson's discussion is simply not serious. He ignores the relevant literature and the analysis is entirely too brief.

11. Wilson is faced with the same problems as Skinnerian behaviorists. If one eliminates the concept of mind, how does one explain the actions of the experimenters? The philosopher of science David Hull suggests that "a sociobiological analysis of the sociobiologists themselves might prove not only instructive but also entertaining. How did Wilson become the head honcho? What sorts of submissive behavior do others lower in the sociobiological dominance hierarchy exhibit to deflect his aggressive behavior? Do others in Wilson's research group behave like juveniles, or like females in estrus?" (Hull, 1980, p. 81). Donna Haraway nicely suggests the same thing when she refers to "the field primatologists' niches and money-foraging behaviors" (Haraway, 1989, p. 121). For an excellent analysis of what is lacking in Wilson's early works, see the discussion of reason and genes by Peter Singer (Singer, 1981, pp. 87–147).

12. In a 1990 article on "Biology and the Social Sciences" Wilson, although describing sociology as the social science he finds "the most alien and least interesting," says that "sociology is truly the subject most remote from the fundamental principles of individual behavior." Its subjects "probably have the greatest discrepancies between genetic and cultural fitness and hence are most likely to display emergent properties not predictable from a knowledge of individual psychology alone" (Wilson, 1990, p. 259). Edward Wilson meets Clifford Geertz (1973). One could hardly fathom why the controversy over sociobiology occurred at all. If, however, a subject matter is alien to one's perspective, it is, by definition, not taken into account.

13. Darwin's world, by way of contrast, is a very friendly place. Although this is counter to the common sense perception of the survival of the fittest image of Darwinism, a reading of Darwin's discussion of the origins of morality in *The Descent of Man* shows otherwise. "Looking to future generations" says Darwin, "there is no cause to fear that the social instincts

will grow weaker" (Darwin, 1981 [1871], p. 104. For Darwin there was no conflict between the social instincts (i.e., our human biogram) and morality. He believed that our moral sense was ultimately a result of our biological history. Humans can't avoid reflection. Our morality is "aboriginally derived from the social instincts" (Darwin, 1981 [1871], p. 97). I also find it interesting that Darwin clearly stated the principles of reciprocal altruism exactly one hundred years before Robert Trivers' well-known discussion (1971). Darwin wrote in 1871 that "each man would soon learn from experience that if he aided his fellowmen, he would commonly receive aid in return" (Darwin, 1871, p. 169). See also the interesting discussion of Darwin's moral theory by Richards (1987, pp. 110–126).

14. Although Eiseley's use of "man" as a generic marker for humankind is typical of the time when he was writing, his holistic style of analysis is certainly less androcentric than was that of most of his anthropological contemporaries.

15. In his autobiographical work *Biophilia* (1984), Wilson refers to "my own taxonomist's eye" (Wilson, 1984, p. 4). He also states that "I feel most at home with a jumble of glittering data and the feeling they might be fitted together for the first time in some new pattern" (Wilson, 1984, p. 65). To be fair to Wilson, however, *Biophilia* also refers to humanity as the poetic species and contains many passages which demonstrate that Wilson's personal views of nature are actually similar to Eiseley's lyricism. One simply wouldn't know that from a reading of *Sociobiology*.

Wilson also makes a statement in *Biophilia* concerning species analogies which would seem to devalue much of his earlier work: "Although the rules of sexual choice, diet selection, and social behavior are to some extent shared with a few other species, the overall pattern is particular to *Homo sapiens*. Not only symbolization and language, but also most of the basic cognitive specializations are unique" (Wilson, 1984, p. 114, emphasis added). Cultural anthropologists and sociologists would certainly agree, but where does this leave the myriad interspecies comparisons suggested throughout *Sociobiology*? As I have previously argued, it seems clear that a concentration on other primates is warranted. Wilson does make the suggestion in *Biophilia* that research on the pygmy chimpanzee among all the species on earth "deserves the highest priority" (Wilson, 1984, p. 128).

16. Huxley did present a clearer argument which is similar to the position which I will outline in Chapters IV and V. He wrote that "social organization

does canalize and concentrate the psychological forces of human nature in different ways, so that society can act either as an organ of frustration or an organ of fulfillment. Once we have grasped that fact, it is up to us to make the attempt to improve its design" (Huxley, 1957, p. 196). This is a very different and more coherent position than assuming the natural progress of evolution.

17. As I will argue in Chapter IV, it makes a considerable difference whether one is analyzing wants or needs. The assumption of their equality leads to much unnecessary confusion.

18. It is clear that a similar phenomenon of appealing to the proper authority plays a large part in sociology, as the countless quotations from Marx and Weber indicate. An exclusive reliance on authority figures limits creative thought. Of course one has to start somewhere and Marx and Weber are incredibly significant sources. The logical alternative is the absurdity of August Comte's cerebral hygiene: one avoids all contamination from the thoughts of others by simply not reading them (Ritzer, 1988, p. 15).

19. Richards, for example, is particularly critical of Stephen Gould and argues in his book *The Meaning of Evolution* that Gould's Darwinism is an example of "the ideological uses of history" (Richards, 1992, pp. 167–180).

20. For an excellent discussion of the similarities and differences between Spencer and Darwin, as well as their relationships to both Thomas and Julian Huxley, see John C. Greene (1981) *Science, Ideology and World View*. (Berkeley: University of California Press).

21. The kinds of attitudes which qualitative distinctions generate is exemplified by a recent story in *The New York Times* on Haiti's elite. The article quotes a Mr. Denis who states that "if a man works for me, and I lift something heavy from my car instead of allowing him to lift it for me and bring it in the house, then I insult him. Because he feels it is his duty" (Bragg, 1994, p. 8a).

22. See the discussion in Tooby and Cosmides, 1992, p. 110.

23. As is the case with the skeptical postmodernists, one might ask the social constructionist why his or her own writings should be taken seriously? Logically, why shouldn't we only look at *how the social constructionist came to write about* the particular question he or she is concerned with? In other words, the validity of the sociological analysis is not the important issue. Of course someone else might then do the same for the second analysis with no end in sight for this *reductio ad absurdum*.

24. Stout argues that truth as warranted assertability is "refuted by familiar cases in which we are warranted in asserting a proposition at a given time but later discover the proposition to have been false" (Stout, 1988a, p. 298). Surely, however, Dewey's own works suggested, indeed were predicated on, the same idea. Stout, for example, thinks pragmatism is "never having to say you are certain" (Stout, 1988a, p. 297. Dewey in *The Quest for Certainty* wrote that validity is "tested by results and not by correspondence with antecedent properties of existence" (Dewey, 1929, p. 147). He also argued that "there are as many kinds of valid knowledge as there are conclusions wherein distinctive operations have been employed to solve the problems set by antecedently experienced situations" (Dewey, 1929, p. 197). Dewey would have no problem in accepting the fact that what is true at one point—given the best available information—could be falsified at a later date. His whole philosophy assumed as much.

25. The public response to the research of Eaton, Shostak and Konner demonstrates the gap in understanding which exists even among well-known and respected journalists. For example, Ellen Goodman wrote in *The Boston Globe* that "I am convinced that the average Paleolithic person was the very role model of good health when he died at the ripe old age of 32." Other newspaper headlines were "Check Ads for Specials on Saber-toothed Tigers" and "Cave Man Takes a Healthy Bite Out of Today's 'Civilized' Diet." Even *The Washington Post* ridiculed the findings (Konner, 1990, p. 43).

As the authors pointed out in great detail, the major finding of their research was that the kinds of diseases which people died from in Paleolithic times—infectious diseases, as well as trauma—were different from the degenerative diseases evident today. According to *Vital Statistics*, of the fifteen leading causes of death in the United States, heart disease produces the leading share of the total (34.1%), cancer is second (23.1%), and cerebrovascular diseases are third (6.8%) (United States Department of Health and Public Services, 1993, p. 11). While we have generally eliminated the infectious diseases, trauma, and accidents which killed our ancestors, Eaton, Shostak and Konner argue with much justification that a more natural diet similar to practices in the Paleolithic would greatly reduce our leading causes of death. Perhaps our sophisticated perspective cannot accept the possibility that primitive humans could possibly teach us anything. Living among the !Kung in the Kalahari Desert for his dissertation research convinced Konner that this particular conceit was fundamentally mistaken (Konner, 1990, pp. 19–28, 39–46, 99–111, 209–222).

26. It is interesting how rapidly the skeptical postmodernist necessarily abandons theoretical assumptions in what Dewey called "the meaning of the daily detail" (Dewey, 1920, p. 212). That is, if all narratives have equal validity and performativity is not an acceptable criterion, why take one's car to a mechanic when it doesn't start? Presumably anyone else could do as well since all privileged information is equally suspect. From past experience, however, we know that the mechanic is more likely to get the car running again, as opposed to, say, our neighbor who is willing to take a look. Our neighbor, unfortunately, does not have the same experience and background as the mechanic. With respect to fixing our car, the knowledge and experience of the mechanic are more instrumentally warranted.

27. One can argue, of course, that action occurs because it is forced. By eliminating any concern with shared human needs and basing his theories on exclusively rational considerations, Gewirth is open to the criticism that his rationalistic approach ignores problems of social control and coercion.

28. The theoretical approach of biocriticism is similar in this regard to the institutional economics of Clarence Ayres (1961) and Marc Tool (1985). Tool, for example, argues that GNP and marginal utility are theoretically deficient concepts for economic analysis because they provide no way of distinguishing between, say, the economic contributions of the tobacco industry and that of HMOs. GNP assumes the qualitative equality of all fiscal activities. Tool, in contrast, argues that "direction is forward which provides for the *continuity of human life and noninvidious recreation of community through the instrumental use of knowledge*" (Tool, 1985, p. 293, emphasis in original). Biocritique extends this analysis by detailing a theory of human needs which need to be met in order for the qualities of life which Tool values to exist in the first place. For further analysis, see Wendell Gordon and John Adams (1989) *Economics as Social Science: An Evolutionary Approach*.

29. In their use of the term intervention, postmodernists have appropriated a term which would seem to be contrary to their expressed reliance on local standards and decentering critiques. One intervenes given overwhelming force or military superiority—a typically androcentric activity. Intervention has masculine connotations of force—a strangely traditionalistic notion for postmodernists critical of all logocentric narratives.

30. It is interesting to note that in Tocqueville's original formulation he distinguished between mores in the strict sense and different notions and "various opinions, the whole moral and intellectual state of a people" (Tocqueville, 1835/1969, p. 287). He was more interested in the original Roman use "for customs in the broadest and richest sense of the word, including the notion that customs served welfare, and had traditional and mystic sanction" as opposed to "the French *moeurs* which is trivial compared with mores" (Sumner, 1960 [1906], p. 48). Tocqueville, in other words, was contrasting habits of the heart with a broader and more inclusive concept which he wished to use in his own work. Although habits of the heart seems an especially felicitous characterization of mores, it appears that its use by Bellah et al. does not follow Tocqueville's usage. They, as well as Tocqueville, are interested in "the whole moral and intellectual state of a people" as opposed to "mores in the strict sense" (i.e., habits of the heart).

31. By the good life of personality Bourne meant exactly the same kind of internal virtues and friendships which MacIntyre and Bellah advocate. As he wrote of friendship in *Youth and Life*: "One achieves a sort of transfiguration of personality in those moments. In the midst of the high and genial flow of intimate talk, a pang may seize one at the thought of the next day's drudgery, when life will be lived alone again; but nothing can dispel the ease and fullness with which it is being lived at the moment" (Bourne, 1977, p. 112).

32. To be fair to Bellah and his co-authors, their recent volume *The Good Society* (1991) does contain a more political orientation and does make use of the work of John Dewey and Walter Lippmann, but their analysis still has a somewhat ethereal quality. For example: "In this book we have repeatedly suggested the need for a new paradigm, which we can now call the pattern of cultivation. This pattern would not mean a return to the settlement forms of the early nineteenth century, but it would be the attempt to find, in today's circumstances, a social and environmental balance, a recovery of meaning and purpose in our lives together, giving attention to the natural and cultural endowment we want to hand down to our children and grandchildren, and avoiding the distractions which have confused us in the past" (Bellah, et al., 1991, p. 271). The obvious question is how do we go about pursuing these lofty goals? Writers like Lewis Mumford proposed the same kinds of goals but were very sketchy on the procedural details. *The Good Society* is eloquent in its description of the good life but deficient in information on getting there.

Bellah and his co-authors offer a great many generalities: "In a society as obsessively concerned with money as ours, money is a major form of distraction" (Bellah, et al., 1991, p. 264). The contrast is evident when comparing Bellah's observations to Etzioni's. Etzioni offers some specific suggestions for implementing communitarian reforms. For example, he suggests that parents' social security numbers should be printed on their children's birth certificates "so that it would be possible to find either parent if he or she left the child" (Etzioni, 1993, p. 83).

33.   As I have previously argued, there is no single language of individualism. In the United States today there is a multiplicity of different languages. Similarly, there is no single republican tradition or community of memory. We talk about the same themes, but all have our own variations. What I am proposing with biocritique is that we recognize our commonalities, as well as the differences.

34.   In *Looking Backward* (1993) Derek Phillips persuasively argues that the presumably communitarian features of 19th-century American life have been greatly exaggerated and idealized in the communitarian discourse (pp. 24–80). Thus, for example, "fewer than 10 percent of the inhabitants of old Virginia had the right to vote" (Phillips, 1993, p. 73). The public good was rather narrowly defined and it was a singularly picayune public.

35.   In this regard, as I argued in Chapter One, his use of the term underclass is particularly unfortunate. His own terminology leads to the kinds of particularistic and negative categorizing which he believes effective efforts at social reform need to avoid.

36.   See the convincing arguments in Tooby and Cosmides, 1992.

37.   On a possible dyslexia gene, see *Newsweek*, October 24, 1994, p. 66. On the possibility of a gene which may help to unclog arteries, see Levy (1994).

38.   This ignores, of course, the likelihood of contemporary racism negatively affecting any child from Haiti. For the purposes of this example, I am assuming the racism will not be a factor.

I am likewise assuming in this example that gender is not a significant discriminatory factor. In spite of these unrealistic assumptions, it is easy to accept a thought experiment which suggests that the socialization and opportunities later available to a baby brought from Haiti could possibly be the same as the ones available to any other child raised in the same family in the United States.

One of the benefits of travel to Latin America for North Americans is the likelihood of experiencing vastly different racial situations and categories. As any traveler to Latin America discovers, the "racial" categories we use in the United States are culturally specific.

BIBLIOGRAPHY

Alexander, Jeffery C. "Looking for Theory: Facts and Values as the Intellectual Legacy of the 1970s." *Theory and Society* 10.2 (1981): 279 –292.

_____. *Positivism, Presuppositions and Current Controversies.* Berkeley, CA: University of California Press, 1982.

Allman, William F. *The Stone Age Present.* New York: Simon and Schuster, 1994.

Alper, Joseph; Beckwith, Jim; and Miller, Larry. *Sociobiology Is a Political Issue.* Cambridge, MA: Science for the People, 1978.

Ardrey, Robert. *The Territorial Imperative.* New York: Atheneum, 1966.

Ashley, David and Orenstein, David Michael. *Sociological Theory: Classical Statements.* Boston: Allyn and Bacon, 1990.

Axelrod, Robert. *The Evolution of Cooperation.* New York: Harper Collins, 1984.

Ayres, Clarence. *Toward a Reasonable Society.* Austin: University of Texas Press, 1961.

Barash, David. *The Whisperings Within.* London: Penguin, 1979.

Barkow, Jerome; Cosmides, Leda; and Tooby, John. *The Adapted Mind.* New York: Oxford University Press, 1992.

Barlow, George W. and Silver, James, eds. *Sociobiology: Beyond Nature/Nurture.* Boulder, CO: Westview, 1980.

Bellah, Robert. "The Idea of Practices in Habits: A Response." In *Community in America: The Challenge of Habits of the Heart*, edited by Charles H. Reynolds and Ralph V. Norman, 269-288. Berkeley, CA: University of California Press, 1988.

Bellah, Robert; Madsen, Richard; Sullivan, William M.; Swidler, Ann; and Tipton, Stephen M. *Habits of the Heart.* New York: Harper and Row, 1985.

_____. *The Good Society*. New York: Random House, 1991.

Benedict, Ruth. *Patterns of Culture*. New York: New American Library, 1934.

Berger, Peter and Luckmann, Thomas. *The Social Construction of Reality*. Garden City, NJ: Doubleday, 1966.

Berke, Richard L. "Anger and Cynicism Well Up in Voters as Hope Gives Way." *New York Times* (October 10, 1994): A1, A7.

Berman, Marshall. *All That Is Solid Melts Into Air*. New York: Simon and Schuster, 1982.

Bernstein, Richard J. *The Restructuring of Social and Political Theory*. Philadelphia, PA: University of Pennsylvania Press, 1976.

Berryman, Phillip. *Liberation Theology*. New York: Random House, 1987.

Blake, Casey Nelson. *Beloved Community*. Chapel Hill, NC: University of North Carolina Press, 1990.

Blute, Marion. (1976). "Review Symposia, Sociobiology: The New Synthesis, *Contemporary Sociology* 5.6 (1976): 727–731.

Bork, Robert. *The Tempting of America*. New York: Simon and Schuster, 1990.

Bottomore, Tom and Nisbet, Robert, eds. *A History of Sociological Analysis*. New York: Basic Books, 1978.

Bouchard, Thomas; Lykken, D.; McGue, M.; Segal, N.; and Tellegen, A. (1990). "Sources of Human Psychological Differences: The Minnesota Study of Twins Reared Apart." *Science* 250.4978 (October 12, 1990): 223–250.

Bourne, Randolph. *War and the Intellectuals*. New York: Harper and Row, 1964.

_____. *The Radical Will: Selected Writings, 1911–1918*. New York: Urizen, 1977.

Boyne, Roy. *Foucault and Derrida*. London: Unwin Hyman Ltd., 1990.

Bragg, Rick. "Behind Ouster of Aristide: Haiti's Tiny Elite." *New York Times* (August 18, 1994): Al, A8.

Braybrooke, David. *Meeting Needs*. Princeton: Princeton University Press, 1987.

Brinkerhoff, David and White, Lynn K. *Sociology*. 3rd ed. St. Paul, MN: West, 1991.

Bronowski, Jacob. *Science and Human Values*. New York: Julian Messner, 1956.

Brooks, Van Wyck. *America's Coming of Age*. New York: B. W. Huebsch, 1915.

Brown, Donald. *Human Universals*. New York: McGraw – Hill, 1991.

Bryant, Christopher G. *Positivism, Social Theory and Research*. New York: St. Martin's, 1985.

Burhoe, Ralph. (1992). "On Huxley's Evolution and Ethics in Sociobiological Perspective." *Zygon*, 23.4 (1992): 417 – 429.

Burkitt, Denis. *Eat Right*. New York: Arco, 1979.

Callebaut, Werner. *Taking the Naturalistic Turn*. Chicago: University of Chicago Press, 1993.

Campbell, James. *The Community Reconstructs*. Urbana: University of Illinois Press, 1992.

_____. *Understanding John Dewey*. Chicago: Open Court, 1995.

Caplan, Arthur, ed. *The Sociobiology Debate*. New York: Harper and Row, 1978.

Cavalieri, Paola and Singer, Peter. *The Great Ape Project*. New York: St. Martin's, 1993.

Cela-Conde, Camilo. "The Challenge of Evolutionary Ethics." *Biology and Philosophy 1* (1986): 293 – 297.

Chasin, Barbara. *Sociobiology: A Sexist Synthesis*. Cambridge, MA: Science for the People, 1977.

Cheney, Dorothy and Seyfarth, Robert. *How Monkeys See the World*. Chicago: University of Chicago Press, 1990.

Collins, Patricia Hill. "The Social Construction of Invisibility." In *Perspectives on Social Problems* (vol. 1), edited by James A. Holstein and Gale Miller, 77–93. Greenwich, London: AI Press, 1989.

Collins, Randall. *Conflict Sociology*. New York: Academic, 1975.

_____. *Theoretical Sociology*. New York: Harcourt Brace Jovanovich, 1988.

Crippin, Timothy. "An Evolutionary Critique of Cultural Analysis in Sociology," *Human Nature* 31.4 (1992): 379–412.

_____. "Toward a Neo-Darwinian Sociology." *Sociological Perspectives* 37.3 (1994): 309–335.

Cruse, Harold. *Plural but Equal*. New York: Morrow, 1987.

Cummings, Michael R. *Human Heredity*. St. Paul: West, 1991.

Darwin, Charles. *The Autobiography of Charles Darwin*. New York: Norton, 1958. (Original Work published 1887)

_____. *Expression of the Emotions in Man and Animals*. Chicago: University of Chicago Press, 1965. (Original Work published 1872)

_____. *The Descent of Man, and Selection in Relationship to Sex*. Princeton, NJ: Princeton University Press, 1981. (Original work published 1871)

_____. *The Essential Darwin*. Boston: Little, Brown and Company, 1984.

Dash, Leon. "Rosa Lee's Story." *The Washington Post* (October 10-16, 1994): 15–38.

Dawkins, Marian. *Through Our Eyes Only? The Search for Animal Consciousness*. Oxford: W. H. Freeman, 1993.

Dawkins, Richard. *The Blind Watchmaker*. New York: Norton, 1986.

_____. *The Selfish Gene*. Oxford: Oxford University Press, 1989.

_____. "Gaps in the Mind." In *The Great Ape Project*, edited by P. Cavalieri and P. Singer, 80–87. New York: Norton, 1993.

Degler, Carl L. *In Search of Human Nature*. New York: Oxford, 1991.

Dewey, John. *Reconstruction in Philosophy*. Boston: Beacon, 1920.

_____. *The Quest for Certainty*. New York: G. P. Putnams, 1929.

Diamond, Jared. *The Third Chimpanzee*. New York: Harper Collins, 1992.

Diggins, John. *The Promise of Pragmatism*. Chicago: University of Chicago Press, 1994.

Dunbar, R. I. M. "What's in a Classification?" In *The Great Ape Project*, edited by P. Cavalieri & P. Singer, 109–112. New York: Norton, 1993.

Durham, William. *Coevolution*. Stanford: Stanford University Press, 1991.

Durkheim, Emile. *Sociology and Philosophy*. Glencoe, IL: The Free Press, 1953. (Original work published 1924)

_____. "The Dualism of Human Nature and its Social Conditions." In K. H. Wolf (Ed.), *Emile Durkheim, 1858–1917*, edited by K. H. Wolf, 325–340. Columbus, OH: Ohio State University Press. 1960. (Original work published 1914)

_____. *The Rules of Sociological Method*. New York: The Free Press, 1966. (Original work published 1895)

Duster, Troy and Garrett, Karen, eds. *Cultural Perspectives on Biological Knowledge*. Norwood, NJ: Ablex Publishing Company, 1984.

Eaton, S. Boyd; Shostak, Marjorie; and Konner, Melvin. *The Paleolithic Prescription*. New York: Harper and Row, 1988.

Eckland, Bruce. "Darwin Rides Again." *American Journal of Sociology* 82.3 (1976): 692–697.

Edel, Abraham. *Ethical Judgment*. New York: The Free Press, 1955.

_____. *Exploring Fact and Value*. New Brunswick: Transaction, 1980.

Edey, Maitland and Johanson, Donald. *Blueprints: Solving the Mystery of Evolution*. Boston: Little Brown, 1989.

Ehrlich, Paul R. *The Population Bomb*. New York: Ballantine, 1971.

Eiseley, Loren. *The Immense Journey*. New York: Random House, 1959.

_____. *Darwin's Century*. Garden City, NJ: Doubleday, 1961.

_____. *The Night Country*. New York: Charles Scribner, 1971.

Eitzen, D. Stanley. "Teaching Social Problems: Implications of the Objectivist-Subjectivist Debate." *SSSP Newsletter 16*, (1984): 10–12.

Eldredge, Niles. *Time Frames*. New York: Simon and Schuster, 1985.

Eldredge, Niles and Grene, Marjorie. *Interactions: The Biological Context of Social Systems*. New York: Columbia University Press, 1992.

Etzioni, Amitai. "Basic Human Needs, Alienation and Inauthenticity." *American Sociological Review* 33.6 (1968): 870–885.

_____. *The Spirit of Community*. New York: Simon and Schuster, 1993.

Evans, Richard I. *Konrad Lorenz: The Man and His ideas*. New York: Harcourt, Brace and Janovich, 1975.

Faia, Michael A. *What's Wrong With the Social Sciences?* Lanham, MD: University Press of America, 1993.

Fernald, Anne. "Human Maternal Vocalizations to Infants as Biologically Relevant Signals: An Evolutionary Perspective." In *The Adapted Mind*, edited by J. Barkow, L. Cosmides, and J. Tooby, 391–428. New York: Oxford University Press, 1992.

Ferrante, Joan. *Sociology: A Global Perspective*. Belmont: Wadsworth, 1992.

Foucault, Michel. *Discipline and Punish*. New York: Random House, 1979.

Fouts, Roger S. and Fouts, Deborah H. "Chimpanzees' Use of Sign Language. In *The Great Ape Project*, edited by P. Cavalieri & P. Singer, 28–41. New York: Norton, 1993.

Fox, Robin. *The Search for Society*. New Brunswick: Rutgers University Press, 1989.

Friedenberg, Edgar. *The Vanishing Adolescent*. New York: Dell, 1959.

Friedman, Milton. *Capitalism and Freedom*. Chicago: University of Chicago Press, 1962.

Friedrichs, Robert W. *A Sociology of Sociology*. New York: The Free Press, 1970.

Fromm, Erich. *The Sane Society*. New York: Holt, Rinehart, 1955.

Gandy, Ross. *Twenty Keys to Mexico*. Cuernavaca: Center for Bilingual and Multicultural Studies, 1990.

Garcia, Ismael. *Justice in Latin American Theology of Liberation*. Atlanta: John Knox Press, 1987.

Geertz, Clifford. *The Interpretation of Cultures*. New York: Basic Books, 1973.

Gerth, Hans and Mills, C. Wright. *Character and Social Structure*. New York: Harcourt, Brace & World, 1953.

Gewirth, Alan. *Reason and Morality*. Chicago: University of Chicago Press, 1978.

_____. *Human Rights: Essays on Justification and Applications*. Chicago: University of Chicago Press, 1982.

_____. "The Problem of Specificity in Evolutionary Ethics." *Biology and Philosophy 1* (1986): 297–305.

Giddings, Franklin H. *Principles of Sociology*. New York: Macmillan, 1896.

Goodall, Jane. *The Chimpanzees of Gombe*. Cambridge: Harvard University Press, 1986.

Gordon, Wendell and Adams, John. *Economics as Social Science: An Evolutionary Perspective*. Riverdale, MD: Riverdale Press, 1989.

Gould, Stephen. *Ever Since Darwin*. New York: Norton, 1977.

_____. "Sociobiology and the Theory of Natural Selection." In *Sociobiology: Beyond Nature/Nurture?*, edited by George Barlow and James Silverberg, 257–269. Boulder, CO: Westview, 1980.

_____. "Unenchanted Evening." *Natural History 9* (1991): 4–14.

Gove, Walter. "Sociobiology Misses the Mark: An Essay on Why Biology but Not Sociobiology Is Very Relevant to Sociology." *American Sociologist* 18.3 (1987): 258–277.

Gray, William. "Evolution and the Meaning of Life." *Zygon* 22.4 (1987): 479–496.

Greene, John. *Science, Ideology, and World View*. Berkeley, CA: University of California Press, 1981.

Gregory, Michael; Silvers, Anita; and Sutch, Diane, eds. *Sociobiology and Human Nature*. San Francisco, CA:Jossey-Bass, 1978.

Griffin, Donald. *Animal Minds*. Chicago: University of Chicago Press, 1992.

Gruber, Howard. *Darwin on Man*. New York: Dutton, 1974.

Gubrium, Jaber. "For a Cautious Naturalism." In *Constructionist Controversies*, edited by G. Miller and. Holstein, 55–67). New York: Aldine De Gruyter, 1993.

Gusfield, Joseph. "Taking the Starch out of Social Problems." Paper presented at the annual meeting of Society for the Study of Social Problems Symposium on Social Theory, Cincinnati, Ohio, August 1980.

_____. "I Gotta Be Me." *Contemporary Sociology* 15.1 (1986): 7–9.

Hall, Edward. *The Silent Language*. New York: Fawcett, 1959.

Haraway, Donna. *Primate Visions*. New York: Routledge, 1989.

_____. *Simians, Cyborgs and Women*. New York: Routledge, 1991.

Harding, Vincent. "Toward a Darkly Radiant Vision of America's Truth: A Letter of Concern, an Invitation to Re-creation." In *Community in America: The Challenge of Habits of the Heart*, edited by C. H. Reynolds and R. V. Norman, 67-83. Berkeley, CA: University of California Press, 1988.

Harrington, Walt. *Crossings*. New York: Harper Collins, 1992.

Harris, Marvin. *The Rise of Anthropological Theory*. New York: Thomas Y. Crowell, 1968.

_____. *Our Kind*. New York: Harper Collins, 1989.

Herrnstein, Richard J. and Murray, Charles. *The Bell Curve*. New York: The Free Press, 1994.

Hickman, Larry. *John Dewey's Pragmatic Technology*. Bloomington, IN: Indiana University Press, 1990.

Himmelfarb, Gertrude. *Darwin and the Darwinian Revolution*. New York: Norton, 1968.

Hofstadter, Richard. *Social Darwinism in American Thought*. Revised ed. New York: George Braziller, 1959.

Holbach, Paul Henri. *The System of Nature*. New York: B. Franklin, 1970.

Holden, Constance. "The Genetics of Personality." *Science* 237.4815 (1987): 598–601.

Hollinger, David. *Postethnic America*. New York: Basic Books, 1995.

Honneth, Axel and Joas, Hans. *Social Action and Human Nature*. Cambridge: Cambridge University Press, 1988.

Hook, Sidney. *John Dewey: An Intellectual Portrait*. Westport, CN: Greenwood, 1971. (Original work published 1939)

Horkheimer, Max. *Eclipse of Reason*. New York: Seabury, 1947.

_____. *Critical Theory*. New York: Herder and Herder, 1972.

Horkheimer, Max and Adorno, Theodor W. *Dialectic of Enlightenment*. New York: Seabury, 1972.

Horowitz, Irving L. *The Decomposition of Sociology*. New York: Oxford University Press, 1993.

Hrdy, Sarah Blaffer. *The Woman That Never Evolved*. Cambridge: Harvard University Press, 1981.

_____. "Raising Darwin's Consciousness: Females and Evolutionary Theory." *Zygon* 25.2 (1990): 129–137.

Hubbard, Ruth and Wald, Elijah. *Exploding the Gene Myth*. Boston: Beacon, 1993.

Hudson, W. D, ed. *The Is/Ought Question*. London: Macmillan, 1969.

Hughes, William. "Richards' Defense of Evolutionary Ethics." *Biology and Philosophy 1* (1986): 306–315.

Hull, David L. "Sociobiology: Another New Synthesis." In *Sociobiology: Beyond Nature/Nurture?*, edited by G. W. Barlow and. Silverberg, 77–96. Boulder, CO: Westview, 1980.

Hume, David. *Treatise of Human Nature*. Oxford: Oxford University Press, 1959. (Original work published 1739)

Huxley, Julian. *Religion Without Revelation*. New York: New American Library, 1957.

Huxley, Thomas. "Evolution and Ethics." In *Evolutionary Ethics*, edited by M. H. Nitecki and D. V. Nitecki, 29–80. Albany, NY: State University of New York Press, 1993. (Original work published 1894)

Jameson, Fredric. "On Habits of the Heart." In *Community in America: The Challenge of Habits of the Heart*, edited by C. H. Reynolds and R. V. Norman, 97-112. Berkeley, CA: University of California Press, 1988.

_____. *Postmodernism, or the Cultural Logic of Late Capitalism*. Durham: Duke University Press, 1991.

Johanson, Donald and Edey, Maitland. *Lucy: The Beginnings of Humankind*. New York: Simon and Schuster, 1981.

Johanson, Donald; Johanson, Lenore; and Edgar, Blake. *Ancestors*. New York: Random House, 1994.

Jones, Steve. "A Brave, New, Healthy World?" *Natural History* 103.6 (1994): 72–74.

Junker, Louis. *The Social and Economic Thought of Clarence Ayres*. Unpublished Ph.D. Dissertation, University of Wisconsin, Madison, 1962.

Kanrowite, B. "Sociology's Lonely Crowd." *Newsweek* (February 3, 1992): 55.

Kaufmann, Walter. *Critique of Religion and Philosophy*. Princeton: Princeton University Press, 1978.

Kaye, Howard. *The Social Meaning of Modern Biology*. New Haven, CT: Yale University Press, 1986.

Kellner, Douglas. *Critical Theory, Marxism and Modernity*. Baltimore, MD: Johns Hopkins, 1989.

Kitcher, Phillip. *Vaulting Ambition*. Cambridge: MIT, 1985.

_____. *The Advancement of Science*. New York: Oxford University Press, 1993.

Konner, Melvin. *The Tangled Wing*. New York: Henry Holt, 1982.

_____. *Why the Reckless Survive*. New York: Viking, 1990.

_____. *Childhood: A Multicultural View*. Boston: Little, Brown and Company, 1991.

Kozol, Jonathan. *Savage Inequalities*. New York: Crown, 1991.

Krutch, Joseph Wood. *The Measure of Man*. New York: Bobbs-Merrill, 1954.

_____. *The Great Chain of Life*. Cambridge: Houghton-Mifflin, 1956.

Kuhn, Thomas. *The Structure of Scientific Revolutions*. Chicago: University of Chicago Press, 1970.

Kuper, Adam. *The Chosen People*. Cambridge: Harvard University Press, 1994.

Lasch, Christopher. "The Communitarian Critique of Liberalism." In *Community in America: The Challenge of Habits of the Heart*, edited by C. H. Reynolds and R. V. Norman, 173-184. Berkeley, CA: University of California Press, 1988.

Lawrence, Jill. "Americans Are Growing Bitter, Survey Finds." *Kalamazoo Gazette* (September 21, 1994): A1, A2.

Leakey, Richard. *The Making of Mankind*. New York: Dutton, 1981.

Leakey, Richard and Lewin, Roger. *Origins*. New York: Dutton, 1977.

Lenski, Gerhard. "Rethinking Macrosociological Theory." *American Sociological Review 53* (1988): 163–171.

Lerner, Richard. *Final Solutions*. University Park, PA: Pennsylvania State University Press, 1992.

Levins, Richard and Lewontin, Richard. *The Dialectical Biologist*. Cambridge: Harvard University Press, 1985.

Levy, Doug. "Family's Mutant Gene May Unclog Arteries.: *USA Today* (October 17, 1994): A1.

Lewontin, Richard. *Biology as Ideology*. New York: Harper Collins, 1991.

Lewontin, Richard; Rose, Steven; and Kamin, Leon. *Not in Our Genes*. New York: Random House, 1984.

Lieberman, Lenoard. "A Discipline Divided: Acceptance of Human Sociobiological Concepts in Anthropology." *Current Anthropology* 30.5 (1989): 676–682.

Lloyd, Elizabeth. *The Structure and Confirmation of Evolutionary Theory*. Princeton: Princeton University Press, 1994.

Lorenz, Konrad. *King Solomon's Ring*. New York: Time-Life, 1952.

Lumsden, Charles J. and Wilson, Edward. *Promethean Fire*. Cambridge: Harvard University Press, 1983.

Macedo, Donaldo. *Literacies of Power*. Boulder, CO: Westview, 1994.

MacIntyre, Alasdair. *After Virtue*. 2nd ed. Notre Dame, OH: University of Notre Dame Press, 1984.

Mannheim, Karl. *Ideology and Utopia*. New York: Harcourt, Brace & World, 1936.

Marcuse, Herbert. *Eros and Civilization*. New York: Random House, 1955.

_____. *One-dimensional Man*. Boston: Beacon, 1964.

Maryanski, Alexandra. "The Pursuit of Human Nature in Sociobiology and Evolutionary Sociology." *Sociological Perspectives* 3.3 (1994): 375 –389.

Masserman, Jules; Wechkin, Stanley; and Terris, William. "Altruistic Behavior in Rhesus Monkeys." *American Journal of Psychiatry 121* (1964): 584-585.

Mattera, Philip. *Prosperity Lost.* New York: Addison-Wesley, 1990.

Mauss, Almond L. "Beyond the Illusion of Social Problems Theory." In *Perspectives on Social Problems*, edited by A. Holstein and G. Miller, 19 –39. Greenwich, London:AI Press, 1989.

Mayr, Ernst. *One Long Argument: Charles Darwin and the Genesis of Modern Evolutionary Thought.* Cambridge: Harvard University Press, 1991.

Mazur, Allan. "On Wilson's Sociobiology." *American Journal of Sociology* 82.3 (1976): 697 –700.

Mazur, Allan and Robertson, Leon. S. *Biology and Social Behavior.* New York: The Free Press, 1972.

McKibben, Bill. *The Age of Missing Information.* New York: Random House, 1992.

Mead, George Herbert. *Mind, Self and Society.* Chicago: University of Chicago Press, 1962. (Original work published 1934)

Means, Richard. L. "Sociology, Biology and the Analysis of Social Problems." *Social Problems* 15.2 (1967): 200 –212.

Megone, C. B. "What Is Need?" In *In Need: Meeting Needs in an Affluent Society*, edited by A. Corden, E. Robertson and K. Tolley, 12 –30. Aldershot: Avebury, 1992.

Merton, Robert. *On Theoretical Sociology.* New York: The Free Press, 1967.

Midgley, Mary. *Beast and Man: The Roots of Human Nature.* Ithica, NY: Cornell University Press, 1978.

_____. "Gene-Juggling." *Philosophy 54* (1979): 439 –458.

_____. "Rival Fatalisms: The Hollowness of the Sociobiology Debate." In *Sociobiology Examined*, edited by A. Montagu, 15–38. New York: Oxford University Press, 1980.

_____. *Animals and Why They Matter*. Athens, GA: University of Georgia Press, 1983a.

_____. "Human Ideals and Human Needs." *Philosophy 58* (1983b): 89–94.

_____. *Wickedness*. London: Routledge & Kegan Paul, 1984.

_____. *Evolution as a Religion*. London: Methuen, 1985.

_____. *Science as Salvation*. London: Routledge, 1992.

_____. *Can't We Make Moral Judgments?* New York: St. Martin's, 1993.

Miles, H Lynn White. "Language and The Orangutan: The Old Person of the Forest." In *The Great Ape Project*, edited by P. Cavalieri & P. Singer, 42–57. New York: St. Martin's, 1993.

Miller, Gale and Holstein, James, eds. *Constructionist Controversies*. New York: Aldine De Gruyter, 1993.

Mills, C. Wright. *The Sociological Imagination*. New York: Grove, 1959.

Moore, G. E. *Principia Ethica*. Cambridge: Cambridge University Press, 1903.

Myrdal, Gunnar. *Objectivity in Social Research*. New York: Random House, 1969.

Nachmias, David and Nachmias, Chava. *Research Methods in the Social Sciences*. New York: St. Martin's, 1981.

Neuhaus, John. "Reification, Politics and the Postmodern Turn." *Pomo Magazine* 1.1 (1995): 30-34.

Nisbet, Robert. *The Quest for Community*. New York: Oxford University Press, 1953.

Nitecki, Matthew H. and Nitecki, Doris V. *Evolutionary Ethics*. Albany: State University of New York Press, 1993.

Nussbaum, Martha. "Human Functioning and Social Justice." *Political Theory* 20.2 (1992): 202–246.

Nussbaum, Martha and Sen, Amartya. *The Quality of Life*. Oxford: Clarendon, 1993.

Oates, David. "Social Darwinism and Natural Theodicy." *Zygon* 23.4 (1988): 439–454.

Ogburn, William. *On Culture and Social Change*. Chicago: University of Chicago Press, 1964.

Orians, Gordon H. "Habitat Selection: General Theory and Applications to Human Behavior." In *The Evolution of Human Social Behavior*, edited by. Lockard, 49–66. New York: Elsevier, 1980.

Orians, Gordon H. and Heerwagen, Judith H. "Evolved Responses to Landscapes." In *The Adapted Mind*, edited by. Barkow, L. Cosmides, and Tooby, 555–579. New York: Oxford University Press, 1992.

Orr, David W. *Ecological Literacy*. Albany: State University of New York Press, 1992.

Patterson, Francine and Gordon, Wendy. "The Case For the Personhood of Gorillas." In *The Great Ape Project*, edited by P. Cavalieri & P. Singer, 58–77. New York: St. Martin's, 1993.

Patterson, Francine and Linden, Eugene. *The Education of Koko*. New York: Holt, Rinehart and Winston, 1981.

Pfeiffer, John E. *The Creative Explosion: An Enquiry Into the Origins of Art and Religion*. New York: Harper and Row, 1982.

Pfohl, Stephen. *Images of Deviance and Social Control*. 2nd. ed. New York: McGraw-Hill, 1994.

Phillips, Derek. *Toward a Just Social Order*. Princeton: Princeton University Press, 1986.

_____. *Looking Backward*. Princeton: Princeton University, 1993.

Pinker, Steven and Bloom, Paul. "Natural Language and Natural Selection." In *The Adapted Mind*, edited by. Barkow, L. Cosmides, and. Tooby, 451–493. New York: Oxford University Press, 1992.

Plotkin, Henry. *Darwin Machines and the Nature of Knowledge*, Cambridge: Harvard University Press, 1994.

Polanyi, Michael. *Personal Knowledge*. New York: Harper and Row, 1962.

Popper, Karl. *Conjectures and Refutations*. New York: Harper and Row, 1963.

Poster, Mark. *The Mode of Information*. Chicago: University of Chicago Press, 1990.

Postman, Neil. *Technopoly*. New York: Random House, 1992.

Powell, Steward. M. "Clinton Tests Idea of Character Education." *Kalamazoo Gazette* (July 10, 1994): A7.

Quine, W. V. O. *Two Dogmas of Empiricism*. Cambridge: Harvard University Press, 1961.

Rachels, James. *Created From Animals: The Moral Implications of Darwinism*. New York: Oxford University Press, 1990.

Rajchman, John. *Michel Foucault: The Freedom of Philosophy*. New York: Columbia University Press, 1985.

Rapaport, Anatol and Chammah, A. *Prisoner's Dilemma*. Ann Arbor: University of Michigan, 1965.

Rapaport, Anatol and Dale, P. "The End and Start Effects in Iterated Prisoner's Dilemma." *Journal of Conflict Resolution 10* (1967): 363–366.

Reich, Robert B. *Tales for a New America*. New York: Random House, 1987.

Remming, Gunter. *Road to Suspicion*. New York: Appleton-Century-Crofts, 1967.

Restak, Richard. *The Brain*. New York: Bantam, 1984.

_____. *The Brain Has a Mind of Its Own*. New York: Crown, 1991.

Reynolds, Charles H. and Norman, Ralph V., eds. *Community in America: The Challenge of Habits of the Heart.* Berkeley, CA: University of California Press, 1988.

Rhoads, John. *Critical Issues in Social Theory.* University Park: Pennsylvania State University Press, 1991.

Richards, Robert J. "A Defense of Evolutionary Ethics." *Biology and Philosophy 1* (1986a): 265–293.

_____. "Justification Through Biological Faith: A Rejoinder." *Biology and Philosophy 1* (1986b): 337–354.

_____. *Darwin and the Emergence of Evolutionary Theories of Mind and Behavior.* Chicago: University of Chicago Press, 1987.

_____. "The Moral Foundations of the Idea of Evolutionary Progress: Darwin, Spencer and the Neo-Darwinists." In *Evolutionary Progress*, edited by M. H. Nitecki, 129–148. Chicago: University of Chicago Press, 1988.

_____. "Dutch Objections to Evolutionary Ethics." *Biology and Philosophy 4* (1989): 331–343.

_____. *The Meaning of Evolution.* Chicago: University of Chicago Press, 1992.

_____. "Birth, Death and Resurrection of Evolutionary Ethics." In *Evolutionary Ethics*, edited by M. H. Nitecki and D. V. Nitecki, 113–131. Albany, NY: State University of New York Press, 1993.

Richardson, Laurel. "Postmodern Social Theory: Representational Practices." *Sociological Theory* 9.2 (1991): 173–179.

Riesman, David. "Introduction." In *The Vanishing Adolescent*, edited by Edgar Friedenberg, 7–16. New York: Dell, 1959.

Ritzer, George. *Sociological Theory.* New York: Random House, 1983.

_____. *Contemporary Sociological Theory.* New York: Random House, 1988.

Robertson, Roland. *Globalization.* London: Sage, 1992.

Rodseth, Lars; Wrangham, R. W.; Harrigan, A. M.; and Smuts, B. B. "The Human Community as a Primate Society." *Current Anthropology* 32.3 (1991): 221–254.

Rolston, Holmes, III. *Philosophy Gone Wild*. Buffalo: Prometheus, 1986.

_____. "Biophilia, Selfish Genes, Shared Values." In *The Biophilia Hypothesis*, edited by S. R. Kellert and E. O. Wilson, 381–414. Washington, DC: Island Press, 1993.

Root, Michael. *Philosophy of Social Science*. Cambridge: Blackwell, 1993.

Rorty, Richard. *Philosophy and the Mirror of Nature*. Princeton: Princeton University Press, 1979.

Rosenau, Pauline Marie. *Post-modernism and the Social Sciences*. Princeton: Princeton University Press, 1991.

Ruse, Michael. "Sociobiology: A Philosophical Analysis." In *The Sociobiology Debate*, edited by A. Caplan, 355–375. New York: Harper and Row, 1978.

_____. *Philosophy of Biology Today*. Albany: State University of New York Press, 1988.

Ruse, Michael and Wilson, E. O. "Moral Philosophy as Applied Science." *Philosophy 61* (1986): 173–192.

Rushton, J. Phillips. "A Revolutionary Theory of Health, Longevity, and Personality: Sociobiology and R/K Reproductive Strategies." *Psychological Reports 60* (1987): 539–549.

_____. "Do R/K Reproductive Strategies Apply to Human differences?" *Social Biology* 35.3–4 (1988a): 337–340.

_____. "Race Differences in Behavior: A Review and Evolutionary Analysis." *Personality and Individual Differences* 9.6 (1988b): 1009–1024.

Russell, Bertrand. *A History of Western Philosophy*. New York: Simon and Schuster, 1945.

Sagan, Carl and Druyan, Ann. *In Search of Forgotten Ancestors*. New York: Random House, 1992.

Sahlins, Marshall. *The Use and Abuse of Biology*. Ann Arbor: University of Michigan Press, 1976.

Sanderson, Stephen and Ellis, Lee. "Theoretical and Political Perspectives of American Sociologists in the 1990s." *The American Sociologist* 23.2 (1992): 26–42.

Savage-Rumbaugh, Sue and Lewin, Roger. "Ape at the Brink." *Discover*, 15.9 (1994): 91–98.

Schneewind, J. B. "Sociobiology, Social Policy, and Nirvana. In *Sociobiology and Human Nature*, edited by M. S. Gregory, A. Silvers, and D. Sutch, 225–239. San Francisco: Josey-Bass, 1978.

Schutz, Alfred. *Collected Papers I*. The Hague: Martinus Nijhoff, 1962.

_____. *Collected Papers II*. The Hague: Martinus Nijhoff, 1964.

Seeley, John. R. "Social Science? Some Probative Problems." In *Sociology on Trial*, edited by M. Stein and A. Vicich, 53–65. Englewood-Cliffs, NJ: Prentice-Hall, 1963.

Seidman, Steven. "The End of Sociological Theory: The Postmodern Hope." *Sociological Theory*, 9.2 (1991): 131–146.

_____. *Contested Knowledge*. Cambridge: Blackwell, 1994.

Sharp, Ronald. *Friendship and Literature*. Durham: Duke University Press, 1986.

Shepard, Roger N. "The Perceptual Organization of Colors: An Adaptation to the Regularities of the Terrestrial World?" In *The Adapted Mind*, edited by Jerome Barkow, Leda Cosmides, and John Tooby, 495–532. New York: Oxford University Press, 1992.

Shorris, Earl. *Latinos*. New York: W. W. Norton, 1992.

Singer, Peter. *The Expanding Circle*. New York: Farrar, Straus & Giroux, 1981.

Skinner, B. F. *Beyond Freedom and Dignity*. New York: Random House, 1974.

Spector, Malcom and Kitsuse, John. *Constructing Social Problems*. Menlo Park, CA: Cummings, 1977.

Stark, Werner. *The Sociology of Knowledge*. London: Routledge & Kegan Paul, 1958.

Stout, Jeffrey. *Ethics After Babel*. Boston: Beacon. 1988a.

_____. "Liberal Society and the Languages of Morals." In *Community in America: The Challenge of Habits of the Heart*, edited by C. H. Reynolds and R. V. Norman, 127-146. Berkeley, CA: University of California Press, 1988b.

Sumner, William Graham. *Folkways*. New York: New American Library, 1960. (Original work published 1906)

Sutton, H. Eldon and Wagner, Robert. P. *Genetics*. New York: Macmillan, 1985.

Symons, Donald. "On the Use and Misuse of Darwinism in the Study of Human Behavior." In *The Adapted Mind*, edited by J. H. Barkow, L. Cosmides, and J. Tooby, 137–159. New York: Oxford University Press, 1992.

Tennant, Neil. "Evolutionary v. Evolved Ethics." *Philosophy 58* (1983): 289–302.

Terrace, Herbert. S. *Nim, a Chimpanzee Who Learned Sign Language*. New York: Random House, 1979.

Thomas, Laurence. "Biological Moralism." *Biology and Philosophy 1* (1986): 316–325.

Tiger, Lionel. *Men in Groups*. New York: Random House, 1969.

Timasheff, Nicholas. *Sociological Theory*. New York: Random House, 1957.

Tiryakian, Edward. "Biosocial Man." *American Journal of Sociology* 82.3 (1976): 701–706.

Tocqueville, Alexis de. *Democracy in America*. Garden City, NJ: Doubleday, 1969. (Original work published 1835)

Tooby, John and Cosmides, Leda. "The Psychological Foundations of Culture." In *The Adapted Mind*, edited by. Barkow, L. Cosmides, and. Tooby, 19–136. New York: Oxford University Press, 1992.

Tool, Marc. *The Discretionary Economy*. Boulder, CO: Westview, 1985.

Townsend, Sue. *The Adrian Mole Diaries*. New York: Grove, 1986.

Trigg, Roger. "Evolutionary Ethics." *Biology and Philosophy 1* (1986): 325–335.

Trivers, Robert. "The Evolution of Reciprocal Altruism." *Quarterly Review of Biology* 46.1 (1971): 35–57.

Turner, Jonathan. "Toward a Sociological Theory of Motivation." *American Sociological Review 52* (1987): 15–27.

United States Department of Health and Public Services. *Vital Statistics of the United States*. Vol. II, Part A. Hayettsville, MD, 1993.

Van den Berghe, Pierre. L. *Man in Society*. New York: Elsevier, 1975.

_____. "Why Most Sociologists Don't (and Won't) Think Evolutionarily." *Sociological Forum* 15.2 (1990): 173–185.

Viorst, Milton. *Fire in the Streets*. New York: Simon and Schuster, 1979.

Walzer, Michael. "The Communitarian Critique of Liberalism." *Political Theory* 18.1 (1990): 6–23.

Weber, Max. "Science as a Vocation." In *From Max Weber: Essays in Sociology*, edited by H. Gerth and C. W. Mills, 129–156. New York: Oxford University Press, 1946. (Original work published 1919)

Weiss, Mark and Mann, Alan E. *Human Biology and Behavior*. Boston: Little, Brown and Company, 1981.

Wellborn, Stanley N. "How Genes Shape Behavior." *U.S. News & World Report* 102.14 (1987): 58–62.

West, Cornel. *The American Evasion of Philosophy*. Madison, WI: University of Wisconsin Press, 1989.

White, Leslie. *The Evolution of Culture*. New York: McGraw-Hill, 1959.

_____. *The Science of Culture*. New York: Farrar, Straus & Giroux, 1969.

_____. *The Concept of Culture*. Minneapolis: Burgess, 1973.

Wiener, Norbert. *The Human Use of Human Beings*. Garden City, NJ: Doubleday, 1954.

Williams, George. C. "Huxley's Evolution and Ethics in Socio-biological Perspective." *Zygon* 23.4 (1988): 383–407.

Williams, Patricia. "Evolved Ethics Re-Examined: The Theory of Robert Richards." *Biology and Philosophy* 5 (1990): 451–457.

Willis, Delta. *The Hominid Gang*. New York: Viking, 1989.

Wills, Christopher. *The Runaway Brain*. New York: Basic Books, 1993.

Wilson, Edward. *Sociobiology: The New Synthesis*. Cambridge: Harvard University Press, 1975.

_____. "Forward." In *The Sociobiology Debate*, edited by A. Caplan, pp. xi–xiv. New York: Harper and Row, 1977.

_____. *On Human Nature*. New York: Bantam, 1978.

_____. "A Consideration of the Genetic Foundation of Human Social Behavior." In *Sociobiology: Beyond Nature/Nurture?*, edited by G. W. Barlow and. Silverberg, 295–306. Boulder, CO: Westview, 1980.

_____. *Biophilia*. Cambridge: Harvard University Press, 1984.

_____. (1990). "Biology and the Social Sciences." *Zygon* 25 (1990): 245–262.

_____. *The Diversity of Life*. New York: W. W. Norton, 1992.

Wilson, Janelle. *Lost in the Fifties: A Study of Collected Memories*. Unpublished Ph.D. Dissertation, Western Michigan University, Kalamazoo, 1995.

Wilson, William. *The Truly Disadvantaged*. Chicago: University of Chicago Press, 1987.

Woolgar, Steve and Pawluch, Dorothy. "Ontological Gerrymandering." *Social Problems* 32.3 (1985): 214–227.

Wrong, Dennis.   "The Oversocialized Conception of Man in Modern Sociology." *American Sociological Review 26* (1961): 184–193.

Wuketitus, Franz. "Darwinism: Still a Challenge to Philosophy." *Zygon* 23.4 (1988): 455–467.

INDEX